Good Ideas
from Questionable
Christians and
Outright
Pagans

An Introduction to Key
Thinkers and Philosophies

Steve Wilkens

InterVarsity Press
Downers Grove, Illinois

InterVarsity Press
P.O. Box 1400, Downers Grove, IL 60515-1426
World Wide Web: www.ivpress.com
E-mail: mail@ivpress.com

InterVarsity Press® is the book-publishing division of InterVarsity Christian Fellowship/USA®, a student movement active on campus at hundreds of universities, colleges and schools of nursing in the United States of America, and a member movement of the International Fellowship of Evangelical Students. For information about local and regional activities, write Public Relations Dept., InterVarsity Christian Fellowship/USA, 6400 Schroeder Rd., P.O. Box 7895, Madison, WI 53707-7895, or visit the IVCF website at <www.ivcf.org>.

Scripture quotations, unless otherwise noted, are from the New Revised Standard Version of the Bible, copyright 1989 by the Division of Christian Education of the National Council of the Churches of Christ in the USA. Used by permission. All rights reserved.

Cover design: Cindy Kiple

Cover image: Giraudon/Art Resource, N.Y.

ISBN 0-8308-2739-0

Printed in the United States of America ∞

Library of Congress Cataloging-in-Publication Data

Wilkens, Steve, 1955-
    Good ideas from questionable Christians and outright pagans/Steve
Wilkens.
        p. cm.
Includes bibliographical references.
    ISBN 0-8308-2739-0 (pbk.: alk. paper)
    1. Philosophy and religion. 2. Christianity—Philosophy. I. Title.
    BR100.W495 2004
    102'.427—dc22
                                            2003020590

P	19	18	17	16	15	14	13	12	11	10	9	8	7	6	5	4	3	2	1
Y	19	18	17	16	15	14	13	12	11	10	09	08	07	06	05	04			

For Zoe Sophia:
May you embrace wisdom
with the vigor with which you pursue life.

CONTENTS

INTRODUCTION
What's a Nice Christian like You Doing in a Place like Athens?

It happened many years ago, but my memories of the moment are still vivid. I was waiting for my first introduction to philosophy class to begin. I was apprehensive about what would happen over the next sixteen weeks of the course. Actually, *apprehensive* is not a strong enough word; I was flat-out scared. This is probably not an unusual state of affairs for many students anticipating an introductory philosophy class, but my situation was somewhat different. I was the instructor! It is a bit unusual for a person to teach an introductory college course he or she has never taken, and it is not a route to teaching that I would suggest. However, there is a story behind this story.

The fear I experienced while waiting for my introductory philosophy class to begin was not a new emotion. Fear of philosophy had been there during my college years. While no one ever said it explicitly, a message had been quite effectively communicated from all the sources I relied on for good advice: stay away from philosophy. It isn't the type of thing that is good for a Christian. In fact, it is downright dangerous. It may not be on any list of official psychological disorders, but I had a severe case of "philosophobia." I was not sure why my fine Christian college offered such a course, but I was certain that I should let nothing interfere with my faith. Philosophy, I was certain, would do that. My goal, after getting my degree, was to go to graduate school and eventually teach Bible or theology. I would not let philosophy mess up those plans. Fortunately, I could get my degree without an introductory philosophy class. I did have to take philosophy of religion, but since it had "religion" in the title, it seemed as if it would be safe as long as I did not take the philosophy part too seriously.

My dream of graduate school on my way to a teaching career began to come true. I made it through my master's degree and entered a Ph.D. program in systematic theology. Somewhere in this process, a couple of interesting things happened. First, I discovered that I could not do theology without a fairly solid grasp of philosophy. The two disciplines kept intersecting, so I had to learn on my own what I could have started learning during my college days. Second, as my explorations of philosophy continued, I found out how wrong my early impressions of this field of study were wrong. Philosophy actually helped me think through theological issues with greater clarity. I learned from it. It was more than just learning from it, however. I became a convert to the value of philosophy for Christians.

This brings us back to the beginning of my story. Colleges offer a lot more philosophy classes than theology courses, and as a freshly minted Ph.D. with no teaching experience, I couldn't get too picky about what jobs I took. I started teaching philosophy courses while I waited for a "real" job in theology. Eventually, as I grew to have an increasing respect for philosophy and its value to Christians, I landed a full-time philosophy position at a Christian university. Perhaps it is testimony to God's sense of humor that a college student with philosophobia would, a decade later, enter a career teaching philosophy to students with the same fears he had.

CHRISTIANITY AND PHILOSOPHY

Nervousness within the church about the proper role of philosophy, if it should have a place at all, is nothing new. A well-known quote by Tertullian, a Christian intellectual who wrote at the beginning of the third century, reveals this. He asks, "What indeed has Athens to do with Jerusalem? What concord is there between the Academy and the Church?" (*On Prescription Against Heretics* 7). These questions are intended to be rhetorical, with the assumed answer that Athens, which is representative of Greek philosophy, has nothing to do with the church. However, Tertullian asked these questions in a historical context in which other prominent Christians were finding great utility in expressing Christian ideas within a framework of Greek philosophical language and categories. They obviously would not have answered these questions in the same way; nor would many Christian thinkers up to the present.

One might ask why people like Tertullian would question whether Christians should pay attention to ideas from Athens, but today the burden of proof in Christian circles is generally assumed to lie on the other side of this debate. Why would Christians think that philosophy would have something to say that Christians ought to hear? Since the title of this book indicates that I find some of the ideas from "questionable Christians" and "outright pagans" to be good ones, I'll attempt a few reasons for giving them a hearing. Before we get to this, however, let's make certain we understand the two categories that I work with.

The "questionable Christians" referred to in the title are thinkers who identify themselves as Christians. Thus, this label applies to Augustine, Aquinas, Descartes and Kierkegaard. So if these four are self-identified Christians, why are they referred to as "questionable?" I want to be very clear that I do not find their Christian commitment questionable. However, while the "questionable" label does not represent my view, my opinion is not universally shared within the Christian world. For some, the assumptions behind Tertullian's rhetorical questions explain the tone of doubt. The very fact that they engaged in philosophical discourse at all makes their faith subject to scrutiny. For others, their conclusions raise questions about whether they deserve to be designated as Christians. The fact that Augustine, Descartes and Aquinas fall within the Catholic tradition may make them suspect to some Protestants, and Kierkegaard's Protestantism may cause certain Catholics to be wary. For most, however, it is the basic unfamiliarity with ideas that come from times that are, in some cases, centuries removed from our time that make us wonder whether they are relevant to twenty-first-century Christians.

"Outright pagans" refers to the remaining six philosophers surveyed here who make no claim at all to Christian faith. Some might cut a little slack for the first three—Socrates, Plato and Aristotle—since they all died a few centuries before Jesus appeared on the scene. It would be a little unfair to blame them for not embracing the faith. Many Christian readers would have more problems with the last three in this group—Nietzsche, Sartre and Marx. Not only are they non-Christians, but they are intentionally anti-Christian in their beliefs. Nevertheless, I will maintain that they all have some wisdom that can be of benefit to anyone.

Now that we have the tags straight, why should Christians care what philosophers have to say? I hope some of the reasons will be apparent as you ponder the ideas of the thinkers in the book, but I will start with four preliminary reasons. Perhaps we might begin with a simple observation. We do not find it illegitimate for Christians to learn any number of things—from sociology to auto mechanics—from people outside the faith, even if we might have learned the same things from fellow believers. Christians do not have a corner on truth in all its different facets, and, if God is the ultimate author of what is true, the conduits through which it passes on the way to us do not seem to be that important. Moreover, we recognize that some non-Christians have great wisdom about how to conduct certain aspects of their life. My challenge in this book is that you examine the ideas of some of the most influential thinkers in western intellectual history and draw your own conclusions about whether they offer any insight for living.

Second, over the years, I have read too many essays by college students and heard too many sermons from preachers declaring some philosopher a complete fool without having any real clue as to what that philosopher actually said. Many people outside the church have a stereotype of Christians as uninformed idiots, and experiences like this strongly reinforce that image. Disagreeing with someone's ideas is not bad, but uninformed disagreement is irresponsible and an embarrassment. If we are going to weigh in on an issue, we have a duty to do so honestly and intelligently.

This leads to a third reason for Christians to think through important philosophical issues. There are certain essential questions that every human should think through, and philosophers have had something to say about these matters for centuries. If we are going to address these questions thoughtfully, we cannot help but bump into others who struggle with the issues that go square to the heart of life. What does it mean to be free? Why does evil exist? How should we think about ethics? Can we know anything with certainty? Moreover, these questions all converge at a point that marks what is perhaps the most basic issue of human existence. Each philosopher, either directly or indirectly, addresses the question of how one might get the most out of life. Unless we believe that we are the only ones who have this matter nailed down, we might want to see if we can find some good ideas in others who have wrestled with the big questions.

Finally, I think there are good reasons to listen to certain philosophers precisely *because* of their opposition to Christianity. Too often, Christians develop blinds spots and are unable to recognize our weaknesses and flaws. Even when we are aware of problems, we may be reluctant to air our dirty laundry for all to see. Some Christians consider highlighting shortcomings a kind of disloyalty. However, because Christianity's opponents have no such loyalties, they are honest about what they perceive as wrong in Christian circles. And they are often dead right. Any time someone tells us the truth about ourselves, we ought to pay attention. There are numerous examples in Scripture of leaders who should have pointed out deficiencies to God's people but failed in their task. Often in these situations, God used the armies of pagan nations to get Israel's attention and put them back on track. Given this history, I don't see why God cannot use the intellectual arrows from pagan philosophers to accomplish the same goal.

THE SCOPE AND STRUCTURE OF THE BOOK

The scope of this book is extremely modest. This is a selective introduction to a few key philosophers. We will not even get to all the marquee names in the philosophical constellation, not to mention completely ignoring many very stimulating junior varsity philosophers. Even with those we examine, only a few bits of each philosopher's thought, usually from one, or at most a few, of their writings will be considered. And these few ideas we do look at will often receive only a quick glance. In short, this is not intended as a complete overview of philosophy, but a taste.

The structure of this book involves a rather odd combination. On the one hand, I have avoided footnotes and endnotes that can sometimes get in the way of the main ideas. On the other hand, I use numerous direct quotes from the sources themselves. Fortunately, most of the sources drawn from have standard forms of reference. Therefore, the reader can go to these reference points and find the information, if not the exact wording, regardless of the translation or edition. In those works that do not have standard references for locating information, I provide page numbers and a note about the translation I have used.

There are several reasons that I make such extensive use of quotes. First, if we let these philosophers speak in their own voices, it keeps us honest. As much as possible, I want to let them do the talking without filtering too much of what they have to say. More important, by drawing on quotes from these philosophical sources, I want to encourage you to look at the primary sources for yourself. Most people assume that Plato, Aristotle and Descartes will go way over their head. This is not at all the case. While you cannot read them like you read *People* magazine, they are more accessible to mortals than you might imagine, and are often more understandable than the texts that are supposed to explain their ideas.

A final reason for the heavy reliance on quotes is that I have discovered that you gain more insight into the mind of a person if you not only listen to what they say, but the way they say it. This last point provides a good opportunity for a reminder. A common mistake when we enter conversations with those outside our own circles is that we listen only to vocabulary and not to the meaning of what is said. When the words or forms of expression do not match with the ways we are used to hearing ideas communicated, we become suspicious. This creates a problem for Christians when they read philosophers, or almost any other specialized area of study, because they do not write in "Christianese." However, if we get beneath the surface, we might find substantial areas of agreement, and even when we do not, we gain some insight into ideas that have influenced the beliefs of people around us.

In addition to the survey of philosophical ideas, each chapter will conclude with a few evaluative thoughts. Since I find such at least some area of agreement with each philosopher surveyed, I highlight what I see as useful insights. I also raise questions that may represent gaps in that individual's thought. In the end, however, much is intentionally left open-ended. In a lot of cases, I would love to give you what I believe to be the "right" answers. I do have strong opinions on and, I think, creative responses to many of these big issues. However, this might shut down the thinking process too early and would be a disservice to you. My hope is that you will marvel at the mysteries of life for a while, chew on these ideas, think them through and pursue the answers yourself. In short, the intent is that you participate in the process rather than experience it vicariously. Decisions about your beliefs are too important to delegate to others. Thinking, like other aspects of life, was designed as a participant activity, not a spectator sport.

One of the greatest tragedies of the universe is that so many people treat life as a spectator sport and lead what might be called "accidental lives." An accidental life is a life that just happens. Like a twig in a river that is pushed downstream by a current or swirls in shallow pool, many people are propelled by events down the path of least resistance. The reason this is so pitiful is that life is so amazingly valuable and precious, and so many never really decide what to do with it. I have developed a love for philosophy, in large part because it begins with the assumption that we should not stumble through life on default mode, but should consciously and thoughtfully engage it and decide what we will value and where we will go.

Because life is so valuable, I am convinced that no thoughtful Christian should answer the Athens/Jerusalem question before gaining a fairly solid idea of what "Athens" has to say. To do otherwise is to make a decision before you have all the information, which is never a good idea. I did make such an uninformed decision in my undergrad years, and you can probably guess that one of the purposes of this book is to help others avoid my mistake. I have come to believe that Athens and Jerusalem—the life of philosophy and the life of faith—are not at all antithetical. They are not the same, but they are not opponents. In fact, my hope is that you will find that philosophy, with its tough thinking about important questions, is quite at home within the life of a Christian.

1

SOCRATES I

Why Ask Why?

Maybe I should not reveal my biases right from the start, but it is my opinion that Socrates is one of the best teachers you could consult if you want some solid lessons in the art of life. Life did not just happen to him. He latched on to every event, every person and every conversation as an opportunity to add to his considerable stockpile of wisdom. He wanted everything that life had to offer and he pursued it with vigor. Moreover, it is my evaluation that this pursuit paid off with a set of beliefs that, for the most part, were valuable possessions. In short, I believe that both the way Socrates lived life and the end product of his endeavors are useful instruction for the person who wants to squeeze the most out of their earthly journey. Of course, all this got Socrates killed, but we will deal with that minor detail in the next chapter.

If you know something about the way philosophy is usually done, Socrates' method may come as something of a surprise. First, philosophers tend to write their ideas down, but Socrates himself did not write anything. We get bits and pieces of Socrates' ideas from a few writers of the time, but the bulk of what we know about his teachings comes through his famous disciple, Plato. This leads to interesting questions about how much of philosophy found in these writings should be attributed to Socrates and what reflects the more developed thought of Plato. Most specialists generally agree that the ideas presented in chapters one and two represent the views, if not the exact words, of Socrates, while the words placed in the mouth of Socrates in chapter three represent the thought of Plato, which he builds on the basic ideas of his master.

A second (and related) feature of Socrates' method is that he did not teach in long heavy monologues. Instead, he entered into conversations, or dialogues as they are usually called. The dialogues, which engage a wide variety of people ranging from close friends to complete strangers and people whose views are sometimes diametrically opposed to those of Socrates, generally begin with a question or theme. When Socrates' dialogue partner takes a position on the question, Socrates subjects this answer to a series of probing questions. Through this approach, commonly referred to as the "Socratic method," conclusions are sometimes achieved. However, in many other dialogues the effect is something like tugging on a dangling thread. When you pull hard enough, things fall apart. And this is where the dialogue ends. We have many questions, but no answers.

At this point, Socrates' approach may simply confirm what many people think about philosophy and philosophers in general. It is all questions and confusion, but no answers. This is not the conclusion Socrates would want you to draw. He firmly believed there were answers to be found, and, despite what he will say in the next chapter, he believes that he knows some of these answers. However, the Socratic method reflects at least two of his beliefs. First, he wants to make certain that we do the search for ourselves. If he tells his dialogue partners what they ought to believe, their views never become their own because they did not work for it. Second, his method is kept open-ended to remind us that we should not stop looking for more truth, even after we think we have found it. This is one of the reasons he writes nothing down. When we commit something to paper, it often leaves us with the impression that we are done. The dialogical method reminds Socrates that the quest for truth is an on-going process and that he should be open to any source—friend, stranger or opponent—who might bring him closer to the best possible answers.

This chapter will examine the Socratic method in action with two goals in view. First, we will watch how Socrates tests potential answers to big questions in the give and take of conversation (although it will be difficult to reproduce the feel of the dialogue in our limited space). This method, and the reactions of Socrates' dialogue participants, will be mined to see what might be learned about the search for truth. Our second task will be to engage the enduring questions at the heart of two Socratic dialogues. The first, *Euthyphro*, attempts to define the nature of piety, or holiness. *Theaetetus*, the second dialogue, confronts the question of what constitutes knowledge. Not only are these still open questions, many answers considered in these two dialogues twenty-five hundred years ago still exist in some form today. Thus, we get a chance to see how ideas about these basic questions hold up under Socrates' scrutiny and think through our own views on these topics.

EUTHYPHRO AND THE DEFINITION OF *HOLINESS*

The dialogues recorded in *Euthyphro* and *Theaetetus* occur just prior to Socrates' trial, which we will investigate in the next chapter. As Socrates is waiting to defend himself, he meets Euthyphro, who is waiting for his turn to prosecute a very unusual case: he is bringing his father up on criminal charges! One of the family's slaves had killed another. Euthyphro's father had the murderous servant tied up, thrown into a ditch and dispatched someone to consult a seer about how to handle the situation. By the time word returned, the murderer was dead from neglect. Euthyphro, who fancies himself as a theologian of sorts, views his father's action as an affront to the gods. Obviously, prosecuting one's father for murder is serious step, but Euthyphro believes that his higher duty is to the gods.

On hearing the story and Euthyphro's plan of action, Socrates becomes very interested. Impiety, or dishonoring the gods, is one of the charges for which Socrates will stand trial shortly. Furthermore, in Athenian society, slaves did not amount to much, and one's father was to be revered. Anyone bringing religious charges against their father over a slave must surely know what true piety is. Such solemn steps are "only for a man already far advanced in point of wisdom" (*Euthyphro* 4a). So Socrates cautions him, "You are not afraid that you yourself are doing an unholy deed?" (*Euthyphro* 4e). Euthyphro answers, "If I did not have an accurate knowledge of all that, I should be good for nothing, and Euthyphro would be no different from the general run of men" (*Euthyphro* 5a).

By this point, two things about Euthyphro are apparent: he is sincere, and he is arrogant. Socrates decides to give the young theologian enough rope to hang himself; he offers (ironically) to become Euthyphro's student. If Euthyphro can define holiness, perhaps Socrates can discover whether he is actually guilty of impiety, as he has been charged, and make amends before it is too late. Believing the definition of holiness (or piety) to be a simple question, Euthyphro tells Socrates, "The holy is what I am now doing, prosecuting the wrongdoer who commits a murder or a sacrilegious robbery, or sins in any point like that" (*Euthyphro* 5d). This seems fairly clear at first blush, but Socrates points out that Euthyphro has not answered his question. Giving an *example* of particular actions that are religious does not tell us *why* these actions are religious. Instead, "I wanted you to tell me what is the essential form of holiness which makes all holy actions holy" (*Euthyphro* 6d). This is why Socrates requested a definition. Socrates can only know whether *his* actions, which are different from Euthyphro's own actions, have been holy when he knows the definition of holiness.

Euthyphro recognizes his mistake and gives it another shot: "What is pleasing to the gods is holy and what is not pleasing to them is unholy" (*Euthyphro* 6e). Socrates is delighted. They now have something that looks like a real definition rather than an example, but they must see whether it will help them grasp the essence of holiness. Athenian religious doctrine (which both Socrates and Euthyphro take as a given) envisioned many gods, and these gods frequently disagreed. This divine dissension poses a difficulty that Euthyphro has not recognized, so Socrates brings it to his attention. If the gods disagree, this means that "the same things would alike displease and please them" (*Euthyphro* 8b). This is self-contradictory—an action cannot be simultaneously holy and unholy—so it is not a good definition after all.

Socrates proposes a modified definition of holiness, which Euthyphro accepts enthusiastically: "What the gods all hate is unholy, and what they love is holy" (*Euthyphro* 9d). Socrates now has another question. "Is what is holy holy because the gods approve it, or do they approve it because it is holy?" (*Euthyphro* 10a). If the difference between the two options is unclear to you, it may be of comfort to know that it took some explanation before Euthyphro understood it. This is a "chicken or egg" question. Does the holiness exist first, calling forth the love of the gods? Or does the love of the gods make something holy? Stated otherwise, if the holy is holy because the gods approve it, a thing or action *becomes* holy based on the gods' love of it. On the other hand, if the thing or action *is* holy, this is an intrinsic quality that the gods recognize. The gods do not bring this quality into existence. They simply acknowledge what is already there.

When he believes he finally has the options straightened out, Euthyphro decides that acts are pious *because* the gods love them. Socrates, however, states that this option tells us only about the gods and not the act itself. "Its being loved of the gods is not the reason of its being loved" (*Euthyphro* 10e). We still do not have a definition of holiness. At this point, Euthyphro's arrogance turns to frustration. "Now, Socrates, I simply don't know how to tell you what I think. Somehow everything that we put forward keeps moving about us in a circle, and nothing will stay where we put it" (*Euthyphro* 11b). Translated, this means that Euthyphro accuses Socrates of playing with words. Euthyphro is clearly getting annoyed, and it bubbles to the surface here. There is a change in Socrates' demeanor as well. He drops some of his irony, becomes more direct, and tells Euthyphro, "To my mind, you are languid [a nice word for lazy]" (*Euthyphro* 11e).

To get a fresh start, Socrates suggests attacking the definition of piety from a different angle. He begins with a little elementary logic, pointing out that a statement can be true without its converse also being true. For example, the statement "All ducks are birds" is true, but its converse, "All birds are ducks," is not. Socrates states that it seems to him that all that is holy is also just, but not all matters of justice deal with holiness. Justice is a larger concept that includes piety. So what part of justice is holiness? Which of our duties are holy duties? Euthyphro answers, "The part of justice which is religious and is holy is the part that has to do with the service of the gods; the remainder is the part of justice that has to do with the service of mankind" (*Euthyphro* 12e).

Socrates replies, "What you say there, Euthyphro, to me seems excellent. There is one little point, however, on which I need more light" (*Euthyphro* 13a). The "one little point" has to do with the idea of service. Most forms of service improve those to whom service is rendered. But surely, Socrates says, we do not improve the gods by our actions. Euthyphro agrees, and modifies the idea of service as giving honor and gratitude to the gods. Socrates points out that defining piety as "giving honor and gratitude to the gods" brings us back to a previous answer. It simply restates the idea that "holiness is what pleases the gods," since giving honor and gratitude to the gods would be pleasing to them. But this answer was ruled out earlier. It only tells us what holiness *does* (i.e., pleases or honors the gods), not what holiness *is*.

One more time, Socrates says, "We must go back again, and start from the beginning to find out what the holy is. As for me, I never will give up until I know" (*Euthyphro* 15c). (Euthyphro probably does not doubt the last claim.) However, Euthyphro says, "Another time, then, Socrates, for I am in a hurry, and must be off this minute" (*Euthyphro* 15e). Socrates is left high and dry; he did not get a definition of piety after all that work. What did Euthyphro get out of the conversation? What *should* Euthyphro have received from the dialogue? I suspect that these two questions have different answers, but we will return to this later. For now we will highlight a couple of issues that arise in *Euthyphro* that are relevant for Christians.

DISSECTING EUTHYPHRO

Most people who believe in God's existence also believe that there is a connection between God and goodness (or holiness). What we find to be morally right and wrong must be answered with reference to God. Where things get fuzzy, however, is in the nature of the relationship. How is goodness connected with God? Socrates suspected that Euthyphro was also guilty of fuzzy thinking on the link between God and ethics when the latter argues that things are holy because the gods love them. As we have seen, Socrates states that this solution only tells us about the gods' attitude toward the holy but nothing about why it is holy. Socrates' response can be restated to give it more bite. If holiness, or goodness, is determined by God's love, it seems to make holiness arbitrary. What is good is completely dependent on God's fiat. Thus, we might ask, for example, whether God could have declared the torture of redheads a holy act.

Of course, the expected response (at least from redheads and their friends) is that God would never command such a thing. Why not? Most would probably give one of the two following answers: either (1) God would not (or could not) do such a thing, or (2) torture, even if commanded by God, could not be holy. Regardless of the option selected, Socrates would be quick to point something out. Both answers assume that God loves something *because it is holy*, which is different from saying that something is holy *because God loves it*, the definition we began with.

How does this work? Let's begin with option two first. If torture is wrong, regardless of what God commands, this assumes that goodness has an existence independent of God. But if some things are wrong (e.g., torture of redheads) before God weighs in on the issue, God's moral standing is determined by something external to him. In this case, if God would command the torture of redheads, he would be requiring an immoral act. If we take option one, we have to ask why God would not command torture. To say that God is a good God, and such a God would not violate goodness, brings us back around to the same problem we see above: God's moral status is dependent on his conformity to an external measure. If we argue that a good God *cannot* violate a standard of goodness, this creates a problem with divine omnipotence. God's freedom and ability would be limited by something outside his Being. Thus, Socrates confronts us with a difficult and interesting question; how are goodness and God connected?

If we leave the question at this point, we can see why Euthyphro feels a bit stuck. We might note, however, that Socrates has not necessarily provided all the available options for resolving this question. For example, most Christians would argue that God's decrees about what is good are not limited by some independently existing goodness, but by God's own nature. Thus, the problem of God's freedom may be greatly diminished if his limitations are self-imposed. The point we might take from this is that options beyond those immediately offered to us may assist us in cutting through some difficult questions, but we may have to do some digging to get at them.

The second issue of interest to Christians here concerns the nature and purpose of worship. At one point, Euthyphro defines worship as "a science of sacrifice and prayer" (*Euthyphro* 14c). Expanding on this, he states that by means of the first, we give to the gods; we receive from them by means of the second. In other words, Socrates says, "holiness will be a mutual art of commerce between gods and men" (*Euthyphro* 14e). Putting it in these terms brings to light some issues Christians need to consider. Does our understanding of worship envision God as a type of cosmic vending machine, in which we receive our requests when we figure out what to put in the coin slot? But deeper than this, we should recognize the implications of this idea of worship in relationship to our understanding of God. If God is perfect in himself, what can we offer that would increase God's happiness? If God is changeless, can our worship affect him in any way? Once again, when Socrates helps us unpack the concept of worship, we find that our ideas may lead to unanticipated questions and ramifications.

THEAETETUS AND THE DEFINITION OF *TRUTH*

In the brief introduction to our second dialogue, *Theaetetus*, we learn that the namesake of the writing has been wounded in battle and stricken with dysentery. The odds are that Theaetetus will not survive. The conversants then flash back several years to an event in Theaetetus's youth, in which the mathematician, Theodorus, has just been asked by Socrates about whether he has any particularly promising students. Theodorus gives a high recommendation to Theaetetus, who has just appeared on the scene, and Socrates draws him into the conversation.

The question of the day is "What is knowledge?" Theaetetus' response is that what Theodorus has taught him about geometry is knowledge. Likewise, the craft of the cobbler is knowledge of shoemaking. Theaetetus has made a mistake here, the same one Euthyphro made at the beginning of the previous dialogue. Theaetetus has offered an example of knowledge (what he knows about geometry) rather than a definition of knowledge. Moreover, Socrates points out that this is a circular answer. It amounts to saying that knowledge is knowing something. But what does it mean to "know?"

Theaetetus recognizes the error and takes another stab at the answer; knowledge is perception. "It seems to me that one who knows something is perceiving the thing he knows, and, so far as I can see at present, knowledge is nothing but perception" (*Theaetetus* 151e). Socrates asks whether it would be fair to characterize this idea as a restatement of Protagoras's philosophy, which argues, "Man is the measure of all things" (*Theaetetus* 152a). Theaetetus has read Protagoras and agrees with linking them. Each person has direct awareness of his or her perceptions, and if perceiving is knowing, it follows that the person who perceives is the measure of truth.

Socrates then wants to make certain that Theaetetus understands the implications of "man is the measure"/"perceiving is knowing." First, if perception equals knowledge, what is perceived does not just *seem* to me, but *is* to me. Perception is reality, not just opinion. This leads to a second ramification: "Perception, then, is always of something that *is*, and, as being knowledge, it is infallible" (*Theaetetus* 152c). After all, how would it be possible to tell someone that his or her perception of something is wrong? The perceiver is the only one in a position to know what he or she perceives. Therefore, for example, if coffee tastes bitter (a perception) to a person, the coffee *is* bitter (knowledge of a truth) and this truth cannot be false. Theaetetus agrees that both the reality of what is perceived and our infallibility about knowledge gained through perception follow from the statement that "perceiving is knowing."

Socrates' next step is rather remarkable. He could have taken advantage of Theaetetus's inexperience by asking how two contradictory perceptions of the same thing can both be true. In other words, if I *perceive* a certain object as heavy and you perceive it as light, it would actually *be* both heavy and light, which sounds like nonsense. But instead of critiquing an easily attacked version of "man is the measure" and scoring a quick victory, Socrates tries to cast the theory into a more defensible position. Protagoras, he says, would provide a more complex understanding of perception by acknowledging that no two observers perceive the same thing. That which is heavy to me is different from the object that is light to you. Stated more broadly, my world is distinct to me, just as yours is to you. We are both right about our perceptions of an object's weight because we are not speaking of the same thing. Therefore, the infallibility of my perceptions, and thus also my knowledge, is preserved.

Socrates then adds two further layers of complexity in order to avoid other potential criticisms. First, since an object of perception constantly changes, we should not view an object as static, but as a form of motion. Second, that with which we perceive is also a type of motion. Therefore, a tree we observe is not a static entity, nor is the eye with which we see. Both are dynamic processes. Socrates points out that this allows Theaetetus freedom from dealing with problems such as how an observer can be mistaken about certain perceptions, such as in the case of dreams or hallucinations. The world of the dreamer is different from the world of the "same person" in a waking state. Theaetetus agrees that all this is in accord with Protagoras's position.

Now that Socrates has outlined a fairly complex version of "knowledge is perception"/"man is the measure," he proceeds to critique it. The first question is why, if perceiving is knowing, Protagoras would designate human beings as the standard. "I am surprised that he did not begin his *Truth* with the words, the measure of all things is the pig, or the baboon, or some sentient creature still more uncouth" (*Theaetetus* 161c). Pigs, baboons and tadpoles have sense experience, and would therefore have as much claim to knowledge as any other sentient being. Second, Socrates asks, "Where is the wisdom of Protagoras, to justify his setting up to teach others and to be handsomely paid for it, and where is our comparative ignorance or the need for us to go and sit at his feet, when each of us is himself the measure of his own wisdom" (*Theaetetus* 161e)? If our perceptions yield infallible knowledge, what could we possibly learn from anyone else? Moreover, Protagoras is not in any position to know the contents of any other individual's world. If their universe is different from the one Protagoras inhabits, how can his truth be true for them? A third rebuttal challenges the direct link between perception and knowledge assumed by Protagoras. For instance, we can hear a foreign language spoken or see it written on a page, but we do not understand it. Thus, we can perceive without knowing. Finally, Socrates points out that we can know without perceiving. Shutting our eyes on something we observe does not eliminate our knowledge of what we previously viewed.

When Socrates has finished his critique, Theodorus and Theaetetus agree that the idea that "perceiving is knowing" has suffered several severe blows. However, Socrates hesitates: Protagoras has not had a chance to respond. After all, it may be that these criticisms can be successfully met and answered. However, Protagoras is long dead and cannot defend himself. Socrates offers to rebut his criticisms as Protagoras might, and enlists Theodorus, who is familiar with Protagoras's philosophy, to keep himself honest.

Socrates argues that Protagoras may justify his teaching occupation because, while one may not be able to tell another what is *true* for his or her world, the teacher can guide students toward what is *useful*. Socrates seeks truth, "whereas [Protagoras] should say that one set of thoughts is better than the other, but not in any way truer" (*Theaetetus* 167b). Stated otherwise, Protagoras would shift the question from "What is true?" to "What works?" We each inhabit different worlds, but these worlds can collide when we interact with others. It limits our ability to operate effectively in society if our perception (our truth) causes us to be viewed as strange. Therefore, in order to help them interact in ways that are useful, the teacher may guide students down paths that would benefit them practically. If education is about usefulness rather than truth, Protagoras can justify his role as teacher. Theodorus, speaking on behalf of Protagoras, allows that Socrates has offered an accurate and spirited defense of his predecessor.

Now it is time, once again, to evaluate this modified position, which says that "perception is knowledge of what is useful." At the heart of Socrates' criticism is that, even if Protagoras teaches only what is expedient or useful, he must assume some universal truth about usefulness. Otherwise, the student could say that Protagoras's idea of usefulness, like his concept of truth, applies only to him. Therefore, if Protagoras teaches students how to live effectively, he must admit that the individual does not have an infallible concept of usefulness.

Second, Socrates states, it seems impossible to talk about usefulness without assuming the category of truth. No one would "venture to assert that any enactment which a state supposes to be for its advantage will quite certainly be so" (*Theaetetus* 172b). In other words, our inability to predict with certainty what the future will show to be useful calls the infallibility of perception into question. For example, I may believe that drilling for oil in my back yard will be a successful endeavor. I will only know whether this belief is true or false (or, as Protagoras would state it, useful or useless) in the future. However, if my knowledge of geology is nil and there are no oil wells within forty miles of my house, you might suggest I consult an expert. An expert is a better source than the nongeologist for determining whether a belief will prove out in the future. To state it differently, the specialist is the better measure of the future perceptions (whether you will see oil pumping from your back yard) of an individual than that individual is. Therefore, Socrates concludes, "we may quite reasonably put it to your master [Protagoras] that he must admit that one man is wiser than another and that the wiser man is the measure" (*Theaetetus* 179b).

There is one last element of the thesis that "perception is knowledge" that Socrates wants to pursue. Socrates points out that our individual sense organs are limited to specific types of perception. The eye does not perceive sound nor does the ear perceive color. However, we can contemplate the sensory experience of both organs simultaneously, isolating and comparing the two. Contemplation of different types of perception (which is the same as knowing, according to Protagoras) must therefore be a function of something other than the sense organs, since each receives only data proper to its nature.

When Socrates points this out, Theaetetus concludes that our processing of and reflection on perceptions from different organs must be attributed to the mind. Since reflection is a form of knowledge, the mind, not the senses, must be the source of knowledge. Just one more thing, Socrates says: Don't we speak of knowing certain things that do not rely on the sense organs at all? For example, goodness, justice and other moral qualities emit no color, sound, taste, tactile signals or odors. If knowledge is a matter of perception, how can we know those things to which our physical senses have no access?

All parties in this dialogue now conclude that attempts to resuscitate the idea that perceiving is knowing have failed, and move on to consider other options. In the end, however, Socrates observes that the later attempts to define knowledge also have turned out to be "wind eggs," and Theaetetus agrees. At this point, Socrates has to leave to face his accusers in court, but says, "Tomorrow morning, Theodorus, let us meet here again" (*Theaetetus* 210d). As we will discover in the next chapter, however, Socrates was unable to keep this appointment.

DISSECTING THEAETETUS

Before we review the flow of Socrates' argument in *Theaetetus*, a word should be said about something that pops up early in both dialogues. Both Euthyphro and Theaetetus offer *examples* in their initial answers to their respective questions, but Socrates is interested in *definitions*. What's wrong with examples? Socrates might point out that two very different acts may be described with the same adjective. Convicting a murderer and feeding the poor can be called *just* acts. Whether we recognize it or not, using *just* to characterize both activities, with all their dissimilarities, assumes that they have something in common; something within each of these cases exemplifies justice. Whatever this common "something" is must be known before we see the acts. Otherwise, we would not be able to recognize them as *just* acts. For this reason, Socrates would have little patience with those who state, "This is just an argument about definitions." Until we are clear on the definitions, we haven't agreed on what we are talking about.

Socrates would also tell us that we could never define justice by collecting examples of just acts, because there are innumerable ways to exercise justice. Moreover, it may be that no just act is pure, but is incomplete or mixed with other motives and impulses. If this is the case, only a concept (or definition) can present justice, holiness or any other attribute in complete purity; so, this is where Socrates begins.

When Socrates attempts to get at the definition of knowledge in *Theaetetus*, he encounters a question that cannot be long avoided: "What is the difference between opinion and knowledge?" We find no shortage of opinions on any topic, but opinion, as most define it, can be false. Therefore, distinguishing between knowledge and false opinion is necessary to avoid error. In view of our desire to avoid error, Theaetetus offers a solution that seems to provide certainty: "to perceive is to know." A modern variant of this is the phrase "seeing is believing," and its attractiveness to people is not hard to understand. Perception is immediate and we instinctually rely on it as a guide to truth. Socrates certainly recognizes why "perception is knowledge" would find followers in every generation, but he believes that it becomes problematic when we understand the implications. Some of these are stated explicitly in the dialogue. As we have seen, he points out that "perception equals knowledge" erases the line between *appearance* and *reality* and grants the perceiver infallible knowledge. Thus, right from the beginning we find two troubling features in this theory. First, on occasion, we find it prudent to doubt our senses when perceptual capacities might be impaired by sleight of hand, perspective, distance, sleep, illness, intoxicants or other factors. Second, things that are real for others do not have the same reality to us. If our own perceptions are real and infallible, what are we to make of differing perceptions among infallible perceivers? Most people believe themselves to be right on almost everything, but would draw the line on claiming infallibility. These issues may be enough to give us pause about accepting the idea that perceiving is knowing, but Socrates wants to see if some tinkering can save the theory.

Socrates points out that the problem of contradictory perceptions between individuals might be put to rest by arguing that each individual's world is a private affair. However, this "cure" brings its own set of implications that may be worse than the "disease" of not knowing. While he does not directly mention what an odd state of affairs it would be should each individual inhabit a private universe, Socrates does attack the idea indirectly by fleshing out other ramifications. First, if perception itself brings knowledge, not just any *person*, but any *creature* with sense capacities, qualifies as an infallible knower of reality and the owners of their own personal world. As a result, "seeing is knowing" greatly simplifies the hierarchy of being. Pigs, baboons, tadpoles and thousands of other sentient species have as much claim to knowledge as human beings. However, putting these critters on the same epistemological plane as human beings is a step that few feel comfortable with.

A second problem Socrates raises is that an infallible knowledge within a private universe of perception raises important questions about whether teaching and learning are possible. If perception were a foolproof route to knowledge, as Protagoras claims, it would seem that the only way to learn is to increase our perception. Moreover, no one can help us do this since they do not have access to our world. What use, then, are teachers (one of which is Protagoras)?

As we see in the dialogue, one way to escape the consequences of this is to suggest that we have used the wrong vocabulary. Protagoras says that the categories of truth and reality apply only to private matters because each individual's world is unique. Therefore, social issues must be decided by measures like usefulness, expediency and prudence. This echoes the ideas of many today who argue that the idea of truth is, at best, outmoded or over-ambitious, and, at worst, arrogant. The best we can hope for is finding what works for individuals with divergent truths. But Socrates suggests that changing the vocabulary does not allow us to avoid the category of truth. Not every potential course of action believed to be expedient turns out to be so. Only some things are *truly* useful. In short, it doesn't seem as easy to get rid of truth as Protagoras imagined.

A final implication of hitching knowledge to perception is that it leaves no room for knowledge of the intangible. What is lost when the imperceptible is squeezed out of the realm of knowledge? Socrates notes that perhaps the most obvious loss is moral truth. This may explain why so many people today, who have adopted some form of Protagoras's theory, are willing to relegate ethics to the status of opinion (at least until *they* are wronged). However, if we can only *know* what can be directly accessed through the senses, knowledge of time, gravity, love, God, numbers and a host of other intangibles is impossible. All these things end up in the category of opinion. If you try to get around this by arguing that truth about these entities can be deduced from tangible realities, and thus counted as knowledge, we run into another problem: the rules of deduction are also intangible.

We all believe that we know certain things, and for our sake, I hope we are right. However, Socrates raises some important questions about the process of knowing. While drawing a direct line between our senses of knowledge seems, at first blush, to be an obvious step, Socrates reminds us that this theory comes with a lot of baggage. Not only does Socrates illuminate the fallout from the basic idea that perception equals knowledge, he also shows how certain modifications intended to protect the theory on one front may open it up to greater difficulties on another. The challenge Socrates leaves with us is determining the relationship between the physical senses and knowledge. (Plato will have quite a bit to say about this in chapter three.)

DISSECTING THE SOCRATIC METHOD

Socrates thought of himself as an educator. However, as we have seen, he would probably want us to define education before we got too far in our discussion of whether he was a successful educator. A friend of mine once offered an interesting definition of education. He described it as putting people in a position from which they cannot escape except by thinking. From our quick trip through these two dialogues, Socrates seems to have a similar definition of education. His dialogue partners are invited to think their way out of challenging questions. However, his experience with Euthyphro told him that there was another "escape clause" not covered in this definition. Euthyphro ultimately made his getaway by closing his ears and mind and refusing to think. The two dialogues above offer examples of both means of escape—thinking or running away—and they help us see what the Socratic method can contribute to our pursuit of wisdom.

Socrates challenged the thinking of his dialogue partners with tough inquiries. Theaetetus stayed engaged in the process: listening to the questions, adapting to Socrates' comments, offering alternatives as the course of the dialogue demanded. In other words, he tried to think his way out of the problem. Maybe he felt obligated to hang in there since bailing out would have made him look bad in front of Theodorus, his teacher. But if he had such inclinations, Socrates did not notice. On the other hand, while Euthyphro initially feels confident in his ability to satisfy Socrates' curiosity about the nature of piety, in the end he jumps overboard in frustration.

What accounts for the different responses of these two individuals? One hint comes at the beginning of our second dialogue, when Theaetetus expresses wonder about a particular problem Socrates has illuminated. This attitude excites Socrates, who states, "This sense of wonder is the mark of the philosopher. Philosophy indeed has no other origin" (*Theaetetus* 155d). Wonder is an acknowledgment of the universe's mystery and an admission of our inability to fully grasp what is before us. Wonder opens Theaetetus to philosophical exploration and the hope of discovery. In contrast, Euthyphro is certain that he already knows all the answers. In his opinion, the solution to one of the biggest and most wonder-full questions humanity can confront—What is the nature of the holy?—is already in his back pocket. However, Euthyphro encounters difficulties he did not anticipate. His early answers, by his own admission, came apart at the seams when Socrates yanked at the loose ends, and his later responses kept taking him back the same deficient options. When it became evident that he could not escape Socrates' queries by defining piety and that Socrates was not going to let him off the hook, he had two options. He could admit that he does not know the answer, or he could leave.

So why does Euthyphro leave? It is always tricky to attribute motives to another person, but, being a human for most of my life, I think I can make a pretty good guess. Euthyphro has presented himself to Socrates as an expert in religious matters. Thus, when he could not answer one of the most basic questions about his field of expertise, he was embarrassed. But instead of admitting that he needs to rethink some things, he first accuses Socrates of confusing him with words and then abandons ship.

This may hit uncomfortably close to home. We Christians want to think that we have a solid grip on our religious beliefs. It stings when we get cornered by difficult questions because it makes us, and our faith, look bad. Too often, our reaction parallels Euthyphro's. We become hostile toward the questioner or run for the exits. After a few such situations, we become proficient at avoiding potential interrogators altogether.

While these responses can hardly be characterized as constructive, they reveal something important. We react in this way because we our beliefs are important to us. Therefore, even though many speak as if doctrines, theories and ideas are abstractions with no connection to real life, the impulse to attack the messenger or duck for cover tells us that just the opposite is true: We deeply value our beliefs. We just don't get fired up over things about which we are indifferent. The problem is that these are *defensive* attempts to protect what we find important.

There are constructive ways for dealing with these situations. The best, I believe, is asking ourselves the questions before someone else asks them. If we don't get caught cold, our answers may be more thoughtful and more satisfying to the interlocutor. This also seems to be a more responsible way to be Christian. If our faith matters to us, we should "always be prepared to give an answer [*apologia*] to everyone who asks you to give the reason for the hope that you have" (1 Pet 3:15 NIV). One of the reasons for this book is to help us to anticipate good questions, often coming from outside the Christian ghetto, so we are not an embarrassment to our faith.

Another constructive move would be to recognize (and admit) what we don't know. Christians often have the impression that it is their duty to know all the answers, and when it becomes clear that we do not, we often act in un-Christian ways. Moreover, as ironic as it may seem, willingness to admit that some corners of our universe still are mystery can facilitate one of the greatest, and possibly the most neglected, of the Christian virtues: humility. Socrates tells Theaetetus that, even though they have not adequately defined knowledge, he may have received something even more important. "You will be gentler and more agreeable to your companions, having the good sense not to fancy you know what you do not know" (*Theaetetus* 210c). The illusion of knowledge breeds arrogance, but realism about what we do not know can create gentleness and humility.

A third positive response is to respect truth. It may sound harsh to put it in these terms, but the difference between Euthyphro and Theaetetus is a matter of honesty. The impression we get from Euthyphro's responses is that he did not want to know whether his beliefs were true. So when he gets backed into a corner, he does not respect truth enough to rethink his views. He probably walked away with his idea of "truth" intact, but truth maintained by walking away from fair questions is cheap and dishonest.

The actions of Socrates provide a nice counterpoint to this. We know from other dialogues that he believes that "man is the measure" is a dangerous doctrine. In *Theaetetus*, however, he refuses to attack a straw man. Instead, unless we ascribe some ulterior motives to him, Socrates develops "man is the measure" in what he thought was its most robust and defensible form, even though he thought it was a thoroughly wrong-headed notion. There is a lesson here for Christian apologists, who too often set up a caricature of their opponents' positions, kick it over and claim victory for "our side." An honest search for truth compels us to entertain the option that our opponents might know something we don't. If we are unwilling to take an adversary's best shot, we lack integrity.

Finally, it would be good to take a look at Socrates' practice of asking questions.

Since we see these dialogues from the perspective of the one who must respond to Socrates' questions, he comes off as a frustrating, and possibly obnoxious, individual. It wears us out to answer one question after another. If we can see it from Socrates' perspective, however, we may be a bit more charitable in our evaluation. He is frustrated himself. He really does want to find all the truth about piety, knowledge and a raft of other issues. Since he values the truth, his frustration leads him to continual questioning. To someone who does not have Socrates' hunger for truth, his scrutiny can come across as badgering. To those who love truth, it is a moral and intellectual imperative.

Socrates' intense quest for wisdom might be a helpful corrective to the church's tendency to discourage people from asking hard questions. Those who question get tagged as contentious or lacking in faith. Maybe this is backwards. Maybe we should be less tolerant of those who accept everything without a murmur and view those who bring up tough issues as honest inquirers after the truth. Not everyone has intellectual hurdles to cross on the way to faith, but many do. Unless we confront their questions head-on, we will perpetuate a common perception that Christianity cannot stand up to real questions. To suggest something really radical, perhaps, rather than simply addressing questions that people have, we should actually raise the questions ourselves. This might keep us from becoming "languid," like Euthyphro. Moreover, beliefs, like everything else we own, are more important to us if we earn them through hard work rather than having them given to us.

One final point on questions. Socrates does not claim any more insight on the proper definitions of holiness and knowledge than Euthyphro and Theaetetus. However, he is ahead by another scoring system. He knows the right questions. Anyone can come up with a list of random queries, but Socrates is smart enough to ask questions that help people recognize where their answers lead them or how their proposals affect other responses they have given. He can do this because he has taken the time and energy to think out the issues of holiness and knowing before the dialogues. It may be that teaching (and knowing) has a lot more to do with recognizing relevant questions than it does with knowing all the answers. Socrates, like the others in this book, is an excellent teacher because he raises good, honest and difficult questions about the way we think and live. Whether we actually learn anything from Socrates and the others, as the actions of Euthyphro and Theaetetus demonstrate, depends on us.

2

SOCRATES II
Are Beliefs Worth Living (and Dying) For?

In the previous chapter, we saw two examples of Socrates in dialogue. In both cases a topic was raised; potential solutions were tested, modified and retested; and, because no unshakable answers were found, Socrates and his partners suspended judgment pending better answers. This is certainly a worthwhile way to approach philosophical subjects, but Socrates did not view philosophy merely as a process of working through intellectual puzzles. In his view, our philosophy should shape the way we live and guide our decisions, and Socrates has some important decisions before him. Earlier, we met Socrates just before he went before a jury. As we pick up the story, he stands before the court as a defendant, and his choices have life-or-death consequences. What he says about his beliefs (and *how* he says it) will determine the outcome. This is not armchair philosophy; it's the real thing.

APOLOGY I: SOCRATES' DEFENSE
Our information about Socrates' trial comes from a work called the *Apology* (*apology*, in this context, means "defense"). As we read Socrates' defense before the court, we should be aware of a couple of important details.

First, we are not reading an official court transcript. Instead, we have Plato's recollections of the trial, and he is certainly not an unbiased source. Second, Plato does not provide any account of what Socrates' accusers say in court. Their claims can only be gleaned from Socrates' responses to them (or Plato's representation of Socrates' responses). While we will never have an exact picture of what happened in court on that day, we already know that Socrates had a tendency to irritate people, and the story in the *Apology* is consistent with this.

The *Apology* picks up after Socrates' accusers have laid out their charges. When he opens his defense against the accusations, Socrates comes across as one who suspects that things will not turn out well if he follows his conscience. Apparently, this does not bother him. In fact, he says things that are intentionally inflammatory. Socrates begins by complimenting his accusers for their skillful presentation, but tells the jury that "scarcely a word of what they said was true" (*Apology* 17a). His own words, he says, will not be up to the standards of rhetorical skill displayed by his accusers. He will rely instead on the power of truth, not oratorical style. It is not hard to pick up the innuendo here.

Socrates must respond to two sets of charges made against him—earlier accusations and later, formal charges. The earlier charges state, "Socrates is guilty of criminal meddling, makes the weaker argument defeat the stronger, and teaches others to follow his example" (*Apology* 19b). According to Socrates, these accusations consist of rumors and already-formed impressions of him that have been around for years. Fighting them will require that he argue "against an invisible opponent" (*Apology* 19d), but he vows to address them as adequately as he can.

His first line of defense is to separate himself from the Sophists, with whom he seems to be confused in the popular view. The Sophists were a new school of philosophers who collected fees for teaching the art of persuasive speech (Protagoras, mentioned in the previous chapter, is of this philosophical persuasion). His statement about relying on the force of truth rather than rhetorical skill was his first step in putting distance between himself and the Sophists. He then points out that, unlike the Sophists, he has never collected money for his conversations. He refers to the Sophist, Evenus, whose teaching fee was five minas (a mina was about three months' wages for a laborer). Socrates sarcastically states that this is a very small amount for true wisdom, making it very clear that he does not believe wisdom is a commodity to be sold and that he doubts Evenus has anything worth buying.

In response to the last part of the charge against him—that he teaches others to follow his example—Socrates tells a story. A friend named Chaerephon approached the Oracle of Delphi with an enquiry: Is any person in Athens wiser than Socrates? When the god's answer comes back that Socrates was the wisest, Socrates is baffled. He claims to know nothing, so how could he be the wisest? Thus, Socrates tells us, "After puzzling about it for some time, I set myself at last with considerable reluctance to check the truth of it" (*Apology* 21b).

In order to prove the Oracle wrong, Socrates interviewed people with a reputation for wisdom, starting with the politicians. Given what we saw in the previous chapter, it is not surprising that Socrates, after questioning them, discovered that the city leaders only thought they knew what they were talking about, but were actually clueless. He next goes to the poets. While the poets wrote inspiring works, Socrates concludes that they "deliver all their sublime messages without knowing in the least what they mean" (*Apology* 22c). They create beauty, but do not understand beauty itself. The last group queried was the skilled craftspersons. Socrates admits that they were are technically proficient, but they also did not have understanding. Knowing *how* to do something is different from knowing *why.*

These investigations led Socrates to two conclusions about the Oracle's pronouncement that he was the wisest of the Athenians. First, he concludes that the Oracle was correct. Even though Socrates is in the same boat with everyone he spoke with—he knows nothing—he is ahead in an important way. He at least knows that he knows nothing. This is better than being ignorant without an awareness of one's ignorance. The second conclusion addresses the charge more directly. Socrates cannot be guilty of teaching falsely because, knowing nothing, he does not teach. He only asks questions in search of wisdom. Instead of pretending to know something that he teaches to others, Socrates says that "real wisdom is the property of God, and this oracle is his way of telling us that human wisdom has little or no value. It . . . [is] as if he would say to us, the wisest of you men is he who has realized, like Socrates, that in respect of wisdom he is really worthless" (*Apology* 23ab). This explains Socrates' practice of questioning others. "When I think that any person is not wise, I try to help the cause of God by proving that he is not" (*Apology* 23b).

After Socrates finishes his response to the first set of accusations, he turns to the second, more formal, charges. These state that Socrates "is guilty of corrupting the minds of the young, and of believing in deities of his own invention instead of the gods recognized by the state" (*Apology* 24b). Socrates first takes on the charge that he had corrupted the youth of Athens. He questions Meletus, one of his accusers, about who corrupts or improves the youth. Meletus replies that the jurors, the members of the Council, the Assembly members, indeed, the entire population of Athens all exert a positive influence on the youth. Socrates alone is a corrupter.

If the situation Meletus describes were true (that everyone in the city except Socrates properly trains the next generation), this would be a great world. However, Socrates points out that Meletus does not actually believe what he says. If, for example, Meletus wanted to have a horse trained, he would not turn the job over to just anyone. He would find an expert with the necessary skills. By analogy, if the youth are more valuable than horses, should we not get the best training for them? How could Athens's young receive proper training if we let just anyone do it? Socrates concludes by saying to Meletus, "You have never bothered your head about the young, and you make it perfectly clear that you have never taken the slightest interest in the cause for the sake of which you are now indicting me" (*Apology* 25c).

Socrates then asks Meletus whether his corruption of the young was intentional or unintentional. Meletus answers that Socrates' acts were intentional. Socrates states that it would be foolish to intentionally corrupt anyone. "Am I so hopelessly ignorant as not even to realize that by spoiling the character of one of my companions I shall run the risk of getting some harm from him?" (*Apology* 25e). If, on the other hand, the damage Socrates inflicted on the young was unintentional, it would not be a crime. Moreover, responsible citizens would have taken him aside and corrected him. However, Socrates points out, Meletus and the other accusers did no such thing. For years, Socrates was willing to talk with anyone and have his ideas critiqued, but Meletus and his friends deliberately avoided him. Once again, then, Socrates states that those who bring the charges are not really interested in protecting the youth of Athens. They have some other motive behind their actions.

Socrates now turns to the second formal charge, impiety (which he discussed with Euthyphro in chapter one). In their presentation of this charge, Socrates' opponents claimed that Socrates is an atheist. Socrates asks for clarification of this charge. Does Meletus mean that Socrates embraces religious ideas that are out of the mainstream, or that he disbelieves in divine beings altogether? Meletus states that the latter is the case. With this, Meletus has trapped himself in a contradiction. He had earlier asserted that Socrates believed and taught others "to believe in supernatural activities" (*Apology* 27c). Socrates points out the obvious: it is impossible to conceive of divine activities without the existence of supernatural beings, so how can he be an atheist?

As he completes his formal defense, Socrates anticipates punishments that could be imposed on him if he is found guilty. The death sentence is one possibility. However, Socrates is not intimidated by it. "To be afraid of death is only another form of thinking that one is wise when one is not; it is to think that one knows what one does not know. No one knows with regard to death whether it is not really the greatest blessing that can happen to a man, but people treat it as though they were certain that it is the greatest evil" (*Apology* 29ab). He then gives advance notice that he will not accept a punishment that requires him to stop his philosophical activities. "I owe a greater obedience to God than to you, and so long as I draw breath and have my faculties, I shall never stop practicing philosophy in exhorting you and elucidating the truth for everyone that I meet" (*Apology* 29d).

His closing comments before the jury votes provide insight into how Socrates views his mission. Whether they know it or not, the Athenians need someone who needles them. In fact, Socrates views his persistent questioning as something of a divine commission. "God has specially appointed me to this city, as though it were a large thoroughbred horse which because of its great size is inclined to be lazy and needs the stimulation of some stinging fly. It seems to me that God has attached me to this city to perform the office of such a fly, and all day along I never ceased to settle here, there, and everywhere, rousing, persuading, reproving every one of you. You will not easily find another like me, gentlemen, and if you take my advice you will spare my life" (*Apology* 30e). Socrates concludes that few will vote to spare his life because his task is rather unpleasant for those he is called to serve. His job is to bug them, and no one likes to be bugged.

APOLOGY II: THE VERDICT

The vote was close. If only thirty jurors out of the five hundred had voted otherwise, Socrates would have been back on the street. But the majority voted guilty, and we now enter the sentencing phase of the trial. The crimes for which Socrates has been found guilty had no predetermined sentence. Socrates' accusers have asked for the death sentence and Socrates must suggest an alternative. The jurors cannot entertain a third option. They either choose death, as Socrates' accusers are requesting, or whatever punishment Socrates proposes.

Since death is the prospect if Socrates cannot give a more acceptable choice, most people would think that he should drop the confrontational approach we saw in the first part of the trial. That is not Socrates' style. As he thinks out loud about what penalties he might choose, he continues to say things that will get their dander up. Socrates' first suggestion is maintenance in the Prytaneum. The Prytaneum was a state-owned dining hall reserved for dignitaries and Olympic athletes. Thus, Socrates was suggesting that he ought to be "punished" for his crimes by receiving free meals with Athens's most honored citizens at a high class cafeteria. After all, he is convinced that he performs a great, if unappreciated, service to Athens and ought to be rewarded accordingly.

Socrates predicts that the jury would probably vote for exile if he would ask for it. Anything to get rid of him. However, by forfeiting the opportunity to encourage Athens to seek justice and goodness, he would be shirking his God-given duty. If he lives, he must continue to challenge the Athenians to think through their beliefs, because "life without this sort of examination is not worth living" (*Apology* 38a). Therefore, even though banishment would be acceptable to the court, Socrates cannot in good conscience suggest it. He then settles on a fine as the appropriate punishment. From his own resources, he thought he could afford a mina, the equivalent of three or four months' pay for a skilled craftsperson. However, on the advice of friends who are willing to pay the fine for him, Socrates' final suggestion for punishment is thirty minas. The court must now decide between this fine and death.

APOLOGY III: THE SENTENCE

The jury has decided on the sentence and Socrates is now zero for two; he has been condemned to death. In his final opportunity to address the court, he begins with two thoughts directed at those who voted for conviction. First, he says that he was convicted, not because he was guilty or put up an inadequate defense, but because he refused to pander to the jury. The jurors vowed to consider the facts of the case, and they violated their oath because they felt insulted by him. Thus, the persuasive, but false, rhetoric of his accusers has won out over truth for the moment. While one might suspect that this is just a bit of whining on the part of someone who has lost a case, Socrates' accusations have some warrant. More jurors voted for the death sentence than for a guilty verdict! The conclusion, then, is that at least some of them had no qualms about executing a person they had earlier determined to be innocent.

While Socrates may have lost in the court, he predicts that those who voted for conviction will suffer more than he. Dying as a result of the unjust acts of others is, in the end, not as difficult as living with an injustice you have committed. Furthermore, getting rid of one gadfly does not solve the problem because others will continue to do what he has done. He suggests that a more effective way for the Athenians to deal with critics is to become good people rather than punishing the messengers.

Finally, Socrates addresses those who voted for acquittal. They should not be grieved by the death sentence because "Death is one of two things. Either it is annihilation, and the dead have no consciousness of anything, or, as we are told, it is really a change—a migration of the soul from this place to another" (*Apology* 40cd). If the first is the case, death is like a dreamless sleep and holds nothing to be feared. If the second is true, the good person's soul will migrate to a world in which the great reside. Should this occur, Socrates says, "above all I should like to spend my time there, as here, in examining and searching people's minds, to find out who is really wise among them, and who he thinks that he is" (*Apology* 41b). The bottom line for him is that "nothing can harm a good man either in life or after death" (*Apology* 41c). His last request is that his friends look after his young sons. Above all, they should be corrected if they value money or fame above wisdom.

PHAEDO I: THE SOUL

The *Apology* tells us what Socrates did at his trial but only provides a few clues as to why he did them. Perhaps the biggest question is why he seems so unconcerned about his death sentence. *Phaedo,* a dialogue that occurs just before Socrates' death sentence is to be carried out, gives us a glimpse into the reasons behind his calmness. Because the setting of *Phaedo* is just before Socrates' death sentence is to be carried out, it should not surprise us that a central topic is the nature of death. Nor should it surprise us that

Socrates and his companions agree that they need to define death before they can discuss it intelligently. In this case, they agree on a definition. Death is a state in which "the soul exists in herself, and is parted from the body and the body is parted from the soul" (*Phaedo* 64c).

This answer presupposes some ground already covered in the dialogue. It was previously determined that the human being is a composite of two different parts—body and soul. These two components have different characteristics. The physical body, with its sense capacities, is designed to gather information about other physical objects. The attributes of physical objects—sight, sound, smell, taste and touch—are all imperfect, changeable and temporary, like the body itself.

In contrast, the soul, while real, is not physical. It has none of the characteristics of physical objects nor is it capable of exercising physical activities in itself. Instead, it is an immortal and invisible entity that knows that which is perfect, eternal and nonphysical. We will talk more about these nonphysical things that the soul knows in the next chapter, but they include the concepts behind changeable things. These concepts are not products of objects, but realities that exist separately from physical objects.

This helps illuminate why, in chapter two, Socrates always began by asking for definitions. Physical objects change and are imperfect, but the concepts behind definitions, which are known only by the soul, are enduring and perfect. Therefore, if a philosopher has a choice between putting effort into understanding the temporary and contemplating the eternal, the latter will be the clear winner. This is why, Socrates says, the true philosopher "is entirely concerned with the soul and not with the body. . . . He would like, as far as he can, to be quit of the body and turn to the soul" (*Phaedo* 64e).

We can now understand why Socrates believed he had little to fear from the death sentence. Death affects only temporary things like bodies, not eternal things like souls. If one has no interest in the physical, what is done to the body has no impact. Therefore, while they may kill his body, the jury cannot harm Socrates' soul. How does one kill or damage something they cannot touch? This is why Socrates says at the end of his trial that nothing can harm a good person. Death, rather than doing him injury, actually releases the soul from the limitations of the body.

During the trial, Socrates said that death was either annihilation or the migration of the soul to another location. In *Phaedo* he clearly claims the latter as his position. The body is a prison from which the soul is set free at death. Once emancipated, the soul of one who loves the eternal "departs to the invisible world to the divine and immortal and rational: thither arriving, she lives in bliss and is released from the error and folly of men, their fears and wild passions and all other human ills, and forever dwells . . . in company with the gods" (*Phaedo* 81a). On the other hand, if one's interest is focused on the needs and pleasures of the body during this life, Socrates speculates that his or her soul returns to earth to be embodied once again. In essence, people get what they want. Those who desire freedom from corporeal concerns enter a disembodied existence; those who are hung up on the physical get another physical life.

Because the person who loves wisdom actually looks forward to escaping the restrictions imposed by the body, Socrates says that "philosophy is the practice of death" (*Phaedo* 81a). When we view our physical capacities as inferior and exercise our higher abilities, we are "practicing" for the time when we will be unencumbered by physical desires and needs and can direct our soul's attention to an uninterrupted contemplation of eternal things. Does such a future sound appealing to you? Socrates acknowledges that it would not have much attraction to most people, and it is why few understand his compulsion to self-examination. They are distracted by the immediate concerns and demands of the temporary and physical. For those who have had a taste of the higher things, however, the fleeting pleasures of the physical realm hold little luster.

CRITO: CONTEMPLATING JAIL BREAK

With this background in place concerning Socrates' ideas about the soul, death and immortality, we can pick up the story line in *Crito*. Crito, a close friend, comes early one morning with the news that the ship that must arrive before Socrates can be executed has been sighted. The death sentence will be carried out in a day or two. However, there is another possibility. It was commonly known by all the parties involved that if the right amount of money found its way into the right hands, people would turn their heads while Socrates made an escape. After all, executing an old man for nonviolent activities is messy business, and everyone would be happier with a solution that would get Socrates out of their hair.

Crito plays all the angles to convince Socrates to let his friends bribe the jailers and get him out of town. They have more than enough money to make it happen. Moreover, Crito says, Socrates would contribute to injustice by staying. He was unjustly convicted, and good people do not let injustice stand. Since everyone knows that Socrates' friends can get him out, it will look like they did not care enough to put up the money if the execution goes forward. Crito has friends in another city who will harbor him, and Socrates will have the freedom to philosophize there. These are powerful reasons, but Crito waits until the end to bring out the big guns. He now asks, Don't you care what happens to your wife and three young sons? "What sort of chance are they likely to get? The sort of thing that usually happens to orphans when they lose their parents" (*Crito* 45d). Crito wraps up his arguments with a thinly veiled insult about Socrates' courage.

Socrates does not immediately respond to Crito's specific points. Instead, he wants to determine whether these reasons hold water. "I am and always have been one of those natures who must be guided by reason, whatever the reason may be which upon reflection appears to me to be the best; and now that this fortune has come upon me, I cannot put away the reasons which I have before given: . . . and unless we can find other and better principles on the instant, I am certain not to agree with you" (*Crito* 46bc). In essence, Socrates wants to face death in the same way he lived life. That requires that he make his decisions rationally. He then invites Crito to help him evaluate the arguments for escaping. Crito is not really in a position to refuse.

Socrates points out that not all opinions are of equal value. Some are good and others are worthless. How do we decide whose opinions are worth listening to? Do we not want to give heed to the views of the most qualified rather than simply following the majority? Crito agrees that popular opinion is different from truth and the majority is often wrong. At the same time, Crito reminds us, the majority has the power to put a person to death. Socrates now plays his ace card; it is "not life, but a good life, [that] is to be chiefly valued" (*Crito* 48b). If we value physical life, it is prudent to maintain good public relations. On the other hand, if the life of the soul is more important than biological longevity, what really matters is a *good* life. Since what is right is a different question than what works, "the only question which remains to be considered is, whether we do rightly either in escaping or in suffering others to aid in our escape" (*Crito* 48d).

Now that they are asking the right question, they can decide whether Crito is correct in encouraging Socrates to bail out of Athens. Socrates begins by eliciting an agreement from Crito on a principle that should sound familiar to Christians: "One must not even do wrong when one is wronged" (*Crito* 49b). If this principle is true, they must decide if escaping causes harm to anyone. Socrates points out that we should distinguish between the laws themselves and the way these laws are administered. Socrates and Crito agree that the laws of Athens are good and necessary and have not harmed Socrates. Instead, the harm has come through the unjust *administration* of good laws. His escaping cannot change how bad people use the legal system. Furthermore, if he runs away, Socrates argues, it will send a message that laws can be ignored. The idea that one can flout the law damages society. Therefore, Socrates and Crito agree that Socrates' escape will injure others. The irony here is that Socrates, who faces a death sentence because he is supposed to have corrupted the youth of Athens, refuses to flee because doing so would corrupt the youth of Athens.

Next, Socrates argues that the state plays a role similar to that of parents. Even though parents or governments are imperfect, they teach us what is right and wrong, protect us, and fulfill other important functions that people need. Socrates says that the government of Athens has provided many good things to him over his long life. To flee in the face of an injustice would be ingratitude, much like dishonoring one's parents. Moreover, Socrates has been free to leave Athens at any time. The fact that he has remained and enjoyed its benefits requires that he also take the bad when it comes. In other words, his presence in Athens implies a contract, and every contract involves both rights and responsibilities. We cannot simply take the rights; accepting the rights requires that we assume responsibilities toward the state.

Perhaps Socrates' reasoning is not convincing to you, but Crito reluctantly admits that his reasons for escape evaporate when set against the counterarguments for staying. Socrates then concludes the dialogue by saying, "Then give it up, Crito, and let us follow this course [accepting his execution], since God points out the way" (*Crito* 54e). Socrates has signaled his resolve to accept his fate, and there is no turning back.

PHAEDO II: THE DEATH SCENE

The stubborn old man has decided that he will die, so the only thing left to do was get it over with. The last part of *Phaedo* tells us about execution day. Socrates visited with several friends until just before sundown. Socrates then excused himself to bathe. After this, he said goodbye to his sons and returned to his friends. A jail official came to carry out the death sentence. In Socrates' case, execution would be carried out by drinking the extract of a poisonous plant called hemlock. When he drained the cup in one gulp, several of his friends could no longer contain themselves and broke down in tears. Socrates chastised them for what he considered childish behavior. He walked around until his legs felt heavy, then lay down, the numbness gradually moving up his body. When the effects of the poison reached his heart, he died. However, in his ability to reach down through time and provoke us to self-examination, the spirit of Socrates lives on.

DISSECTING THE TRIAL AND DEATH OF SOCRATES

Socrates' ideas give us a lot to chew on. Before we examine them, however, we should look at his methods, because his death sentence seems to be as much the result of *how* Socrates did things as it was the result of *what* he believed. Our idealistic side finds it difficult not to admire people who are willing to die for their beliefs. This level of commitment to a cause is a rare commodity, and for obvious reasons. We all recognize that, when the going gets tough, it is tempting to fudge on our beliefs to save our skin. Socrates stayed in there when things got sticky, and you have to appreciate that. On the other hand, our pragmatic side cannot help but wonder why Socrates refused to flee and save his life when he could have. Moreover, it didn't even have to get this far. His in-your-face strategy during the trial just dared the jury to sentence him to death, and Socrates indicates at several points that he was deliberately trying to get under their skin. One of my students compared Socrates to an obnoxious junior high student who bugs you until you just want to clobber him, and it isn't hard to see the parallels. This tension between our idealism and pragmatism raises an interesting question. Is Socrates foolishly "asking for it," or is there something heroic about what he does? While the difference between a fool and a hero seems easy to discern, the line that separates them may be slimmer than we think.

It would not be difficult to conclude that Socrates was a fool if he was just a cranky old man with a limited life expectancy just itching to get his shots in. This does not seem to be the case, and I am more inclined to accept what Socrates himself says about his motives and beliefs. However, the sincerity with which one holds beliefs does not settle the "hero or fool" question. Even if he is sincere to the point of death, Socrates may simply be a sincere fool. Was there no way for him to be true to his own beliefs without being so aggravating?

It just may be that we cannot neatly separate Socrates' beliefs from the way he communicates his message. Remember that he describes himself as a gadfly who keeps the horse (the state) from getting too comfortable. A horse is prone to complacency, while gadflies are, well, irritating. If Soc-rates is correct that the state (or any other type of organization) has a nat-ural tendency to stick with the status quo rather than go through the pro-cess of examination necessary for the improvement, drastic wake-up measures are required to provoke thought. Thus, Socrates seems to believe that he cannot do his job without bothering people.

One parallel between the teachings of Christianity and Socrates is that self-examination is necessary for growth. Any church, like any state, is an organization. It is *not merely* an organization, but it is an organization. And if, being an organization, a church is likely to stay with what is com-fortable, what happens to its message of self-examination? Does the church need its own gadflies? A quick survey of the Old Testament prophets might help here. God often sent individuals, irritating individ-uals at that, to wake Israel up and get her back on track. These prophets were rarely appreciated by the people in power, and many of them suf-fered a fate similar to Socrates. An important part of the story, however, is that the message of these prophetic outsiders became part of our Bible, warning us against spiritual complacency. This should stand as a re-minder that we should not automatically swat a gadfly, even though this is a natural impulse. If a church becomes a nonprophet organization (par-don my pun), we lose our edge.

While we would do well to listen to gadflies within the church, a word of caution is advisable for those who believe themselves called to that role. The church continues to need prophets, but a prophet is more than just an irritating person. Persecution was the *result* of doing what Socrates or a prophet did, it was never the *goal*. The main thing is the message, and any would-be gadfly better have one. This brings us back to the point that may have been lost in all this. Our evaluation of whether Socrates was a hero or a fool should depend on whether his messages of self-examination, the priority of the soul over the body, the insignificance of popular opinion, and other ideas are worth dying for.

Socrates' call to self-examination might seem difficult to put together with his famous "Socratic ignorance." What if we do our self-audit and discover, as Socrates did, that we know nothing? How can knowing nothing be very useful? If we take Socrates' claim of total ignorance at face value, then it is not helpful. However, Socrates provides hints that he does not believe that his own ignorance is absolute. At minimum, knowing that you know nothing is to know something (which is just the kind of contradiction Socrates loved to point out in others). Moreover, we discover that he professes to know quite a few things. He knows that it is better to do good than to curry public approval, that care of the soul is more valuable than obsession with the body and, among other things, that we should not injure others. So what do we make of this Socratic ignorance?

Socrates' claim to know nothing seems to be a declaration that he has more to learn. The facts we know are less important than what we know about ourselves. If we begin by recognizing that our knowledge is incomplete and listen to others in hopes of improvement, we are in a position to learn and grow. In short, I think we ought to view Socratic ignorance as a call to open-mindedness. In principle, we might affirm an open mind, but probably no Christian has escaped a warning against an open-mindedness so broad that the brains fall out. Some people do take openness to such an extreme that they lapse into total relativism and never commit to anything. However, that is certainly not Socrates' problem. He demonstrates that openness to other ideas does not inevitably lead to skepticism or relativism. Socrates has strong beliefs about what is right and wrong, true and false, and is willing to die for them. At the same time, he still wants to hear what others say in order to learn whatever he can.

How do we combine openness with commitment? Again, Socrates may provide some assistance. He begins by noting that an opinion, in itself, is not worth much. There are lots of them available, and most of them, whether individual or group opinions, are not ideas you would want to stake your life on. Whether an opinion becomes a belief, for Socrates, is determined by the strength of the reasons that support them. Emotions, biases, wishful thinking, group loyalties will not do the trick for him, even though he acknowledges that they can be quite persuasive. Only good reasons—rational arguments—are sufficient grounding for committing ourselves to an idea.

What are Christians to make of Socrates' commitment to reason? Let's look at some alternatives. It is not uncommon for someone to inform me that some philosopher's ideas (sometimes Socrates' ideas) are out to lunch. When I press them, they often cannot articulate why they disagree other than to say that it is incompatible with what they already believe, which is circular reasoning. This only tells me they disagree because they disagree. If I try to break through the circular reasoning and ask why they have embraced their current views, I normally am not given logical arguments in support. Instead, such questions often get answered in terms of what someone else told them was true, family background, feelings, vague intuitions, experiences or some similar foundation.

Socrates, I believe, would make two observations about these substructures for belief systems. First, the supports listed above are inherently conditional and temporary because they build on things that change constantly. Second, he would argue that, because we recognize the shaky nature of these foundations, we have a difficult time acting on beliefs built on them. This reveals what Socrates finds attractive about reliance on reason. If an opinion can be buttressed by strong reasons that are grounded in unchanging truths, it inspires confidence in our actions. Moreover, a rigorous rational examination of ideas allows us to own our beliefs rather than passively absorb them. At the same time, since Socrates is dedicated to the pursuit of truth, he can remain open to persuasion by better arguments if they become available.

I will argue in the next chapter that a commitment to reason as our sole means of salvation encounters problems on two levels. First, it makes reason the only positive impulse in humans, and views other aspects of our life, such as emotions, the senses and our physical desires, as nothing but obstacles to the good life. Second, Socrates assumes that when we think properly, our will automatically aligns itself with our knowledge to allow us to choose and do what is right. Since we all struggle with the contradiction between knowing what is right and actually doing it, I believe Socrates' confidence in reason as the solution to all our problems is difficult to maintain.

Despite these questions, Socrates makes two points that are hard to argue with. First, we should be willing to give reasons for our beliefs, or at least give reasons why we cannot give reasons. Otherwise, all we have done is asserted an opinion without demonstrating why it should be given any more attention than some other opinion. Second, Socrates seems to have something in common with Christians when he argues that a belief system constructed on eternal and unchanging foundations is preferable to one based on transitory things. The trick, of course, is to determine what that eternal ground is and how we discover it.

Socrates' faith in reason is closely linked with his distinction between the soul and the body. It seems obvious why Socrates would believe in the existence of our body, but why would he, and many other philosophers, believe in something they could not see—the soul? We will go into more detail on this in the next chapter, but the reasons behind partitioning the human into separate components boil down to a simple matter. The parts of our body are not radically different from the body parts of many animals. Dissection of a member of our species and an advanced mammal would yield, for the most part, the same organs in the same places. Moreover, the functions performed by the components of the human *body* would be the same as those provided by a animal. However, many of the functions of the human *being*, the person taken as a whole, appear to be very unique to our species. The fact that I could end the last sentence with the words "our species" highlights one distinction. I can pretty safely assume that only humans (though probably not very many of them) will read this book. We also take it for granted that when we speak of other elements that are part of our everyday existence, such as creating art, establishing institutions, voicing religious or political convictions, evaluating acts in moral categories, we are referring to exclusively human activities. Since we possess no unique physical organs that facilitate these unique functions, Socrates believed that there must be an invisible something—a soul—that allows for these purely human activities. Just as Socrates argues that divine activities are impossible without a divine being (or beings), he says that we cannot have nonphysical functions without a nonphysical source.

Socrates' belief that soul and body are two different things goes well beyond the idea that the *person* consists of a body and a soul. The idea that the soul is unaffected by physical death means that personal existence is not threatened, but enhanced, by freedom from the body. When his body dies, he will not stop being Socrates. He will simply be Socrates without a body. Therefore, the body is not a necessary part of who *I* am. This concept of the person is the source of the claim that has intrigued many of my students. His statement that no one can harm a good person sounds strange coming from someone soon to be executed. If execution does not count as harm, what does? However, if the soul is both immune from injury by physical means and the seat of our identity—the real "I"—then how can *I* be harmed by my body's death?

Many Christians find much in common with Socrates on some of the ideas above. It is not unusual that Christians agree that body and soul are two different things, that the death of the body is not the end of our personal existence and that we should not fear that which could harm the body. However, while many Christians share these conclusions with Socrates, the devil is in the details. Christians may have to part ways with Socrates on certain specifics.

First, while Socrates yearns for a freedom in which the immortal soul is released from a troublesome body, Scripture speaks of our future hope in terms of the "resurrection of the body." It seems clear that "body," as it is used in reference to resurrection, means something more than simply a physical container and something more in line with resurrection of the person. Does this signal that Scripture does not follow Socrates in his view that the body is a temporary and bothersome receptacle for a soul? To put it somewhat differently, if a Christian view of life after death includes, rather than excludes, a bodily component, can we follow Socrates in isolating the soul as the seat of our identity?

Second, we should notice that Socrates views the soul as inherently immortal. It survives the death of the body, and, since the body is not a necessary part of our identity, I do not die. Moreover, since the soul is inherently immortal, it continues to live after the body is shed without outside intervention. On the other hand, the idea of resurrection involves a return to life after death. If a person is not really dead, and in Socrates' view there is no real death of the *person*, then how can we speak of a resurrection (see 1 Cor 15)? Scripture also makes clear that resurrection occurs through outside intervention. *God* raises us. In short, even though many Christians use phrases like "immortality of the soul" and "resurrection from the dead" interchangeably, significant differences should be acknowledged.

Third, many Christians find much in common with Socrates when he says that it is impossible for others to harm a good person and that the quality of one's life is more important than the number of years we live. The Bible is full of examples of those who met an early death for the sake of higher things. Scripture is clear that concern for the physical aspect of our life should be secondary to other things. Furthermore, Socrates and Christianity would seem to agree that, while threats of physical harm may make it difficult to maintain our beliefs, no one could force us to change or deny our belief by using physical means. Beneath the surface, however, a parting of the ways occurs. Socrates believes that others cannot harm us because the soul (the person) is inherently immortal. In contrast, Christianity seems to say that the person can be harmed physically, but the hope of resurrection means that this harm is not final. Resurrection is the overcoming of death by life.

Through the centuries, Christian thought has struggled to maintain a balance between two unhealthy extremes. One extreme is to completely write off philosophers as useless or dangerous to Christians. I find it difficult to maintain this position after reading what Socrates has to say. Most Christians find a lot of common ground with his beliefs that physical death is not ultimate, that evil done to an individual is not decisive in that person's fate, that our story is more than just a log of our physical activities, that life is purposeful and that truth rather than popular opinion should guide our lives.

The other extreme, allowing our understanding of Christianity to be determined by a philosophy rather than revelation, is equally dangerous. Scripture is the primary authority of the faith. Although it seems that, given the phobia many Christians have about philosophy, this second problem would be much less common than the first, I have noticed an irony in the Christian world. Sometimes the same people who tell me that philosophy is unnecessary since all their beliefs come from the Bible espouse ideas that are closer to Socrates' philosophy than Scripture. For example, their concept of life after death often sounds a lot more like Socrates' immortality of the soul than resurrection of the person (or body). This does not surprise me because we always use tools available to us to help us interpret Scripture, and one of the interpretive tools commonly used in Christianity's history has been Socratic philosophy. Recognizing this reminds us of a need for balance. It is impossible to come to any text, the Bible included, with no interpretive apparatus, so it is futile to argue that we can leave philosophy behind when we read Scripture. On the other hand, we should also be aware that these interpretive tools are fallible and do our best to avoid confusing Socrates' message with that of Scripture.

One final feature of Socrates' life deserves attention before we leave him. It is improbable that Socrates at the age of twenty ever imagined that he would face a death sentence. Life has interesting twists that cannot be anticipated. At the same time, he was aware that his life would not go on forever and he used philosophy as his "preparation for death." I am not advocating philosophy as the means of salvation, as Socrates did, but I think he was on to something. First, recognizing the transient nature of this life, he sought to discover that which was eternal and order his actions according to it. Second, he took ideas seriously because he took his life seriously.

It is possible to treat our discussions of ideas as an amusing pastime and leave it at that. Socrates recognized that our ideas will shape how we live and, therefore, that living well involves carefully examining our beliefs. This seems to be the proper connection between the two ways of doing philosophy I mentioned at the beginning of the chapter. Socrates used the more peaceful times to develop ideas that are meaningful enough to die for when push came to shove. It seems that if someone can find something important enough to die for, they may also have discovered something significant enough to live for.

3

PLATO

Is a Just Society Possible?

C hapter two mentioned that Socrates' teachings come to us through the writings of his disciple, Plato. We would expect that Socrates' ideas would leave their mark on his student Plato. However, Socrates may well have taught as much through his death as through his dialogues, and it is clear that the execution of Plato's mentor exerted a major influence on his mature philosophy. What we will focus on in this chapter is how Plato connects Socrates' ideas and his death in what is probably Plato's most important dialogue, *The Republic*. *The Republic* fleshes out ideas about knowledge, the soul and reality that are implicit, but undeveloped, in Socrates. These philosophical subjects are discussed against the horizon of Socrates' death, which is rarely mentioned explicitly but is clearly in Plato's mind as he writes. In *The Republic's* conclusion, Plato combines Socratic ideas with the experience of his teacher's execution to suggest a program for restructuring society.

When we examined the dialogues of Socrates in the two earlier chapters, we discovered his interest in definitions. Behind definitions, he believed, we could find truths that were universal, eternal and immutable. In this venture for pure truth, Socrates argued, one had to overcome distractions from the physical world, which contains things that are specific, temporary and changeable. Plato uses the Socratic idea that reality came in two varieties, eternal and transitory, to develop a concept of two different worlds. Everything in the physical realm, despite the tremendous diversity in this huge category, shares a common characteristic: change. All physical objects come into being at some time. Any one of them can be destroyed. Thus, Plato calls the realm that is perceived by the physical senses the "world of *becoming*."

Plato believes that there is a second domain that exists beyond the physical world. This is what philosophers call the metaphysical realm. (The prefix *meta-* means, among other things, "beyond." Thus, *meta*physics describes that which is beyond the physical.) This metaphysical world—what Plato calls the "world of *being*"—contains realities that are unchanging, perfect and beyond our physical faculties. The perfect entities within this world of being are referred to as Forms or Ideas.

THE FORMS

As a way of explaining what Plato means by a Form, we should ask why he believes these intangible, invisible Forms exist at all. Why believe in things that cannot be seen? Perhaps the quickest way to find our way into this metaphysical realm, according to Plato, is via mathematics. For example, if we were asked to draw a square freehand, the final product, no matter how careful we might be, would be imperfect in many ways. The lines would not be precisely straight or equal in length, and the corners would not be the perfect 90-degree angles demanded by the definition of a square. In fact, even the attempt to draw a line assumes imperfection since, according to geometry, a line has only length and not width.

The fact that we know our visible square is imperfect should lead us to a pivotal question. How can we recognize something as imperfect unless we also know the standard used for comparison? To what are we comparing our sorry attempt at a square? We know that it cannot be another visible example of a square, since this is also bound to be flawed. Instead, what we use as a standard of comparison is not a physical thing, but an idea or definition of square*ness*.

It is the definition, idea or concept of squareness that fascinates Plato. Concepts seem to be the sort of thing that we discover rather than create. Moreover, they have a constancy to them. Squareness, for example, does not differ from place to place or over time. Instead, it has a universal and eternal quality that could not be destroyed, even if all physical examples of squares were destroyed. Moreover, it is the ideal of the square that we have in mind that we use to judge the accuracy and precision of the various physical representations of the concept. When we look at it this way, Plato pops the question: If the concept of squareness is eternal, perfect, universal, and the standard by which we judge imperfect and temporal copies, is not the concept or Form of squareness *more* real than what we touch or see?

The idea that conceptual or mental realities are more real than physical objects takes some getting used to since we are comfortable with definitions of *real* that include verification by the senses. If I can see it, hear it, touch it, smell it or taste it, it's real. Right? As the example above demonstrates, Plato does not deny the reality of sense objects. However, behind sensation, the use of our senses to perceive, is a conceptual process about which we are seldom conscious. This is a process Plato attributes to the soul (or mind), which has the ability to understand nonphysical Forms because the soul is also a thing without physical attributes. These Forms, the intangible realities that are grasped by the soul, are what reside in the world of being. Plato would want us to understand that the Forms themselves are different from the concepts we hold about them, but the key thing at this point is to recognize that we are capable of thinking about things that do not originate from objects, are the standard by which we judge the physical examples that correspond to them and are known by some means other than the senses.

THE CAVE

Now that we have outlined Plato's basic distinction between the world of becoming (physical objects) and the realm of being (Forms), he wants to examine the relationship between these two worlds and demonstrate the importance of recognizing these different levels of reality. To do this, Plato creates an interesting little story, the Allegory of the Cave. To set the stage for the story, he asks us to

> picture men dwelling in a sort of subterranean cavern with a long entrance open to the light on its entire width. Conceive them as having their legs and necks fettered from childhood, so that they remain in the same spot, able to look forward only, and prevented by the fetters from turning their heads. Picture further the light from a fire burning higher up and at a distance behind them, and between the fire and the prisoners and above them a road along which a low wall has been built. . . . See also, then, men carrying past the wall implements of all kinds that rise above the wall, and human images and shapes of animals as well, wrought in stone and wood and every material, some of these bearers presumably speaking and others silent. (*Republic* 514a-515a)

The physical situation of these men, imprisoned in the dark depths of a cave, is miserable. Even more wretched is their mental situation. When Plato asks, "Do you think that these men would have seen anything of themselves or of one another except the shadows cast from the fire on the wall of the cave that fronted them?" (*Republic* 515a) the anticipated answer to this last question is "Certainly not." As Plato has set up his allegory, the shackled prisoners have experienced only the shadows of the unseen objects carried above them cast on the cave's back wall by a flickering fire, and the distorted echoes of the workers' voices. Given this, their understanding of the world can be nothing but extremely limited.

Plato would freely acknowledge that the prisoners could provide accurate reports of the shadows and echoes. In other words, they are correct about their perceptions. However, human beings are incapable of stopping at perceptions. We also interpret these perceptions to say what they mean, what they represent and how they are related to each other. If the prisoners construct their interpretations of the world on this faulty, partial raw material, they will inevitably make mistakes. They will attribute the voices of the unseen workers behind them to the shadows. The flickering shadows themselves will be considered the most real of all entities since the prisoners have seen nothing else. Using this sense data, they will develop beliefs about the universe that contain a small nugget of truth, but their overall understanding of the world will be so far off that those who have a more complete perspective could not help but pity them. Just as they see only shadows of the objects carried back and forth at the front of the cave, their idea of truth is, at best, a shadow of the real thing.

ESCAPING THE CAVE

This would be a very depressing tale if it ended here. However, Plato asks us to imagine what might happen if one of these prisoners "was freed from his fetters and compelled to stand up suddenly and turn his head around and walk and to lift up his eyes to the light" (*Republic* 515c). Anyone who has moved quickly from darkness into light will know the answer. This is a painful experience, so we can well imagine how uncomfortable it might be for this prisoner, whose life has passed in almost total darkness, to gaze toward the fire above and the sunlight that filters through the mouth of the cave.

This physical discomfort would be accompanied by another disconcerting experience. Plato asks, "What do you suppose would be his answer if someone told him that what he had seen before [the shadows] was all a cheat and an illusion, but that now, being nearer to reality and turned toward more real things, he saw more truly? And if also one should point out to him each of the passing objects and constrain him by questions to say what it is, do you not think that he would be at a loss and that he would regard what he formerly saw as more real than the things now pointed out to him?" (*Republic* 515cd). Plato's point is that it would be confusing for the prisoner to see the actual objects in all their three-dimensional glory, instead of just their insubstantial shadows, for the first time. In fact, this individual would likely still consider the shadows real and the things themselves to be "a cheat and an illusion."

Plato has a couple of points in mind here. First, we often confuse that which is familiar with what is true. Since this prisoner has spent his entire life in the shadows, it does not occur to him that they might be misleading. Instead, the new will be suspect because, up to this point, it wasn't even on the radar screen. Many of the truths we now take for granted (e.g., that the earth is round and revolving at a high speed) were once unfamiliar and uncomfortable, even thought to be subversive. These are good reminders that we should be a little slower to reject ideas just because they are new. Plato's second point is closely related. The learning process is painful precisely because it requires that we leave a comfort zone and go places we have not been before. Just as entering into full sunlight from a dark room causes our head to ache, encountering unfamiliar ideas often has us reaching for the aspirin. In fact, Plato thinks that true learning demands so much of us that most will attempt to flee enlightenment.

Because our initial response is to escape from that which brings pain, Plato says that the prisoner will want to return to the familiarity of darkness and chains. Thus, he can only find freedom if "someone should drag him thence by force up the ascent which is rough and steep, and not let him go before he had drawn him out into the light of the sun" (*Republic* 515e). If the prisoner is forced out of his chains and pushed from the cave's darkness, does this mean that some sudden epiphany would enlighten him and provide a more focused and detailed understanding of the world? Not so fast, says Plato.

> There would be need of habituation, I take it, to enable him to see the things higher up. And at first he would most easily discern the shadows and, after that, the likenesses or reflections in water of men and other things, and later, the things themselves, and from these he would go on to contemplate the appearances in the heavens and heaven itself, more easily by night, looking at the light of the stars and the moon, than by day the sun and the sun's light. . . . Finally, I suppose, he would be able to look upon the sun itself and see its true nature, not by reflections in water or phantasms of it in an alien setting, but in and by itself in its own place. (*Republic* 516ab)

Plato has outlined two types of ascent. The physical movement from the depths of the cave, past the fire and figurines and out into the sunlight occurs quickly. However, Plato is more interested in the second type of ascent. In this, one has the opportunity to progress from ignorance to enlightenment. In the allegory this ascent is expressed in terms of increasing degrees of light, ranging from flickering shadows in a dim cavern to the direct intensity of sunlight. The role light plays here can be illuminated by an idea Plato explains earlier in *The Republic*.

THE ANALOGY OF THE SUN

Of all the physical senses, sight is generally deemed the most reliable and complete. When we analyze the visual process, two of its facets quickly come to mind. First, we need eyes, along with all the supporting neurological apparatus, in order to see. We also must have objects, with their shapes and colors, to be seen. However, these two elements alone are not enough. We can walk into a totally dark cave with 20/20 vision and still not see what is there. Without light, we are as good as blind. Plato sees the sun as the ultimate source of light and since it, as the origin of light, facilitates a good process—vision—the sun is good. In addition, just as light facilitates vision, the eye recognizes light in a way we cannot know it by means of hearing, touch, taste and smell. "The sun is not vision, yet as being the cause thereof is beheld by vision itself" (*Republic* 508b).

When the connections between the sun and vision are established, Plato reintroduces the issue of proportionality that was such an important feature of the cave allegory. "When the eyes are no longer turned upon objects upon whose colors the light of day falls but that of the dim luminaries of night, their edge is blunted and they appear almost blind, as if pure vision did not dwell in them. . . . But when . . . they are directed upon objects illumined by the sun, they see clearly, and vision appears to reside in these same eyes" (*Republic* 508cd). Plato's point here is simple. When the light is bright, we see clearly. Visual clarity fades, however, when the sun's luminance is imperfectly reflected by something else.

To this point, Plato has said nothing profound. We all know that we cannot see without light, that seeing is good and therefore light is good and that visual acuity diminishes in dimness. In fact, Plato is counting on the ordinary nature of this information to drive home the point of the analogy. "Apply this comparison to the soul also in this way. When it is firmly fixed on the domain where truth and reality shine resplendent, it apprehends and knows them and appears to possess reason; but when it inclines to that region which is mingled with darkness, the world of becoming and passing away, it opines only and its edge is blunted, and it shifts its opinions hither and thither, and again seems as if it lacked reason" (*Republic* 508cd). Thus, Plato's explanation claims that the soul, like the eye, is an instrument of knowing, and the soul's process of knowing requires something analogous to the sun. Provide enough light and the soul acts in a reasonable manner. If illumination diminishes, the soul's abilities are inhibited and we descend from the world of truth into the realm of conflicting and shifting opinions. What is the sun's intellectual parallel that allows our soul to see truth clearly? Plato calls it "the Good." The Good is not what we know (truth) or the part of us that knows (the soul), but is instead the origin of both truth and knowing. Thus, as useful and beautiful as truth itself is, the Good deserves the highest honor and the greatest level of attention since it is the source of truth.

THE DIVIDED LINE

The Analogy of the Sun establishes a parallel between the sun as the eternal source that enlightens physical vision, and the Good, which enlightens the intellectual realm. As we have noted earlier, the physical realm (the world of becoming) is inferior to what Plato calls the intelligible world (the world of being). He now provides a third model, the Simile of the Divided Line, to explain the different degrees of knowledge. In this simile he begins by dissecting a vertical line into two unequal lengths, the higher representing the intelligible world above and the lower the visible realm. He then subdivides each of these sections into two parts.

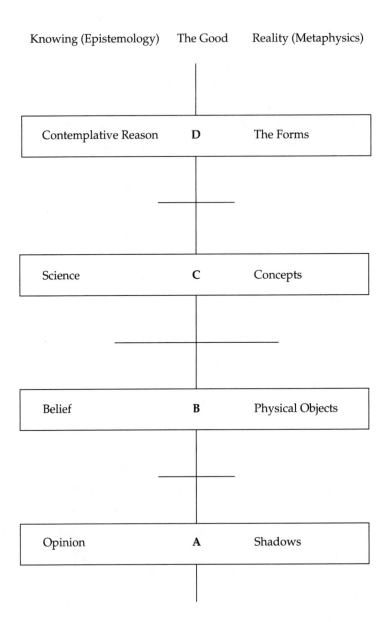

The bottom portion of the line (A) represents what Plato labels as the images. This category contains shadows and reflections. The shadows do exist, but not independently. They are shadows *of* something. The something responsible for the shadows and reflections is found in the next section above (B) where we encounter the objects themselves. Since shadows do not exist without the physical objects, but objects do not require the existence of shadows, the objects have greater reality than the shadows. Moreover, our visual experience with an object adds substantially to what we can learn from shadows. We get color; greater accuracy in determining size, shape and mass; and another dimension—depth. The similarity between these two categories is that shadows and the objects are both perceived by sight. The difference is simply one of the degree of visual acuity. A silhouette leaves us with uncertainty about what we see, but direct vision of the object helps dispel uncertainty. Plato's point about the relationship between a shadow and an object is not difficult to grasp since we are so familiar with the visual realm. The next step, however, requires more explanation.

To get beyond sections A and B, we need to enter a different realm. This level of knowledge takes us beyond the senses and pushes us into the world of conceptual thought. Like the lower half of this line, the top half is also divided into two parts. As Plato explains it, "There is one section of it [C] which the soul is compelled to investigate by treating as images the things imitated in the former division [B], and by means of assumptions from which it proceeds not up to a first principle but down to a conclusion, while there is another section [D] in which it [the soul] advances from its assumption to a beginning or principle that transcends assumption, and in which it makes no use of the images employed by the other section [B], relying on ideas only and progressing systematically through ideas" (*Republic* 510ab).

Plato's rather complicated point is that one form of reasoning gets beyond observation of particular objects by developing hypotheses ("assumptions" in the quote above). As the example earlier in the chapter demonstrated, we do not simply know individual examples of squares.

We also have a general concept of squareness. Squareness is a theoretical construct that we apply to objects and pictures that differ in important ways, even though all are squares. Similarly, we can have concepts of anything that exists in the physical realm: cars, lettuce or ears. Therefore, in section C we have something that straddles the visible and the intelligible worlds. The concepts or theories themselves are not objects of sense, but they can be applied to objects of sense experience. If we have a general definition of *mammal*, for example, we can use this concept to correctly identify an animal we have never encountered as a mammal. Moreover, even though the physical examples of mammals, cars, lettuce or ears can be destroyed, the concepts behind these things are eternal.

If, however, we move from a theory to another level of abstraction, we arrive at section D. Explanation of how this category works is difficult, and even Plato was at something of a loss to describe it fully. To make a beginning of it, however, we might go back to the illustration of the shadow and the object. Just as a shadow is a shadow *of* something, a concept is a concept *of* something that transcends it. What transcends our concept of beauty, for example, is what Plato calls the Form of beauty. Our mental notion of all that comprises beauty is inevitably incomplete in the same way that our knowledge of a physical object is deficient when we see only the shadow. However, the Form of beauty is perfect in the sense that it is not created, not changeable and indestructible. Knowledge on this level does not descend back into the sensible world, but remains within the conceptual realm. Despite the high regard Plato has for the individual Forms, they are still not the ultimate reality. Instead, just as the physical act of seeing requires the sun, the forms of squareness, beauty and anything else originate in the "absolute Form of the Good."

Plato then proceeds to sum up his Simile of the Divided Line. "And now, answering to these four sections, assume these four affections occurring in the soul: intellection or reason for the highest [D], understanding for the second [C]; assign belief to the third [B], and to the last picture-thinking or conjecture [A], and arrange them in a proportion, considering that they participate in clearness and precision in the same degree as their objects partake of truth and reality" (*Republic* 511de).

BACK TO THE CAVE

Plato's Analogy of the Sun and the Simile of the Divided Line provide some useful interpretive keys for his Allegory of the Cave. The prisoner, while chained at the bottom of the cave and observing only the shadows, has a small taste of what the world is like. The shadows are the result of unseen objects projected by a miniscule amount of light. However, because the objects themselves are imperfect and the light dim, the most the prisoner can hope for is what Plato refers to as opinion. In other words, he is trapped in section A on the Divided Line. When the ascent from the cave floor occurs, the light, though still indirect, intensifies and the figurines carried about on the workers' shoulders are seen directly, our prisoner can now know on the level of belief (section B on the Divided Line).

The prisoner reaches a new plateau if he is able to understand the relationship between the light coming both from the mouth of the cave and the flickering fire, the objects and the shadows. He can move from a particular instance in which a shadow is cast by a solid object blocking light to a general theory about how shadows will always result when any solid thing obstructs light from any source, and will be able to use this hypothesis to predict results in various situations. This level is that of science, or understanding (section C). When our freed prisoner reaches section D, he contemplates light itself, undistracted by considerations about different intensity levels or the various instances or sources of light. But the height of all knowing is when one goes beyond the light to mentally dwell on the perfect, immutable, eternal source of it all—the Good—which Plato says is "the cause for all things of all that is right and beautiful, giving birth in the visible world to light, and the author of light and itself in the intelligible world being the authentic source of truth and reason" (*Republic* 517c). We should also note that the increasing levels of knowledge available as one moves from the bowels of the cave into the sunlight is not just a matter of increasing light levels. What we know is also enhanced because that which is known at the top of the ascent, the Forms, possesses greater reality than the physical objects accessible to the senses.

Allegories, by design, stuff a lot of meaning into the various elements within the story. We have already seen how the ascent from the cave symbolizes different degrees of reality and truth. This provides the foundation for Plato's next move, which is to examine what happens to the person who "leaves the cave." At first, the prisoner did not realize he was a prisoner. We cannot know that we lack freedom if we have never experienced it. Now, however, the liberated prisoner realizes that "the region revealed through sight [is like] the habitation of the prison" (*Republic* 517b).

Once emancipation occurs, Plato says that we should "not be surprised that those who have attained to this height are not willing to occupy themselves with the affairs of men, but their souls ever feel the upward urge and the yearning for that sojourn above" (*Republic* 517cd). Obviously, an enlightened individual will be a very different person than when he was a prisoner, and Plato believes that the sun's illumination is so attractive that our prisoner will never want to descend into darkness again. Ignorance is only appealing to the ignorant. Plato also believes that the enlightened person has a second reason not to return to the cave and its shadows. "Do you think it at all strange if a man returning from divine contemplations to the petty miseries of men cuts a sorry figure and appears most ridiculous, if, while still blinking through the gloom, and before he has become sufficiently accustomed to the environing darkness, he is compelled in courtrooms or elsewhere to contend about the shadows of justice or the images that cast the shadows and to wrangle in debate about the notions of these things in the minds of those who have never seen justice itself?" (*Republic* 517de).

The picture of an intellectually enlightened individual forced to deal with those who know only darkness is, on one level, a thinly veiled reference to the fate of Socrates. Socrates knew the higher things and, when "compelled in courtrooms . . . to contend about the shadows of justice," looked like a fool to those trapped in the world of sense experience. Plato believes that, regardless of popular opinion, those who convicted and executed Socrates will be considered the true fools by those who know justice itself. In a more general way, Plato attempts to make the point that the majority will always misunderstand those who have experienced truth and reality in the highest forms. In fact, when those who return to the cave describe what they have experienced, they will be viewed as dangerous.

The image that Plato paints here is worth considering. As we have just mentioned, the philosopher who considers things in themselves will appear odd to those imprisoned in the world of sense, and those who remain in the cave will appear ridiculous and pitiful to the philosopher. Each group functions according to standards that appear crazy to the other side. Therefore, the things that would motivate the prisoners to honor one of their members would be of no account to those who escaped the prison. In short, the differences in what one knows and takes to be real will bring a rearrangement in values and priorities, and what one group understands to be important will be thought foolish by the other. This explains why Plato does not buy into the currently vogue notion that two different ways of looking at things are often equally valid. Instead, he unapologetically asserts that those who have "seen the light" are in a superior position to those who remain in the dark. Darkness, for Plato, is a metaphor for misery, even if those in misery are completely unaware of their misery.

PLATO'S APPLICATION OF THE ALLEGORY OF THE CAVE

At this point, we might ask what value can be found in this abstract discussion of ascending levels of intellectual clarity. This brings us to the practical application Plato has in mind for this allegory. He believes that those who have seen the light should be the political leaders. One may think that philosophers would be the last choice for running a government, but that is exactly what Plato proposes. One of his main points is that the life of the shadows immerses one in the transitory world of the physical and thus makes a person the slave to bodily needs and desires. As a result, what they see as important, just and good for themselves and others is constantly shifting. Or, as Plato puts it, the shadow-dwellers "have no single aim and purpose in life to which all their actions, public and private, must be directed" (*Republic* 519c). In contrast, those who know the eternal things, which Plato likens to the divine, will have a stable, rational understanding of the unchanging and perfect Good. They can ground government in that which is most real, and all will benefit from this strong dose of reality.

Plato's idea that those whose souls direct their lives are those best suited for governing comes into immediate conflict with what we have just mentioned. The vast majority of people do not understand the philosophers. In fact, they seem very odd. Why, then, would the philosopher want to go back into the darkness of the cave and interact with those who do not appreciate or comprehend that which is truly good? Plato's response is that "the law is not concerned with the special happiness of any class in the state, but is trying to produce this condition in the city as a whole, harmonizing and adapting the citizens to one another" (*Republic* 519e).

The sentiment expressed above sounds quite noble. Plato is stating that those who make the laws should be motivated to seek more than just their own happiness (attained by staying among their own) but should use their skill to create a good living situation for all. This nobility is somewhat blunted by the fact that Plato finds it necessary that the philosopher rule "by persuasion and compulsion" (*Republic* 519e), but we will pass over this fact for now. The immediate question is why these philosopher-rulers will have the motivation to work for the good of the whole. Plato's answer is that a true education provides a vision of the big picture in full clarity. This, in turn, generates such a love of the good that benevolence toward all people will be a natural result. In other words, those who think correctly will, as a result, act correctly.

Therefore, Plato says to those whose souls are now free from the darkness of the cave,

Down you must go then, each in his turn, to the habitation of the others and accustom yourselves to the observation of the obscure things there. For once habituated you will discern them infinitely better than the dwellers there, and you will know what each of the "idols" is and whereof it is a semblance, because you have seen the reality of the beautiful, the just and the good. So our city will be governed by us and you with waking minds, and not, as most cities now which are inhabited and ruled darkly as in a dream by men who fight one another for shadows and wrangle for office as if that were a great good, when the truth is that the city in which those who are to rule are least eager to hold office must needs be best administered and most free from dissension. (*Republic* 520cd)

When the focus is on the eternal good of all rather than pursuit of temporary goods, such as wrangling for prestigious offices, political leaders will not repeat injustices such as those imposed on Socrates.

DISSECTING PLATO

Although most Christians would not automatically think of Plato as someone whose philosophy might mirror many Christian ideas, it has not always been that way. In its early history, the Christian church made extensive use of Plato's philosophy as a framework for its theology. I hope it is not difficult to see why the church had such great respect for Plato. Even in this small sample of his thought, we can find broad areas of compatibility between Christianity and Platonism.

One point in common between Christianity and Plato is that both teach that the highest *object* of our knowledge is perfect and divine, and that this perfect reality is also the *source* of all knowledge. The convergence of thought concerning the nature of this ultimate reality is striking. Both Plato and traditional Christianity have ascribed the attributes of perfection, intangibility, eternity, immutability, self-sufficiency and goodness to this ultimate reality. In fact, many early theologians said that Plato's concept of the Good could be easily transposed into a Christian key by removing an *o* and substituting the word *God* (see chapter five).

The similarities between Plato's Good and Christianity's God raise an interesting question, especially when viewed against Plato's background. The religion of Athens that Plato grew up with included many gods who were imperfect in just about every way, so this cannot be the origin of his idea of the Good. Moreover, Plato died about 350 years before Jesus was born, and, although he was certainly aware of Judaism, there is no evidence that Jewish thought influenced his ideas. How, then, is it possible that Plato could come to believe in a perfect, divine Good that shares so many attributes with God?

While the earlier part of his chapter does not explicitly address the reasons that led Plato to believe that the Good existed, one way Plato answers this question is by arguing that the highest object that can be known (the Good) is also the *means* by which we know. In his Analogy of the Sun, Plato says that the perfect light of the Good provides illumination for the mind so that we might know truth. And since the Good is the highest truth to be known, true enlightenment should eventually lead us to the perfect reality that is the source of the light. A Christian version of Plato's argument works in a similar manner. God is perfect in his rationality. As the ultimate source of truth and reason, then, God is the origin of the rational powers of our mind. Therefore, it would seem natural that rational thought will lead us to the highest truth—God. Thus, many Christians are not surprised at all that Plato was able to think his way to a being who shares many attributes of the God of Christianity. Logical thought kicks off a search that brings us back to the origin of all logic.

On the other hand, other Christians are hesitant to attribute such power to human reason. There are at least two reasons for this caution. First, it looks too much like a Tower of Babel scenario, in which people suffer God's judgment for relying on human effort to work their way to God. In response, one might argue that this is not a Babel case where we rely exclusively on our own abilities. Instead, God himself is the one who illuminates the reason so we will come to know of him. Even though human reason is the medium by which God is known, by itself the mind is incapable of "seeing," in the same way that a person cannot see objects in a completely dark cave without a light source. God reveals himself willingly by providing illumination for our mind. In other words, this is revelation, not discovery.

A second reason many Christians are reluctant to say that God can be known by reason is that this seems to leave little room for faith. Where does believing fit in when we have seeing? Although the relationship between faith and reason is a huge issue (and one that will receive significant attention in later chapters), one way of putting them together is hinted at by Plato. You will notice that while he believes that knowledge of perfect entities such as the Forms and the Good is possible, he does not claim that we have perfect knowledge of perfect things. Instead, he believes that our understanding of divine, eternal realities is partial and incomplete in this life. Stated otherwise, on this side of death, we see the perfect and good "through a glass darkly." This knowledge, for both Plato and Christianity, is perfected only in a future life that transcends earthly existence. It may be, then, that the incomplete state of our knowledge of the perfect leaves room for faith. It may be also that faith does not refer exclusively to the use of our intellect, but also requires that we include the will. We will address this below.

Plato's ability to conceive of the Good through logical arguments, apart from reliance on Scripture, raises at least two important questions. Is reason a useful tool for communicating our ideas about the nature and existence of God to those outside the faith? If Plato is correct when he says that the eternal source of truth leads us back to divine truth, we might have more common ground to discuss the nature and existence of God with non-Christians than we normally assume. Second, while Christianity finds Plato's description of the Good an incomplete picture of the fullness of God, no Christian would claim a perfect understanding of God either. Given our own limited comprehension of God, is it possible that Christians can learn truths about God from non-Christians? How we answer the questions above will have significant implications for how we interact with those outside the faith.

Another point Christians have in common with Plato is the idea that human beings are enslaved without truth and that discovering the truth results in a form of salvation. This does not suggest that Plato's concept of salvation is exactly the same as that found in Christianity, but there are several intersections. First, Plato's philosophy seems consistent with Christianity's view that one of the greatest obstacles to salvation is our tendency to be distracted by immediate, lesser goods that appeal to our physical urges and appetites. The physical chains that bind Plato's prisoner are not the most important cause of his enslavement. Even when released from the chains, the prisoner wants to remain in the dark and is thus still enslaved. Christianity also argues that the most profound form of imprisonment is not physical, but spiritual. For both, then, real freedom comes only when "the truth shall set you free."

Christians also agree with Plato that salvation (or enlightenment) changes how we view the world. When Plato's prisoner is pushed out of the cave, new and deeper dimensions of reality unfold before him. This change in the way he sees the world also results in a rearrangement of values. Eternal realities replace the shadows, and become the means by which he now measures everything else. To put it in a more contemporary medium, the cave-dwellers live by the bumper sticker that says, "The one who dies with the most toys, wins." Plato and the Christian would be more likely to say, "The one who dies with the most toys only had toys in the first place." The liberated prisoner who has "seen the light" no longer finds the old things attractive.

Finally, both Plato and Christianity argue that divine enlightenment leads to an obligation to spread the message and serve those who have not experienced this salvation. Plato recognizes that the person who knows the eternal will be strongly tempted to remain in the realm of the eternal Sun and associate only with those who share these values and ideas. In spite of this, he urges them to do as Socrates did. Athens needs what Socrates offered them—a wisdom that comes from knowing the best and highest. At the same time, Socrates' fate reminded Plato that the majority, who remained in the shadows, would not be enthusiastic when told about a dimension of reality that was completely alien to them.

This parallels the impulse of many Christians to remain within the safety of their own groups. We share values and a common way of understanding the world, and that is comfortable. However, we are also called to reach out to those who might not be too excited about hearing our point of view, especially when we portray it as a *better* point of view. Thus, the Christian might readily identify with Plato's Allegory of the Cave when he describes how odd (and dangerous) those freed from enslavement will seem to people who have not experienced this freedom. If nothing else, Plato helps us understand why our system of doctrines and values sounds so foreign to an outsider. It *is* foreign ground.

While I have focused on motifs and ideas in Plato that are compatible with Christianity, we should not overlook the fact that these two systems of thought part ways on important issues. In the previous chapter, it was noted that Christianity does not seem to view the body as negatively as Socrates did. In a related manner, I would argue that Christianity has a more positive view of the physical realm in general than Plato teaches. It is true that both Plato and Christianity view obsession with the physical realm as a hindrance to the development of our higher faculties. However, Plato sees the decision between remaining in the physical world and the contemplation of the eternal, nonphysical forms as an either-or choice. The physical is always a nuisance and a distraction from the Forms. The transient always leads us away from the eternal.

Christianity offers a more positive view of the physical realm. First, the Christian doctrine of creation does not allow us to follow Plato in his denigration of the physical. If God creates the physical realm and declares it good, it cannot be written off. The fact that the psalmist tells us that "the whole earth is filled with his [God's] glory" reminds us that the physical realm can be a receptacle of and a pointer toward the divine, a position that Plato's philosophy makes impossible. Even if we argue that the physical has been spoiled by sin, we should remember that Scripture views it as redeemable by anticipating not only a "new heaven" but also a "new earth " (Rev 21:1). Plato could not imagine that the physical world could be redeemed. Those who seek to be complete must transcend it. These differing views about the value of the material realm help explain why some Christian thinkers find a helpful corrective to Plato in Aristotle's thought (see the next chapter).

Plato's trust in reason as the basis of salvation also marks a departure from Christianity. First, while few deny that humans have a capacity for reason, rationality is not the sum total of human existence. We are social, emotional, spiritual, sensing beings as well. When it comes to establishing the footings for our beliefs, then, why does Plato argue that we put everything aside other than reason? As we saw above, his answer is that reason alone allows us to know what is consistent and permanent, while other potential bases offer only the transitory. Social customs change, experiences differ from person to person, we often fight competing intuitions within ourselves, and sense experience is only momentary. These are all part of the realm of shadows and are thus relegated to the realm of opinion, not truth. Plato would tell us that we should stick with that which is eternal, and only reason provides access to this. However, drawing such a heavy line between reason and other human capacities seems to tell us that everything other than reason is not only useless in the pursuit of truth, but a hindrance. The problem is how we integrate the various facets of our life when Plato's ideal of human existence—the purely rational person—excludes so much that is central to our nature.

Second, Plato does not see reason as only a way to distinguish good opinions from bad ones. Instead, as we have said, it is the means of our salvation. A good person is one who understands eternal realities, and Socrates assumes that when a person understands these eternal realities, he or she will act on them. As he might put it, if we *knew* better we would *do* better. What may be overlooked, however, is the will. *Knowing* what is good, right and eternal does not inevitably lead to *doing* what is good, right and in conformity with the eternal. Since doing is a product of the will, it seems that we frequently experience a short circuit between the reason and the will. This casts doubt on Plato's assumption that once reason has a firm grasp on the truth, our will follows its direction. Similarly, I would guess that most people would not be as confident that the philosopher-kings Plato envisions as the future rulers of Athens would, merely by virtue of their understanding of eternal things, always act in selfless ways for the benefit of the whole.

Finally, Plato is doubtful that any more than a small percentage of people will ever escape the cave because few have the intellectual capacity to rise above the immediate gratification of physical appetites. Since the masses will never understand the enlightened, they will need to be controlled by manipulation. While Christians have doctrinal differences on how many people might be saved, most believe that salvation is at least an option for all. The reason is that Christianity understands salvation, which has its roots in faith, as functioning primarily on the level of will rather than the intellect. Stated otherwise, faith seems to speak about commitment, an act of the will, rather than intellectual belief, a function of the mind. This distinction might provide clues to the relationship between faith and reason. It opens up the possibility that we might have intellectual clarity and assent without faith, or faith without intellectual understanding. We will return to the complicated question of faith and reason in later chapters.

4

ARISTOTLE
Do You Want to Be Happy?

Is it possible for a person who believes that she is happy to be wrong about whether she is, in reality, happy? At first glance, this seems like an odd question. Imagine someone telling you, "No, I'm sorry. Regardless of what you think, you are not happy." The first instinct is to say that one's happiness is not the sort of thing a person could be wrong about. Each individual is in a unique position to know how he or she feels. A second look at the question, however, might lead us to ask whether happiness refers to more than just an emotion. We are, after all, familiar with thinking of large blocks of our life as happy or unhappy, even when these times are interspersed with moments of the contrary feelings. Moreover, when we attempt to gauge the happiness of an extended period of our life, we do not simply add up the duration of pleasant emotions and subtract it from the total duration of unpleasant feelings. In short, we recognize an aspect of happiness that is different from transient emotional experience.

The upshot of the opening paragraph is that our judgments about whether a person can be wrong about their happiness depend on which definition of happiness we use. Are we talking about one's emotional state at the moment, or is it something more like an extended state of being? In the abstract, we might settle the question just by prescribing a definition and going from there. However, we do not live an abstraction. In real life we do not just want to talk about happiness; we want to *be* happy. Since happiness is a big deal for us, an important question is which definition we *should* use as our starting point. Beginning with the wrong target means that we might miss something we want.

The context for this discussion of happiness is provided by what I suspect is a common scenario. Often, when someone is asked why he or she decided on a belief or course of action, the answer is something like, "I just feel this is right." In other words, what one believes or does is directed by feelings or emotions that are thought to lead, ultimately, to happiness. The underlying assumption sometimes seems to be that our emotional state corresponds in some way with truth (or, at least, what is true for us). Those more suspicious of the emotions will respond that how we feel has little to do with what is right or good. The assumption behind this is that our feelings should either be ignored or stuffed into the background when it comes to important decisions. This party will then usually argue that reason should be the arbiter of our actions and ideas.

How do we get past the "emotion versus reason" impasse? Usually, we see little progress beyond this point because the debate is shifted to the realm of personality types. On the one hand, there are "feelers," who rely heavily on the affective side when making decisions. On the other hand, "thinkers" work through the logic of the different options, and then make a rational decision. The presupposition is often that an individual is either a feeler or a thinker and that is that. Nevertheless, while it is hard to ignore that these personality differences exist, it is problematic to think (or feel) that we can resolve the debate by categorization. No one I know is *only* a thinker or a feeler, and experience tells us that we cannot neatly separate thinking and feeling in our own experience. What seems rational to a person is influenced by his or her emotional attachments. My love for my children makes it perfectly reasonable (to me) to believe that they are the most amazing specimens of our species to have ever existed. On the other side of the equation, one's feelings about various events will be shaped by pre-existing beliefs. For example, two people who hear about an abortion obtained by a seventeen-year-old may have very different emotional responses. It is not the incident itself that accounts for this variation. Instead, the difference in preexisting beliefs, for which rational arguments can be offered, explains the difference in the feelings evoked.

Since it does not seem possible or advisable to dispense with either reason or emotion, what is the proper relationship between the two? Aristotle attempts to answer this question against the backdrop of our search for happiness. His discussion of happiness, reason and the meaning of life in *Nicomachean Ethics* has all the intellectual heft you would expect of a first-rate philosopher. However, there is something else you ought to know about this book. It is dedicated to his son, Nicomacheus. Like any decent father, Aristotle wants the best life possible for his son. Therefore, we should remember that Aristotle did not see this work as a dry, intellectual exercise. He wants to provide wise guidance to a beloved son who has important choices to make about life. And Aristotle believes that the difference between a good life and one that fails to bring satisfaction pivots on whether we are wise enough to make the right choices.

PLATO AND ARISTOTLE

The lives of two of history's greatest philosophers are closely intertwined. Aristotle, at the age of seventeen, traveled from his home in Macedonia to study with Plato at the Academy. He studied there for the next twenty years until Plato died. Aristotle's reasons for leaving the Academy are unclear. There is some reason to believe that his departure was the result of disappointment at being passed over to head the Academy.

Five years after his departure, he was called by Philip of Macedonia to become the tutor for his son, Alexander. Alexander, who was about twelve at this time, became better known later as Alexander the Great. While Aristotle might have hoped that Alexander would become one of the enlightened philosopher-kings of a Greek city-state, it didn't work out quite that way. Alexander became the warrior-king who, according to legend, broke down and wept because there were no more worlds for him to conquer. Even though the king did not quite achieve the ideal his teacher envisioned, he treated Aristotle favorably and was instrumental in helping Aristotle establish a school in Athens, the Lyceum. However, upon Alexander's death, Aristotle found himself on the wrong side of the political machine in Athens. He, like Socrates, was charged with impiety. Unlike Socrates, he fled the city, stating that he would not give Athens "the opportunity to sin twice against philosophy."

One can see the influence of Plato in much of Aristotle's philosophy, but Aristotle was far from simply an echo of his teacher. He departs from Plato's thought in fundamental ways. While it is beyond the scope of our interests to look at all the contrasts, one difference should be clear in this chapter. Change, for Plato, obscures reality. In contrast, Aristotle is much more interested in nature because he believed that reality was found in the midst of the shifting, everyday world revealed to us by the senses. Therefore, we do not find in Aristotle the fear and rejection of the material realm that was so much a part of Plato's thought. What Aristotle retains from Plato, however, is a faith in reason to lead us to the best possible life and society.

AIMING AT A GOAL

Nicomachean Ethics begins with an observation: "Every art and every inquiry, and similarly every action and pursuit, is thought to aim at some good; and for this reason the good has rightly been declared to be that at which all things aim" (1.1). We do not simply do things; we do things for a reason. We engage in medical activities to preserve health. Shipbuilding provides seafaring vessels. Economic ventures aim to produce wealth. The good in these activities, then, is not the activity itself, but achieving the goal of the activity. Aristotle's next observation is that not every goal is an end in itself. Some goals are intermediate and support a higher, more ultimate, end. For example, we do not produce bridles just to have a bridle.

Instead, bridles and other equestrian equipment serve the end of horse-manship. Similarly, riding is an intermediate end that serves the purpose of military strategy, and so on.

Since not all goals are of equal importance, Aristotle argues that we should determine what our highest aim is. This is only natural if subordinate goals serve the purpose of the higher ends. If we identify the highest good, this will guide us in ordering all of our activities. It also seems natural that, if lower things support the higher, the highest of all our goals is "that which is always desirable in itself and never for the sake of something else" (*Nicomachean Ethics* 1.7). Aristotle starts his search for what might constitute our ultimate end by evaluating three common contenders—pleasure, honor and wealth. He rejects the idea that pleasure is our highest goal because even ignorant brutes are capable of pleasure. As we will see below, the loftiest aim of human beings must employ our highest capacities. Though many propose that our final end is honor, Aristotle says that, since we receive honor from others, it is not something we control. That which we seek above all else should be the result of our own actions, not the opinions of others. Finally, many believe that accumulation of wealth is the most fundamental aim of the human species. Aristotle rejects this also because money is only useful to the extent that it allows us to pursue other ends.

If pleasure, honor and wealth are not the highest aim of humans, what is? Aristotle believes that our actions provide the answer. The goal we seek above all others, and by means of all our activities, is happiness. When we remember that Aristotle is speaking about the ultimate meaning of our life, his quick and rather dogmatic statement that happiness is the highest pursuit of human existence sounds a bit anticlimactic. It seems we should have to work a little harder at answering the most basic question of life. However, Aristotle would say that the common sense and obvious character of the answer points toward its validity. Why do people seek wealth, pleasure, fame, power or love? Would they do it if they did not think these things would make them happy? They may be mistaken about whether these things will actually bring happiness, but Aristotle says that the desire for happiness is programmed into the structure of our being. We all want it. Moreover, if we ask the question "Why do I want to be happy?" something interesting happens. Our answers bring us right back to where we started. We want to be happy because it makes us happy. It does not seem that we can get any more basic than happiness in our pursuits. Thus, Aristotle says, if we cannot point to some higher purpose behind happiness, it must be an end in itself.

HAPPINESS FOR HUMANS

While Aristotle does not find it necessary to propose a complicated argument to prove that happiness is the final end of human endeavor, he does invest a significant amount of time on the questions of how humans can achieve this goal and what true happiness is. This is necessary because, even though we have a built-in desire for happiness, we can be mistaken about how we get it or exactly what it is we should get. For Aristotle the key to both the "how" and "what" questions concerning happiness is found in function. A flutist, artist or sculptor must function in a particular manner to be considered good at what they do. There are standards for measuring proficiencies in these specific skill areas. Is there likewise a distinctively *human* function that applies to all people regardless of their profession? Does a standard exist that determines whether a human is a *good* human?

Since our question concerns *human* goodness, Aristotle suggests that we should look for some capacity that is unique to the species. Once we locate that, the capacity reveals our purpose. Aristotle says that our defining function is not found in life itself since even plants have this capacity. Nor is our route to happiness located in pleasures that come through the senses. Animals also possess sense abilities and draw pleasure through taste, touch, vision, smell and hearing. Aristotle says that the capacity that sets human beings apart from trees and quadrupeds is rationality, an activity of the soul. If this is our highest faculty, "human good turns out to be activity of soul in accordance with virtue, and if there are more than one virtue, in accordance with the best and most complete. But we must add 'in a complete life.' For one swallow does not make a summer, nor does one day, and so too one day, or a short time, does not make a man blessed and happy" (*Nicomachean Ethics* 1.7).

Aristotle has introduced a number of noteworthy elements—rationality, virtue and durability—in describing the path to and nature of happiness. We will examine these in order. First, he signals his solidarity with Plato, his teacher, by assigning reason to the soul, and gives our mental operations priority over the strictly physical functions of nutrition and sensation. A good plant is one that is capable of drawing nutrition from the soil. A good animal is one whose life is sustained by using its powers of sensation. Good human beings also possess these powers, but as the lower supports the higher, their function is to provide a support system for reason. A good, and therefore happy, person is one whose reason directs use of the body's senses and nutritive powers toward a higher purpose.

A second element in Aristotle's definition of the ultimate human good is the idea of virtue. While a more complete description of virtue will come later, one important feature of the term needs clarification up front. As we use the term today, *virtue* tends to have a strictly ethical sense. Aristotle's definition is broader, and might be translated as "excellence." To know what constitutes the virtue or excellence of something requires that we understand the thing's nature. In other words, a thing that functions virtuously is something that works as it was intended to. For human beings, then, "the virtue of man also will be the state of character which makes a man good and which makes him do his own work well" (*Nicomachean Ethics* 2.3). Thus, Aristotle's concept of virtue is closely linked with recognition of our most powerful capacity. We can only understand and fulfill our purpose in life if we know what is most important or excellent about us. A partial or incorrect comprehension of human nature that draws our energies primarily toward our physical appetites and sensations causes us to fall short of fulfilling the purposes that are proper to our nature. The virtuous person, therefore, is one who is guided by reason.

The final feature in Aristotle's definition of happiness concerns time-frame. True happiness is measured by a lifetime, not a day. This has led many to suggest that the better translation for *eudaimonia* (the term usually rendered happiness) would be "well-being" or "flourishing." Thus, as we see above, the virtue that leads to happiness is described as a "state of character," not a feeling or, as Aristotle calls it, a passion. There are several reasons we should not equate the passions with virtue. First, the types of emotions we experience are not determined by whether we are good or bad people. Both the morally pure and impure feel anger and fear, for example. Second, "We feel anger and fear without choice, but the virtues are modes of choice or involve choice" (*Nicomachean Ethics* 2.5). Thus, when we combine this with the idea that rationality is the premier capacity of human nature and the means by which we achieve the happiness we seek, it becomes clear that Aristotle falls closer to the "thinker" end of the continuum than he does the "feeler" side. However, he does not ignore emotion's role in our pursuit of happiness. Our passions are present in every situation we face. The task of the good person is to bring the emotions under control. We must learn "to feel them [our passions] at the right times, with reference to the right objects, towards the right people, with the right motive, and in the right way" (*Nicomachean Ethics* 2.6).

THE GOLDEN MEAN

Aristotle argues that feeling itself is not wrong. Passions can either be very good and useful, or they can destroy us. The most important factor in determining whether they will play a constructive or destructive role is our success in achieving balance and proportion in our feelings. For example, courage is expected of a good person in a dangerous situation. What makes courage difficult in these circumstances, however, is the feeling of fear. Aristotle does not say that fear itself is bad or wrong. In fact, rational people experience fear when real danger is present, and the proper amount of fear will keep them from doing foolhardy things. A person who "fears everything and does not stand his ground against anything becomes a coward, and the man who fears nothing at all but goes to meet every danger becomes rash" (*Nicomachean Ethics* 2.2). Therefore, the virtue of courage requires that we find a midpoint between excess and deficiency in our feelings of fear.

The need to moderate our passions is required for the development of each specific virtue. Every good characteristic represents an intermediate state (often referred to as the "golden mean") between excess and deficiency. For example, we all have generous impulses. If we become excessively generous, we will not be able to fulfill our financial responsibilities. On the other hand, if we stifle charitable feelings completely, we become miserly. The virtue of generosity is found somewhere between these two extremes.

Aristotle warns us that there is no magic formula for properly locating the intermediate point at which a virtue is found. To illustrate this, he says that a virtuous person satisfies feelings in a moderate way. However, what constitutes a moderate caloric intake for an Olympic wrestler would be excessive for a desk jockey, and the moderate level of food for the latter would be deficient to maintain a wrestler's strength. Just as we can find no general, one-size-fits-all answer for locating the golden mean between the extremes of excess and deficiency, Aristotle argues that the virtuous person will need to calculate the variables to do the right things "to the right person, to the right extent, at the right time, with the right motive, and in the right way." As he sums it up, "It is no easy task to be good" (*Nicomachean Ethics* 2.9).

PRACTICAL REASON

The key to navigating the difficulties of becoming good is found in prudent use of our highest capacity, our reason. Aristotle, however, sees two types of rationality. Contemplative or theoretical wisdom concerns itself with things that do not change. While it is important that we understand these eternal truths, our contemplation of these verities changes nothing. For example, we may spend a lifetime exploring the principles of mathematics, but our contemplation does not create or modify these principles.

This is not the case with what Aristotle calls practical wisdom. Practical wisdom is strategic thinking about things we can change. How should I direct my emotions? What action is called for in this particular circumstance? When should I act? We are able to deliberate about such questions and modify our behavior and the outcomes based on decisions. The "mark of a man of practical wisdom [is] to be able to deliberate well about what is good and expedient for himself, not in some particular respect, e.g., about what sorts of thing conduce to health or to strength, but about what sorts of thing conduce to the good life in general" (*Nicomachean Ethics* 6.5).

As pivotal as reason is, however, Aristotle argues that, in itself, intellect does not bring about choice. Action requires that reason be combined with desire. The intellect provides the aiming mechanism for our choices, while the will supplies the energy. This brings us back once again to the emotions, because the will includes the passional side of our nature. Each situation we encounter is accompanied by feelings, and these emotions provide the energy that propels choice. Fear provides strength in battle. Ambition pushes us toward success. However, as we have seen, emotional energy must be properly channeled so it does not become destructive.

LEARNING VIRTUE

Obviously, Aristotle says that proper control of our emotions does not happen simply because we have certain capacities. A capacity is just the ability to do something. Our intellect and desire provide the opportunity to be morally virtuous, but the opportunity becomes a reality only if we use these powers in the right way. How, then, do we control passions so they serve the purpose of virtue? Aristotle's answer is that certain patterns of behavior must be created and encouraged. In other words, we need to develop good habits. "For the things we have to learn before we can do them, we learn by doing them, e.g., men become builders by building and lyreplayers by playing the lyre; so too we become just by doing just acts, temperate by doing temperate acts, brave by doing brave acts. . . . In one word, states of character arise out of like activities" (*Nicomachean Ethics*

2.1). The process of becoming good, in Aristotle's view, moves from the outside in. When we have done the right things long enough, they become a part of us. Once internalized, virtuous characteristics make virtuous acts our natural response to situations.

Aristotle sees a similar "outside in" movement with pleasure and pain. Since we naturally seek pleasure, those in the process of developing their habits should be rewarded with pleasurable things for good activities, while pain should follow from bad behaviors. Over time, then, pleasure and pain becomes internalized so that emotions such as guilt, shame, joy, sadness and others are matched with certain behaviors. In short, we develop a conscience. However, Aristotle reminds us that conscience itself is just a capacity and, like any other capacity, it can be used well or badly. Conscience is only useful in the development of virtue if it is trained to feel internal pleasure and pain at the right things. Thus, Aristotle says, our choice is not whether moral habits will be established and reinforced by pleasure and pain. This is inevitable. The choice is whether habituation occurs haphazardly or through an intentional process. Only when the conscience has been intelligently trained will people grow to find pleasure in the good and to feel pain when evil occurs. Thus, Aristotle concludes, "It makes no small difference, then, whether we form habits of one kind or of another from our very youth; it makes a very great difference, or rather all the difference" (*Nicomachean Ethics* 2.1).

If proper moral training must be intelligently planned and purposefully executed, who is responsible for the process? Aristotle argues that the quest for human virtue and happiness belongs to the study of politics. The political philosopher "is the architect of the end" (*Nicomachean Ethics* 7.11). Aristotle offers several reasons as to why this is so. First, we should recall that lesser pursuits always serve the higher pursuits. When we survey the disciplines that contribute to the overall well-being of any advanced culture (e.g., military studies, economics, rhetoric), none are comprehensive. Instead, they are aspects of a master science, political philosophy, which encompasses the other areas of knowledge. This master science therefore is concerned with our most fundamental drive: the pursuit of happiness.

Aristotle's second argument for the priority of political theory also expresses the idea that the lower exists to support the higher. We learned earlier that *human* happiness is not obtained by fulfilling the needs of the appetites or pleasing the senses. These physical functions are not a final end, but a means that supports the work of our rationality. Using his definition, Aristotle would say that a person could have wealth, health, good looks, security from crime or military threat, cultural and educational opportunities and friends in abundance, and still be unhappy. However, because the lower provides the foundation for the higher capacities, one cannot be happy without these things. These must be in place before one has the leisure to pursue the contemplative life of rationality. Therefore, since government's job is to provide for our economic, educational, cultural and security needs, society's happiness relies on the skill of the political philosopher.

Finally, those who hold political power play a central role in society's happiness because they are responsible for writing the laws that govern life. Aristotle would quickly point out that happiness is not found in following laws. Happiness is a matter of internal character rather than adhering to regulations imposed by rulers. How, then, does legislation fit into the search for happiness? The first function of law is to restrain evil. In theory, those whose characters are good will have no need for laws because rationality will direct their actions properly. However, being the practical sort that he is, Aristotle recognizes that most people are governed by emotion, not reason. "He who lives as passion directs will not hear argument that dissuades him, nor understand it if he does; and how can we persuade one in such a state to change his ways? And in general passion seems to yield not to argument but to force" (*Nicomachean Ethics* 10.9). In short, if people do not become good by developing the virtues, we must rely on laws to coerce their behaviors. Using regulations as a club to force people to avoid destructive behaviors does not make them good, but it restrains evil within society so that those who desire good can achieve it.

On the more positive side, good laws help train those whose habits are still forming. "To live temperately and hardily is not pleasant to most people, especially when they are young. For this reason their nurture and occupations should be fixed by law; for they will not be painful when they have become customary" (*Nicomachean Ethics* 10.9). In other words, while people do not become virtuous simply by following society's rules, law is the external expression of virtues that should be internalized. Rules function as a temporary stand-in and teacher until the values they embody become part of one's character.

We should notice that Aristotle carefully balances rules and goodness. Good rules are necessary for one to become a good person. However, one does not become a good person simply through consistent adherence to rules and laws, even when following them leads to actions that are consistent with ethical behavior. Making oneself do good things through will-power and fear of punishment or consequences leads to a condition Aristotle calls "continence." Continence is good to the extent that it leads to beneficial behaviors, but is not excellent because it does not tap into the best of our capacities. To move from mere continence to the life of virtue, three additional elements are required. First, as Aristotle has told us, the acts need to grow out of a good disposition or character. In other words, he is not primarily interested in what types of things a person does. Instead, the most important thing is who one is. Continent people can force themselves to do good things, but their goodness is not rooted in their dispositions.

A second requirement of the good person is that "he must choose the acts, and choose them for their own sakes" (*Nicomachean Ethics* 2.4). This gets at the question of motive. Continent people may force themselves to do the right thing out of fear, a desire for honor, peer pressure or simply habits that have been ground into them. Good people are aware of the options available to them and freely choose the good because they love it. Their actions make goodness an end rather than a means to some other purpose.

Toward the end of *Nicomachean Ethics*, Aristotle states, "If happiness is activity in accordance with virtue, it is reasonable that it should be in accordance with the highest virtue; and this will be that of the best thing in us" (10.7). This "best thing in us" is our highest capacity: reason. This leads to Aristotle's third qualification for true goodness: a virtuous person must understand why the good is good. If reason sets us apart from lower species and allows us to comprehend the nature of things, then human excellence cannot be achieved until we rationally grasp the nature of goodness.

The question of goodness introduces a shift in Aristotle's tone. Throughout most of *Nicomachean Ethics*, Aristotle has focused on practical wisdom. In the final section, however, he shifts to the theoretical aspect of our rational capacities: contemplative wisdom. By means of contemplative wisdom, we set our minds on that which is eternal and changeless. This is our highest calling, "since not only is reason the best thing in us, but the objects of reason are the best of knowable objects." Like Plato, Aristotle says that eternal reality is nonphysical and thus transcends our senses. Moreover, we are able to strive for theoretical truth "more continuously than we can do anything." In sum, reason is the human capacity that is most godlike. "If reason is divine, then, in comparison with man, the life according to it is divine in comparison with human life. . . . [We] must, so far as we can, make ourselves immortal, and strain every nerve to live in accordance with the best thing in us; for even if it be small in bulk, much more does it in power and worth surpass everything" (*Nicomachean Ethics* 10.7).

DISSECTING ARISTOTLE

Do you want to be happy? My guess is that you do. What other motivation better explains our actions? However, Christians have often felt awkward about expressing a desire for happiness. While many Christians may agree with Aristotle's contention that we all naturally seek happiness, we might be hesitant to say that this is something we *should* do. If we look at the qualifications Aristotle includes in his definition of happiness, however, we might be somewhat more comfortable with the idea that happiness is a proper object of desire. He clearly does not envision the life of instant gratification and egoistic hedonism as happy. Instead of aiming at the lowest common denominator, Aristotle's *eudaimonia* requires development of the most profound, enduring and complete capacities of our species. This seems consistent with Christianity's emphasis that human flourishing and completeness relies on development of the most godlike capacities in us.

Second, Aristotle's description of happiness as a state of being rather than a fleeting impulse or feeling is consistent with a Christian understanding of our proper goal. Some have suggested that Aristotle's *eudaimonia* is parallel to Jesus' use of "blessed" in the Beatitudes (Mt 5:3-11). In this passage of Scripture, those who are blessed receive a type of fulfillment that transcends momentary feelings and external circumstances. If this parallel is correct, at least on this aspect, Jesus and Aristotle appear to agree that happiness (or blessedness) is something more enduring than temporary sentiments. In fact, it is a state that can exist *in spite of* circumstances that create a contrary feeling.

Finally, both Jesus and Aristotle would say that individuals might very well be wrong about whether they are happy. Happiness, as they understand it, is an objective reality that requires that we conform to a standard. Behind this position is the idea that human beings have a purpose in life that is given by a power beyond them. If poor choices are made, we will not fulfill our purpose, even if we think we are doing OK. On the other hand, if we live in a manner consistent with the purpose for which we are made, we achieve a state of well-being.

In spite of these parallels between Christianity and Aristotle, one important difference should be recognized. First, while Jesus talks about blessedness in the present tense, it is also clear that he finds the highest degree of human completion and beatitude to be a future reality. Aristotle does not consider personal fulfillment and happiness beyond this life. For him, the happiness we should strive for is anchored in this world. This might seem surprising since Aristotle speaks frequently of the importance of nurturing the soul's highest capacities in our pursuit of happiness.

However, Aristotle departs from Plato in an important way in his idea of the soul. For Plato the soul is both inherently immortal and separable from the body. Thus, when the body dies, the soul's life continues. Aristotle, on the other hand, links the soul and body so closely that when the body perishes, the aspect of the soul that is uniquely ours dies also. Therefore, while reason can put us in touch with the eternal, there is no concept of personal immortality in Aristotle's thought and thus no discussion of happiness beyond death.

Because Aristotle wrongly limits consideration of human happiness to this life, it eliminates a dimension of the discussion on this topic that must be included in Christianity. However, Aristotle's this-worldly view of happiness can provide a useful corrective to a common tendency in Christianity, which often follows Plato to the other extreme with his otherworldly focus. Under this Platonic influence, many Christians look at pairs such as body/soul, temporary/eternal and physical/spiritual as either-or choices. We *either* seek satisfaction of the body *or* we nourish the soul. We *either* think about things that are time-bound *or* we contemplate the eternal. Aristotle offers a different path that I find to be more consistent with Christianity. He argues that the key to attaining the good life is not found in choosing heaven over earth or soul over body, but in finding the proper balance between them. Thus, as we saw above, Aristotle claims that happiness cannot be found in money, physical health or great friendships alone. However, he also says that without adequately satisfying the needs of these lower functions, it is difficult, if not impossible, to pursue the highest of our capacities. How easy is it to engage in lofty thought when you are hungry, physically threatened or ill, or when you have a thoroughly disrupted social life?

While Aristotle overstates the case when he says that the higher functions are so dependent on the lower that happiness would be impossible for a prisoner, an impoverished individual or a person with severe physical limitations or some other inhibiting factor, he does bring to light the fact that the different facets of our life are so integrated that when problems exist in one area of our life, it presents obstacles to satisfaction and development in other areas. His solution, then, is that we make certain that each aspect of our life is healthy—the physical, the social, the cultural and the mental—so that the whole person will be healthy. To put it in language that reflects Aristotle's thought, when we achieve virtue (function as intended) in every part of our being, we become virtuous as a person.

In short, Aristotle believes that each human function, when operating properly, contributes something good and necessary to the whole person. While some of the functions play a subordinate role, the lower supports the higher capacities. This seems to present a picture of human nature that is more is line with Christianity than the Platonic model, which tends to view the lower as a persistent nuisance and danger to the higher. Aristotle's concept accommodates the Christian view that God creates us as multifaceted beings. Each one of the layers of our existence requires certain things for its health. This, then, can provide the basis for understanding why feeding the hungry, healing bodies and providing psychological counseling and other such services are not simply good extracurricular activities for Christians. They are part of the core mission for Christians.

This helps explain why chapter two distinguished between a Socratic/Platonic idea of immortality of the soul and the Christian understanding of resurrection of the person. In Scripture, "eternal life" does not refer simply to an existence of endless duration. It is also a qualitative word, indicating a completeness of happiness in every way. Moreover, "eternal life" is found in the present tense in the Bible, denoting a state that begins in the present and comes to completion in the resurrection. Since the person is more than just a soul (contra Socrates and Plato), our mission goes beyond the "saving of souls." The salvation of the person requires that we view ministry to any type of human need as a legitimate and important part of our call as Christians. On the other hand, while Aristotle's thought picks up the present aspect of salvation, it comes up short by not recognizing that human beings, through resurrection, have a future beyond death.

Aristotle's ability to speak of the priority of the soul without excluding the importance of the physical, social, political or educational finds a parallel in his twofold understanding of wisdom. Aristotle agrees with Plato that we should develop our capacity to contemplate the timeless and perfect. As we noted, the last part of *Nicomachean Ethics* extols the virtues of contemplative wisdom, by which we meditate on the eternal, holy things beyond our control. However, Aristotle does not stop there. He also advocates combining theoretical thought with practical wisdom—strategic thinking. I'm not certain that Aristotle does a very good job of showing how these two types of wisdom should fit together, but I think he is onto something when he says that both types are necessary for the best life.

Aristotle's two-fold division of wisdom seems to have a parallel in two different approaches to spirituality in the church today. If you would ask most people today for good ideas about how to grow spiritually, you probably would get an answer that reflects Aristotle's idea of contemplative wisdom. You would be advised to meditate on the enduring, eternal Word of God as given in Scripture and to enter into conversation with the absolute, everlasting God through prayer. These two activities are generally described as spiritual because they take us beyond the fallible, transitory things of this world.

Prayer and Bible reading are certainly important to spiritual development, but that may not be enough. This might sound like some kind of heresy, but take a quick tour of most Christian bookstores and you notice something striking. Count the number of books with titles that begin with something like *Ten Steps to* . . . The popularity of books with such titles betrays a recognition that we have to connect the eternal and unchanging with the actual, gritty circumstances of life. Many of us are familiar with people who have a good theoretical grasp of divine truths and have developed a disciplined life of prayer and Scripture reading, but are strategically clumsy when it comes to translating these truths into action. Their intent is good, but their execution is frequently disastrous and results in misunderstanding, hurt and alienation. It is important to have the tools that can guide us in the who, when, where and how of applying eternal truths to actual situations. In other words, it requires something analogous to what Aristotle calls practical wisdom. If this sounds too much like common sense to be considered "spiritual," it may be that our definition of spirituality is too narrow.

Aristotle's identification of the need to combine practical wisdom with theoretical wisdom also provides a new dimension to many of the ethical discussions I hear among Christians. Christians often lament the loss of absolutes in our culture. The underlying assumption is that if we would just rediscover these absolute moral rules and follow them, our ethical problems would disappear. On one level, I have no beef with this. I agree that there is an objective standard for right and wrong; so does Aristotle. However, he provides a couple of thought-provoking reasons why we might get less than we expect even if we could all agree on a set of moral absolutes.

First, we might agree on the moral absolute that we ought to always act in a loving manner. However, there is not a day that goes by that I do not encounter a situation where I know *that* I should do the loving thing without being clear about *how.* Sometimes love requires punishment; sometimes a gentle hug is called for. Which one of these actions is the best way to apply the moral absolute of love is a tough question. Similarly, Aristotle points out that courage may require that we stand firm against opposition and at other times courage calls us to turn around and walk away. Since even the best absolutes do not apply themselves, the ethical person must possess something analogous to practical wisdom to know what to do with them.

Second, while Aristotle does see a role for rules in ethics, he thinks that the person who simply follows the right rules has not yet become virtuous. He considers rules to be moral guardrails for people who are morally deficient or immature. The rules, which are imposed by outside forces, keep juveniles and bad people from doing bad things. However, not doing bad things because of fear or force, which is what Aristotle referred to as continence, is very different from being virtuous. Aristotle argues that rules have very little use for good people, because good people have no need for them. The actions of virtuous people are guided by an internal moral compass, in which the virtues have become part of their character.

Often, Christians act as if the sum of ethics is conformity to the Ten Commandments. Aristotle brings out a deeper dimension to ethics that can also be found in Scripture. Moral maturity seems to be a matter of doing what is right because we love what is right. This goes beyond the realm of behavior and action. Real virtue, as Aristotle would tell us, operates at the level of beliefs and values that have become incorporated into our dispositions. The downside of this, of course, is that it is much more difficult to become the type of person whose good acts grow out of virtuous character than it is to follow a list of rules. However, Aristotle does seem to have it right when he says that the most fulfilling life can only result from a character that is transformed at the deepest levels.

One thing that seems to separate the wise from the foolish is that wise people never lose sight of a key question: How should I live in order to find fulfillment and completeness? If nothing else, Aristotle pushes us to remember that the most satisfying life does not happen by accident, but requires thoughtful decisions and an understanding of where we ought to go. Not only does *Nicomachean Ethics* remind us that actions have purposes, it warns us that these purposes must be properly prioritized if we are to reach our ultimate goal. I think he does a good job of explaining why so many people never find happiness even though everything they do is geared toward getting it. I also believe that he is basically accurate in his definition of the type of happiness we should want to find. Along the way, Aristotle provides some helpful advice on how to isolate good goals, balance the physical and the mental, maintain equilibrium between theory and practice, and distinguish between being virtuous and simply obeying the rules. The depth of his insights allows us to see why one of the greatest Christian thinkers of history, Thomas Aquinas, finds him to be so close to the target that he simply refers to Aristotle as "The Philosopher." We will look at how this influence plays out in chapter six.

5

AUGUSTINE

Is God Responsible for Evil?

"Sometimes you're the windshield. Sometimes you're the bug." So goes the catchy chorus of a Dire Straits song (later covered by Mary Chapin Carpenter). It often comes to mind when I'm driving on a humid summer evening with insects creating a colorful collage on the windshield. However, life itself can make us ponder the "windshield or bug" fluctuations in life. You can have a long stretch of smooth sailing, then, bam! Something happens that makes you feel like a squished aphid on the grill of a Pontiac. This "something" is intuitively understood to be an intruder, an interruption of the normal course and order of life. The "something" is evil.

There is more than enough evil in the world to go around, and no one gets out of life unscathed by it. It can come in multiple forms—debilitating illness, an untimely death, a betrayal of trust, genocide, criminal victimization or some other manifestation—but it will come. Some personally experience minor doses of evil; others get far more than their share. Regardless of the intensity and quantity, however, the mere presence of evil presents difficult philosophical questions: Is there a purpose behind pain and suffering? What is the source of evil? Why does evil occur to people without any apparent connection with what they deserve? Is there any ultimate justice in the universe?

The philosophical question of why evil exists is intensified for those who hold to a traditional Judeo-Christian view of God. The problem is generally posed in this manner. God is understood to be both good and all-powerful. A God who possesses the first attribute—goodness—would appear to have motive for eliminating evil. Why would a benevolent God allow the existence of something that is diametrically opposed to his nature? This would be understandable if God wanted to destroy evil but, for some reason, was unable to do so. However, a God who also has the second of these attributes—omnipotence—would have the means for getting rid of evil. Presumably, an all-powerful God can do anything. Thus, if God wants to get rid of evil (because he is good) and has the ability (because he is all-powerful), why is evil still around?

This fairly simply statement of the problem should be enough to show how difficult it is to make these three features—God's goodness, God's omnipotence and evil's existence—fit together without throwing logic out the window. They seem incompatible. For this reason, many philosophers have attempted to resolve the issue by eliminating or redefining one or more of these assertions. For example, if God is all-powerful, but is a non-moral being, it would be rather easy to say that God would have no desire to destroy evil, even though the capacity to do so exists. However, eliminating either God's goodness or his omnipotence presents difficulties for the theist. If we get rid of God's goodness or omnipotence, is the survivor something we can call God? On the other hand, if we deny the existence of evil, we appear to have checked out of reality. How can we deny the existence of evil? The presence of evil is, after all, what creates the tension in the first place. So it looks like we are back at square one.

Even with this very sketchy introduction, I think it is clear that the problem of evil is really a whole series of problems and knotty questions. Our first impulse may be to give up before we go any further. I strongly advise against this course of action. First, while we might be able to avoid confronting the abstract philosophical problem of evil, evil itself is unavoidable. Moreover, hiding from a problem, even an intellectual one, never solves it, and usually makes it worse. Because the impact of evil in people's lives is so strong, we ought to be prepared to deal with it. Second, probably no issue presents a greater obstacle to faith than the problem of evil. More often than not, if you ask thoughtful atheists why they reject belief in God, their inability to reconcile God's existence with the ravages of evil is close to the surface. If thinking nonbelievers have to make it through this question to get to Christianity, Christians need to understand the issues and have some response to honest questions generated by evil's existence. This is where Augustine comes in. For a substantial part of his life, he was one of those unbelievers who could not embrace Christianity precisely because he did not find in it a good answer to the problem of evil.

AUGUSTINE'S PILGRIMAGE

When Augustine (354-430) was nineteen he read Cicero's essay titled *Hortensius* (which no longer exists) on the subject of truth. He was so moved by the beautiful portrayal of truth that he committed his life to pursuing it. Of this book Augustine says, "It gave me different values and priorities. Suddenly every vain hope became empty to me, and I longed for the immortality of wisdom with an incredible ardour in my heart. I began to rise up to return to you" (*Confessions* 3.4). Augustine considers his desire for truth the beginning of this return to God. However, this return was a long and twisting journey that led him to reconsider and modify his understanding of God and evil several times.

Augustine's journey began with his birth in Thagaste, a North African city (currently Algeria), in 354. His father was not a Christian until shortly before he died in 370. Although the father's income as a Roman official was modest, he made many financial sacrifices to enable Augustine, who showed great intellectual promise, to have a quality education. Augustine's mother, Monica, was a devout Christian and played a significant role in her son's pilgrimage. However, her prayers that her son would become a Christian would have to wait for some time before they were answered.

As a teenager Augustine decided that Christianity was intellectually second rate and presented a picture of God that was problematic. In particular, the Bible did not answer his question of how a good God could allow evil. In fact, it seemed at points to portray God as the author of evil. Augustine's rejection of Christianity caused his mother great pain, and this was soon followed by two other decisions that increased her anxiety. First, at the age of seventeen he took in a concubine and they had a son together. Shortly after this, Augustine became a follower of a religious sect known as Manichaeism.

As Augustine struggled to establish himself in the academic world as a teacher of rhetoric, Manichaeism provided a resolution to the problem of evil that satisfied him for several years. The Manichaeans asserted that there was not a single good and all-powerful God, but two divine powers that ruled the universe. The principal of light was the good force in the world, and the principle of darkness was the origin of evil. Each principle governed an aspect of the world. The realm of the soul was ruled by the light principle, while the force of darkness dominated the body. This dualism helped Augustine make sense of his own internal moral struggle. The pull to do right was the impulse of a good soul attempting to overcome the evil desires of his body, which was created and ruled by an evil cosmic master.

Gradually, however, questions arose about the intellectual adequacy of Manichaeism, and a conversation with a Manichaean bishop named Faustus only heightened his frustrations. He eventually abandoned this religion. This involved significant risk to Augustine, who had carved out a considerable reputation as a professor of rhetoric, because much of his funding came from Manichaean supporters. He flirted briefly with the philosophy of skepticism, but soon was attracted by Neo-Platonism. One of the major attractions of Neo-Platonism was that it seemed to do what Manichaeism had failed to do: clear up questions about evil.

For Manichaeism, evil is a power that possesses independent reality. Evil comes from the dark principle, which could not be overcome by a well-meaning but limited good god. In short, Manichaeism resolved the problem of evil by denying the existence of an all-powerful good divine being. In contrast, Neo-Platonism solved the problem of evil by denying the separate existence of evil. Evil is not a something, but a lack or deficiency. To state it differently, the attribute of existence, what philosophers call "being," is good. Thus, something that is evil fails to exist in an absolute sense. That which is evil is incomplete or partial; it lacks being. The idea that there are varying degrees of reality envisions a universe in which things are arranged in a hierarchy of being. Some entities possess a great deal of reality; others have only a trace. The only being who is fully real, and thus completely good, is God.

While Neo-Platonism maintains the idea that God is perfect in all ways, its conception of a perfect God differs in a significant way from traditional Christian views. Neo-Platonism's definition of God's perfection does not allow it to speak of God as the creator of the universe. Creating involves acting—doing something—and doing involves a sequence in which change occurs. Neo-Platonism argues that change in a perfect being is impossible. There is only one way to be perfect, and any change in a perfect being would be to imperfection. A change that leads to imperfection, as any change would, is obviously one that any self-respecting perfect being should avoid. Therefore, Neo-Platonists argue, God did not create the world, at least in any intentional way.

If God did not create it, how did this world get here? Neo-Platonism has a creative solution. We can use the sun's illumination to illustrate their answer. The earth receives light from the sun without the sun intending to provide light. The sun just is what it is. However, as a result of the sun's activity, light radiates, or emanates, from it. The closer we are to the sun, the more intense the illumination. If we could travel through the cosmos, we could get far enough from the sun that its light would fade to darkness. In a similar manner, God, as conceived by Neo-Platonism, does not intend to create since creating involves change. God just is, remaining static in his changeless perfection. However, just as light radiates from the sun, God emanates his being. The intensity of being diminishes as the emanations are increasingly distanced from God. Thus, the Neoplatonists would find it proper to say that the world exists as a *result* of God's existence, but is not the intent of God expressed in a decision to create.

Because these emanations vary in distance from God, there is a hierarchy, with those nearest the origin possessing the most reality or goodness. The emanation closest to God is called *nous*, or mind. This level reflects the rationality of God, and provides the logical boundaries within which the universe operates. The next levels of emanation are the world soul, the individual human soul and, on the lowest level, the material realm. Matter, because it is farthest away from God's being, possesses the least amount of reality, or goodness. While a great deal more could be said about Neoplatonic cosmology, we will limit ourselves to one observation: That which is closest to the divine is also that which is most rational. When we move to the level of soul, this realm also possesses reason but is also equipped to assume embodiment. At the lowest level, however, we get irrational matter.

Its followers viewed Neoplatonic philosophy as a means of overcoming the downward pull of the material realm to allow the soul to capture brief glimpses of perfect spiritual beauty and truth. Augustine says that Neo-Platonism provided moments of spiritual satisfaction, "but I did not possess the strength to keep my vision fixed. My weakness reasserted itself, and I returned to my customary condition" (*Confessions* 7.17). Augustine considered Neo-Platonism an important step on his road to Christianity, and it seems that he was able to make an intellectual conversion to the faith before he could make the volitional leap. He needed a conversion of both the mind and the will.

The volitional conversion to Christianity came one day when, in a state of spiritual misery, Augustine heard a young child chant the phrase "Pick up and read." He tells us that he "interpreted it solely as a divine command to me to open the book and read the first chapter I might find" (*Confessions* 8.12). The first passage his eyes fell upon was Romans 13:13-14: "Not in riots and drunken parties, not in eroticism and indecencies, not in strife and rivalry, put on the Lord Jesus Christ and make no provision for the flesh in its lusts." As a result, Augustine writes, "at once, with the last words of this sentence, it was as if a light of relief from all anxiety flooded into my heart. All the shadows of doubt were dispelled" (*Confessions* 8.12).

After Augustine embraced the faith at age thirty-one, he hoped to return to his hometown of Tagaste and spend the remainder of his life in contemplation, prayer and study, but this was not to be. Soon after he returned, he was more or less forcibly ordained, and a few years later became the bishop of Hippo, the main city in the region. His elevation to the bishopric made him responsible for a host of administrative, judicial and ecclesiastical duties during a time when the church was plagued by serious internal dissention and the Roman Empire was crumbling. Augustine died in 430, with the invading Vandals literally at the gates of Hippo.

GOD AS LOVING CREATOR

Augustine's thoughts frequently turned toward the question of evil during the four decades he wrote as a Christian. Many of his ideas about this problem reflect the influence of Neo-Platonism. He agreed with Neo-Platonism that evil was a deficiency rather than a thing that has its own reality. He also borrowed heavily from their belief that entities in this world are arranged in a hierarchy that reflects differing degrees of being. However, because of his commitment to Christianity, Augustine found it necessary to separate himself from Neo-Platonism at two important points. First, Neo-Platonism did not view God as a personal being, stating that personal attributes (or any attributes at all) would limit God. Second, as we have seen above, Neo-Platonism argued that God did not intentionally decide to create the universe. Instead, the world emanates from God as light emanates from the sun. Augustine recognized that Christianity is destroyed if we remove the idea of a personal God who creates. Thus, he had to address the Neoplatonists' rejection of these two doctrines before outlining his solution to the problem of evil.

The Neo-Platonists had argued that creation requires a God who does one thing prior to the world's beginning and another after. This before-

and-after sequence, they claimed, involves change, which is logically impossible for a perfect being. Augustine's response to the Neoplatonists is that they have confused two different things: God's eternity and existence in endless time. An endless time sequence would include an infinite succession of moments, which involves before and after; eternity, in which God exists, is different. As Augustine defines it, "In the eternal, nothing is transient, but the whole is present" (*Confessions* 11.11). Time, which is a succession of moments, is not present in the eternity from which God created, but was itself part of creation. Everything that exists within time has a before and after. However, God's will exists in eternity, in which there is no succession or change of moments. Thus, it makes no sense to ask whether God's will changes after he creates all things, including time. God's decision to create does not involve succession, as our decisions do, so there is no change in God during creation.

Believing that he has explained *how* it is logically possible for a perfect being to create, Augustine must now ask *why* God would create, and it is here that he brings in his concept of God as a personal being. He agrees with the Neoplatonists that God is a perfect being, but disagrees on the definition of perfection. Perfection is more than pure being that is endlessly contemplating itself. Instead, perfection, for Augustine involves a being that, although completely self-sufficient, intentionally goes outside himself in love. God is not complete by virtue of total self-absorption, but by perfectly and intentionally sharing himself in love. In short, the attribute of love sums up what it means to be perfect. From this definition, then, Augustine believes we can find God's motive for creation. Love, by its nature, always looks outward, so it is within the nature of God to express his love in the act of creating. The love by which God creates is evident within the universe at creation because, at several points in the process of creation, he declares the product good (Gen 1:4, 10, 18, 21, 25).

With these two corrections in place, Augustine now modifies other Neoplatonic ideas to present a Christian response to the problem of evil. The first Neoplatonic idea he borrows from is the idea that existence itself is good. To the extent that something has reality, it is good. This does not mean that anything that exists is inherently good, that each existing entity possesses good from itself. Instead, Augustine says, "all of nature, therefore, is good, since the Creator of all nature is supremely good. But nature is not supremely and immutably good as is the Creator of it" (*Handbook* 4.12). Thus, Augustine tells us that only God is inherently good. Created things derive their goodness from the immutable and perfect goodness of their Creator.

THE DIFFERENCE BETWEEN GOOD AND PERFECT

We might have a difficult time understanding how evil comes into the picture if everything God has created is good. One necessary piece of this puzzle requires that we make a critical distinction between two things that are often confused. God is both good and perfect. In contrast, all created things, human beings included, are good and imperfect. To say that something is imperfect does not mean that it has a moral flaw. Even the ideal human being, for example, will not have the power of knowing everything (omniscience) or of being in all places (omnipresence) and all times (infinity) at once. These attributes (and others) are the attributes possessed by God alone and are the characteristics of perfection. If a human being had these perfections, she or he would not be a human because, by definition, humans are imperfect. What Augustine means by the goodness of created things, then, is that they are good according to their species; they function in a manner that God has ordained for them.

The distinction between goodness and perfection then leads to the next piece of the puzzle. God in his perfection is incorruptible and unchanging, and thus cannot lose his goodness. Created things, however, are corruptible. "Thus the good in created things can be diminished and augmented. For good to be diminished is evil" (*Handbook* 4.12). This lays the foundation for the concept of evil that Augustine will develop. Things that are corruptible are not in themselves evil; they are only potential evil. Evil occurs when that which is corruptible actually becomes corrupted. The concept of evil as spoiled or diminished goodness shows how far Augustine has moved away from the Manichaean philosophy he had embraced in his younger years. Then, he had thought of evil as a separate power that stood in opposition to good. Now, he says, "evils . . . have their source in the good, and unless they are parasitic on something good, they are not anything at all" (*Handbook* 4.14).

The idea that evil is not a thing itself, but a corruption of and parasite on goodness is a bit difficult to wrap one's brain around since that is not the way we normally talk about it. Augustine explains it in this manner: "In animal bodies, for instance, sickness and wounds are nothing but the privation of health. When a cure is effected, the evils which were present (i.e., the sickness and the wounds) do not retreat and go elsewhere. Rather, they simply do not exist any more. . . . Thus, whatever defects there are in a soul are privations of a natural good. When a cure takes place, they are not transferred elsewhere but, since they are no longer present in the state of health, they no longer exist at all" (*Handbook* 3.11). Good can exist without evil, but evil only exists where there is goodness to corrupt.

The concept of evil as a privation or defect of the goodness that God has invested in his creation is a pivotal idea in his attempt to solve the problem of evil, but we need to further investigate the idea of creation to round out the picture. We have seen that God's goodness is combined with the attributes of perfection, and while creation is good, it does not possess these perfect characteristics. Similarly, there are categories of created things whose attributes distinguish them from other classes of created entities. Within these variations of attributes, he sees a hierarchy. Inanimate objects such as bricks and buckets have only characteristics such as size, color, shape and weight. Objects in this category are inferior to entities that own these same qualities, but also have life. However, even among living beings there is a pecking order. Bacteria and cacti, which possess biological life, are inferior to critters like aardvarks and gorillas, which have sense capacities. The latter, in turn, have less reality than humans, who not only possess sensation but also rational and volitional functions. We can think and choose. Angels have will and rationality, but they surpass humans in goodness because they are immortal beings. However, all these various types of creatures share a characteristic. They are creatures: created beings. Their Creator gives whatever good they have. God alone, who is the creator of all, possesses full reality, or perfect being.

Augustine acknowledges the goodness that resides in each created thing, but also states, "If I were to regard them in isolation, I would indeed wish for something better" (*Confessions* 7.13). How can we improve on good things? Augustine says, "All things taken together are better than superior things by themselves" (*Confessions* 7.12). This is why, after creation was complete, "God saw everything that he had made, and behold; it was very good" (Gen 1:31). The individual features of creation are good, but the whole picture, when combined, is *very* good. Creation is not simply a random collection of things, but an interconnected organization of entities that serve different purposes. The lower aspects of creation are given to serve the higher things. The earth supports life, plant life supports animal life, animals serve humans, and humans and angels are created to serve God. When everything comes together as intended, each part fulfilling the role for which it was created, the result is a totality that surpasses the individual parts in beauty and goodness.

PERVERTED LOVE

The picture we get in the early part of Genesis, then, is one in which all things are properly ordered and all creation glorifies God and is therefore very good. The perfection of creation bears with it the critical question of evil. If evil is not created by God and is not a part of the original state of the universe, where does it come from? The answer is found, ironically, in love. It was mentioned above that one element that allows human beings to hold the highest position on earth in the "great chain of being" is our capacity for reason and will. Reason is important because, if used properly, it helps us to know how we should choose. Choice—will—provides the ability to direct our affections toward one thing or another. Thus, reason and choice facilitate and support our capacity to love. However, Augustine would tell us that we do not simply have the ability to love. We cannot help but love. Because we are made in the image of God, whose essence is love, we do things for the same reason God does. Every human action is motivated by love. Moreover, because all things come from God, it is proper that we love all that he has made.

Thus far, it is hard to see where the problem arises if our love of objects, others, self and God is good. The difficulty arises when love becomes disordered. Because we are imperfect, we are able to use our God-given ability to love in an improper manner. When we do this, evil results. More precisely, evil occurs when love for that which is higher in being becomes obscured by desire for the lower. Even the most corrupt person never loses the capacity to love. The problem is an improper priority given to what is loved. Augustine offers the example of how an act as evil as murder might be explained as disordered love. "A man committed murder. Why? Because he loves another's wife or his property; or he wanted to acquire money to live on by plundering his goods; or he was afraid of losing his own property by the action of his victim; or he had suffered injury and burned with desire for revenge. No one would commit murder without a motive, merely because he took pleasure in killing" (*Confessions* 2.5).

It will, no doubt, sound strange to identify love as the motive of something as ugly as murder. However, Augustine points out that every action has a motive. A motive only makes sense when we determine what benefit will come through a considered action, and what we would consider a benefit is determined by what we desire (or love). Therefore, out of love for self, we might have a motive for killing others who have harmed us. For the love of property, a person might murder those who possess what they want or threaten what they have. What makes these actions evil is that they violate the proper order and harmony that God established for his creation. To love things more than people perverts the measure of goodness with which God has invested the various objects of his creation. Love of self more than others fails to acknowledge that God is owner and lord of all creation.

An interesting feature of describing evil as a deficiency or misuse of love is that any human action can be evil if distorted from its purpose within the order of things. Murder is universally condemned, but even those things that are considered good can be perverted. Augustine uses friendship as an example. "Human friendship is also a nest of love and gentleness because of the unity it brings about between many souls. Yet sin is committed for the sake of all these things and others of this kind when, in consequence of an immoderate urge toward those things which are at the bottom end of the scale of good, we abandon the higher and supreme goods, that is you, Lord God, and your truth and your law. These inferior goods have their delights, but not comparable to my God who has made them all" (*Confessions* 2.5).

The point that Augustine is attempting to bring home above is that the goodness that all things receive from God should lead us back to the source of that goodness. The ugliness of evil, then, is intensified because it always involves the rejection of God. God, the supreme and perfect good, is loved less than those things that he has created. To state it differently, evil results in loving the good that God has invested in lesser things more than the perfect goodness that God possesses. As Augustine later analyzed his early life, "You [God] were with me, and I was not with you. The lovely things kept me far from you, though if they did not have their existence in you, they had no existence at all" (*Confessions* 10.27). Evil, then, is not a love for bad things. Instead, evil results when we get lost in the beauty and value of good things to the extent that we neglect what is best.

One of the satisfying elements of Augustine's understanding of evil is that it moves us beyond the "just say no" approach to sin by explaining why we should say no. We should avoid evil because it harms us; it leaves us incomplete and unhappy. This is because the amount of satisfaction that can be drawn from anything is determined by the degree of being it possesses. Thus, the gratification we receive when we love lower objects is short-lived and meets the needs of our lower functions only. Love of higher things by means of our most complete abilities, those which distinguish us from animals and plants, generates greater happiness. The higher things have more to give. However, no finite object or person can fulfill our deepest need for happiness. Finite entities can provide only finite satisfaction. Only an infinite object of love can satisfy our spiritual desire. Since the spiritual aspect of our life represents the highest human capacity, our first love should be our love of God. If love of God does not take priority over all other loves, we will consequently be incapable of loving anything else properly since we will expect from these lesser things what they are unable to deliver. Therefore, when we invest our life in the lower things, we ultimately damage ourselves.

If we are able to see beyond differences in vocabulary, we will find that much of what Augustine says here echoes Aristotle. Both argue that we naturally seek well-being or fulfillment. They agree that, while the things that satisfy our biological needs are good, they become evil when we allow them to supersede the higher goods that bring fulfillment to our loftier abilities. There is no argument between Augustine and Aristotle on the idea that happiness is discovered in a properly aligned life in which the higher things are given priority. However, Augustine brings several important elements to the discussion of evil and the good life that are lacking in Aristotle's view.

First, Aristotle does not have a doctrine of absolute creation in which a divine power begins with nothing and calls a universe into existence. The universe and all its components are eternal. It simply undergoes a constant reconfiguration. Moreover, the divine force that Aristotle envisions is not a personal entity. Both of these elements make it more difficult to understand why and how ethics can be part of the world's structure. Augustine's view better explains how love, goodness and happiness become features of human existence. A perfect creator would be expected to create things that have a purpose. If God's essence is love, it would make sense that what he creates is good and that the highest aspects of the created order would find fulfillment in the giving and receiving of love.

A second difference is that Augustine does not view rationality as the highest of our capacities, as Aristotle does. Augustine agrees with Aristotle that reason plays a vital role in helping us prioritize the various needs that compete for attention so we can make intelligent choices in our search for happiness. Failure to make logical choices about what is truly important and what is secondary can wreck a life. However, reason by itself does not bring us to happiness and salvation. Instead, as an aiming mechanism, reason serves the higher function—love. It is in properly expressing love that we ultimately reach our God-given telos. Experience seems to confirm the priority of love over reason. Perhaps we have all known people who have a firm intellectual grasp on the nature and ways of the universe, but have serious deficiencies in their ability to love and be loved. Such a life is far from complete.

LOVE AS AN ACT OF THE WILL

A final difference is that Aristotle is confident that we will want to do what a properly trained intellect tells us is right and good. Augustine says that while we *should* want to do what is rational, this is not always the case. Our will can go in a separate direction from our mind. This brings us to the final piece of the puzzle in Augustine's understanding of evil. Evil does not occur because of a fault in our understanding, but a flaw in the will. Since what we love is a matter of choice, and choice is determined by the will, Augustine's concept of evil as disordered love identifies our will as the place where the problem arises. Evil does not occur in plants, animals or minerals. Thus, as Augustine tells us, greed is not a problem in gold. Gold is simply an object without the capacity to choose. We, on the other hand, can choose whether we will make our love for gold a higher priority than our love for its owner (which occurs when we steal another's gold) or if we will realize that, as physical objects, gold and all other forms of wealth cannot meet our deepest needs.

Since human beings are the only earthly creatures that have will, only human beings can do evil. Stated in a different manner, we recognize that love requires freedom. Actions that are coerced cannot be loving acts. Only free beings are capable of loving, and only loving beings are capable of loving in a disordered manner. Therefore, humans are the only earthly beings that can do wrong. However, while we are the only *earthly* beings with will, we are not the only volitional creatures. Angels also must choose how they will love. This means that Augustine does not view Satan, an angelic being, as inherently evil. As a creation of God, he is good. He becomes evil by spoiling the goodness given to him by God when he attempts to place himself on God's level and perverts the proper order of love.

This is Augustine's point of departure when he interprets the Genesis account of the entrance of sin into the world. Adam and Eve did not fall into evil because the tree from which they ate was evil. Instead, "every tree also which God planted in Paradise is assuredly good. Man did not therefore strive after an evil nature when he touched the forbidden tree; but by deserting what was better, he committed an evil deed" (*Concerning the Nature of Good* 34). Adam's desertion of the better ultimately comes down to a matter of pride. When he ignores God's command not to eat from the tree, he puts himself in a position that is rightfully God's rather than submitting to the divine will. Thus, Augustine sums up our degeneration into sin: "For its [the will's] defections are not to evil things, but are themselves evil; that is to say, are not towards things that are naturally and in themselves evil, but the defection of the will is evil, because it is contrary to the order of nature, and an abandonment of that which has supreme being for that which has less" (*City of God* 12.8).

By referring to love as the motivation behind creation, Augustine believes he has acquitted God of the charge of creating evil. All that God creates is good. Evil enters, not by choosing that which is already evil, but in the way we choose. We do not turn to evil, but evil occurs in our turning away from the greater good and toward those things that are lower. However, even when we distort the God-given order of love, we cannot ultimately get away from God. As Augustine puts it, "In their perverted way all humanity imitates you [God]. Yet they put themselves at a distance from you and exalt themselves against you. But even by thus imitating you they acknowledge that you are the creator of all nature and so concede that there is no place where one can entirely escape from you" (*Confessions* 2.6). Exalting ourselves, acting pridefully, is a perversion of a proper love of the self. The irony that Augustine points out is that we are only capable of distorted self-love because God has made us with the capacity to love. Thus, even in our corruption, we bear the evidence of being created in the image of a loving God.

Dissecting Augustine

I like a lot of things about Augustine. He not only writes from an impressive intellect, but does so on a broad array of issues. His ideas dominated the theology of the Catholic Church for centuries and remain a touchstone for Roman Catholic thought up to the present. But we should not confine his influence to Catholicism. His theology was pivotal for the Protestant Reformation, and you will still find Protestant theological works packed with favorable references to Augustine. Moreover, he combines his intellectual agility with deep Christian devotion, commitment to the well-being of the church and solid administrative skills. That is a rare combination. However, one of the things I enjoy most about Augustine is his uncompromising dedication to the pursuit of truth.

I would hope that everyone has a strong desire for and love of truth, but for a scholar the quest for truth takes on a special dimension. Ideas are a scholar's stock-in-trade. Truth is what they have to offer others. For scholars to admit, then, that they are wrong is, in a very real way, to say that they have failed in their life's mission up to that point. This makes it all the more impressive that Augustine, whose identity prior to his conversion was so closely linked with his views on truth, was willing to admit that his ideas were fundamentally wrong at (at least) two different points in his life. You have to admire someone whose commitment to searching out truth is so strong that it overcomes the fear of admitting error.

I also find that two additional aspects of Augustine's biography hold some relevant messages for us. First, one of the reasons we recounted Augustine's various attempts to untangle the question of evil is that Manichaeism, which provides Augustine with his first resolution of the problem, is not a long-dead philosophy. Many Christians today are functional Manichaeans. It is not unusual for Christians to speak as if good and evil are two distinct and equal powers under the governance of two essentially equal beings, God and Satan. Thus, when I ask a Christian where evil comes from, the answer usually given is that Satan causes it. However, this view, without some important qualifications, puts the Christian in an extremely awkward position. For example, if God is good, why would he create an evil being who would ruin the goodness of creation? Doesn't this make God the author of evil? Moreover, if an evil being was part of creation, how could God declare all of creation good? If Satan is not a creation of God, how can something exist that God didn't make?

Augustine's later position on evil is a direct denial of a Manichaean-type dualism that puts God and Satan on an equal plane. Satan's evil is not something present at creation. Instead, he, like us, was created good and became evil by turning away from God. In addition, like us, he has no independent power against God. Even his ability to rebel comes as a result of God granting him the ability to love the lower over the higher. In other words, in Augustine's response to the Manichaeans, we also find a critique of a problematic position that many Christians hold.

Second, Augustine has a take on the value of non-Christian philosophies that seems to be more useful than the Christianity-is-true-so-your-ideas-are-not approach we so often see. In contrast to this, Augustine saw Neo-Platonism as the tool that God used to draw him to Christianity. Even well after his conversion, he says that "in all the platonic books God and his Word keep slipping in" (*Confessions* 8.2). Neo-Platonism's concepts of God as perfect, of reality being arranged in a hierarchical structure and of evil as a nonentity are retained and used in his Christian explanation of evil. Augustine's fruitful use of this non-Christian thought system shows the value of getting beyond the false dichotomy of "either true or false" and demonstrates that good ideas are worth hanging on to, regardless of their source.

At the same time, even though Augustine finds a great deal of common ground with the Neoplatonists, he does not hesitate to modify or reject their views when they run counter to Christian doctrine. Thus, Augustine parts ways with Neo-Platonism on the concept of creation. The world is not simply an emanation of an impersonal Absolute. Instead, the God of the Bible freely chooses to create out of the motive of love. We would expect a Christian to view Scripture as the final authority. But the way that Augustine uses Christian belief to modify philosophical ideas takes us well beyond the typical Christian approach. He does not simply say that Neo-Platonism is contrary to the teaching of Scripture on creation, and thus we should blindly accept Scripture. Instead, he goes beyond "the Bible says so" to show how Scripture's teaching makes sense and how it fits together with other related doctrines.

Augustine's desire to demonstrate the logic of Christianity brings up the final thing of value I find in his biography. When certain falsehoods get repeated often enough, a lot of people start to believe them. One such falsehood I have heard often is that no one has ever been argued into faith. The fact is that Augustine was, in large part, brought to Christianity through the strength of rational arguments (and he is far from the only one). This is not to say that other important elements were not also present. Having a mother like Monica who prayed for her son for years does not hurt, and many Christians provided Augustine with good examples of the life of faith. But these alone were not enough. Augustine was the sort of person who would not send his heart to a place where his head could not also go. In order for him to commit his life to Christianity, certain intellectual questions had to be resolved. Fortunately for him (and for us) he encountered people of faith who were intellectually prepared to honestly and patiently answer some tough questions.

I have offered evaluative comments on Augustine's ideas in the body of this chapter to a greater extent than in previous chapters. However, there are a couple of additional features in his ideas about evil that should be mentioned. First, it seems that his attempt to satisfy his questions about evil highlights an interesting feature of human nature. Notice how quick we are to ask questions about why evil occurs in the world. However, we seldom ask why *good* happens. Why do we assume that we should experience goodness and love? Why do we talk about the "problem of evil" but not the "problem of goodness"? Why do we naturally view evil as a problem? These may be some of the best unasked questions of life. Augustine tells us that we cannot understand why we would see evil as a problem in the first place unless we get a handle on why we expect goodness in life. His answer, as we have seen, is that God creates us to love what is good. We also recognize, if only unconsciously, that all that exists is good and should be loved.

If Augustine is right about the essential goodness of creation and our inability not to love, the ramifications are significant. It indicates that God has created us in such a way that we cannot help but search for him. Whenever we love something, and we cannot help but love, the natural direction this love should take us is toward the origin of that love—God. This is how Augustine understood his journey as he reflected on it later in life when he said, "Our hearts are restless until they find their rest in Thee" (*Confessions* 1.1). Just as disease is a disorder of a healthy body, evil creates "dis-ease" where peace and goodness should be. We instinctively recognize evil as an intruder. Thus when we desire to rid ourselves of evil and seek goodness, what we actually seek is God, even if we don't realize that he is the goal of our search. God's ultimate hope for us, to use our love in a way that completes us and glorifies him, is ingrained.

My guess is that some Christians have a very difficult time with Augustine's view that to the extent that something exists—to the extent that it is a nature—it is good. This may appear to clash with the concepts of original sin and total depravity, and the idea that sin has infected all creation. Thus, in order to give proper attention to the idea that sin leaves nothing untouched, I have heard many Christians says that we are inherently evil. This obviously does not fit with Augustine's idea that the nature of all things is good, so far as it is a nature and exists, and that for this reason all things are proper objects of love.

Augustine would have at least three responses to the idea that people are inherently evil. His first comment would be that the belief that human beings are inherently good does not contradict the idea that sin touches and ruins everything. Few people have accused Augustine of understating the effects of sin. Second, Augustine would state that any claim that we are intrinsically evil generates problems with the idea that God is our Creator. Why would God create us with an evil nature if he is good and loving? Third, Augustine would ask, If evil is a basic part of our nature, why would God desire to save us? If he saves *us* and we are innately evil, then we will be evil in the state of salvation. That hardly seems logical. If, on the other hand, salvation means that we lose our nature, it would not be *our* salvation. After all, our nature is who we are.

While I think Augustine gives us a great place to start on the very difficult problem of understanding evil, we should not think that we have finally put the question to rest. With this brief introduction, we have only touched the tip of the iceberg. For example, while we recognize that love requires freedom of choice and that true freedom seems to require the possibility of rebellion against God and the evil that it brings, why would God allow even the possibility of evil and all the pain it would bring? And if we put this together with the idea that God can do all things, why did he not choose to create a world where all would properly use their freedom to love in a positive manner? Moreover, since God knows all things, he certainly knew that we would love in a disordered manner. Why, then, doesn't God stop it before it happens? One might argue that evil in some way paves the way for a greater good, but some things are just so horrible that we wonder what good could possibility justify it. Moreover, Augustine's answer has addressed only evil that results from the misuse of the will. However, how are we to understand things such as disease, natural disasters, accidents and other events that cause so much death and pain but cannot be directly traced to willful acts? Such a list of seemingly intractable problems could go on for some length. While there may well be some good answers to these questions, the complexity of the problem of evil is so great that we should be careful about thinking that we have all the answers nailed down.

Writing about Augustine in a short space is frustrating. For one thing, he produced volumes of material, and so much of it is worth talking about. To be forced by space constraints to pick out only one topic among so many leaves me feeling that I have cheated the reader. Second, Augustine's treatment of evil, love, creation and happiness is the basis for so many of his other ideas. To stop here is akin to shutting off the projector twenty minutes into a compelling movie. From this brief introduction, we get only hints of how he will use the foundation laid here to develop his ideas on sin, grace, salvation, free will, predestination and a host of other very important areas. From this brief introduction, however, I hope you get a small taste of the fertile mind of a person so drawn to truth that he wrestles with what is perhaps the most difficult question that confronts human beings and, in the process, discovers a God of love.

6

AQUINAS

Can Nature Lead Us to God?

The famous Yankee philosopher Yogi Berra once stated that you can see a lot of things just by observing. If we go to the idea behind the mangled semantics, it is hard to disagree with Yogi; some things don't require a Ph.D. and a lifetime of research to figure out. They are apparent even to casual observers. One of those obvious facts is that human beings are far more likely than not to believe in God or gods. Even today, which may be the least religious time in human history, the vast majority of this planet's inhabitants still align themselves with some religious tradition. And the vast majority of these religious adherents embrace the idea that there is some type of supernatural being. Interestingly, even the majority of people who do not identify with any particular religious tradition still believe in God's existence. Most polls tell us that around 95 percent of Americans accept as truth that there is a God. This is not to deny that important differences exist among the world's religions and that conceptions of God can vary significantly. My simple point is this: most human beings believe that we cannot say all that needs to be said about our universe and its significance if we speak only of nature. Instead, they will argue that the world's story is incomplete without bringing in the supernatural.

OK, so human beings are religious and believe in God. What is so important about that? If nothing else, it raises questions about why so many people have invested belief in something that transcends our senses. With a few minor exceptions, most religions do not conceive of divine beings as visible, yet they still believe that supernatural beings exist. Why, then, is there such universal belief in a being that is not directly visible or accessible to any of our senses? If you ask most Christians why *they* believe in God, it is probable that they will refer to Scripture. Most Christians feel confident that God wants us to know about his existence, and the most obvious means by which would we expect God to reveal this information is through Scripture, which Christians take to be God's Word.

If Christians believe that God makes his existence known through the Bible, how do we square this with an almost universal awareness of the supernatural? Is Scripture the only avenue by which God makes his existence known? If so, why does God's existence seem to be common knowledge? Is this common knowledge possible because of a common source of information that all people may draw on to learn basic truths about God? Thomas Aquinas argues that not only does such a mutual starting point exist, but also that God designed us so that all could know of his reality. The means by which this happens, he says, is reason.

THOMAS AQUINAS (1225-1274)

Thomas Aquinas was the youngest son of a wealthy, noble family who lived near Naples. It was not unusual in that time for prominent families to direct younger offspring toward an ecclesiastical vocation. To this end, young Thomas was enrolled at the age of five in the Benedictine school at the abbey of Monte Casino. Though Benedictine monks took a vow of poverty, the order itself was well-established, wealthy and powerful, and his family probably hoped that in time Thomas would assume leadership of the prestigious monastery at Monte Casino. In his early teens, turmoil at the monastery school forced Aquinas to move to Naples temporarily to continue his education. While there, he established friendships with several Dominican monks, and this led to an important turning point in his life. The Dominicans were a relatively new order, formed in part because of the perception that other orders had forsaken their duties to the poor. While the Dominicans stressed a frugal existence, they also developed a reputation for intellectual rigor. Impressed by this combination of missionary zeal and academic vitality, Thomas eventually decided to join the Order of Preachers, as the Dominicans were known.

This choice did not set well with his family, who viewed the Dominicans as a major backward step in social status. In response, Thomas was kidnapped by his older brothers and held captive in the family castle while they tried to talk some sense into the young man. One colorful legend claims that his family hired a woman to seduce him in hopes that he would forsake his vow of celibacy. While the actual details of the family's deprogramming strategy are lost to history, it is clear that Thomas's determination to remain with the order was firm. When his family realized that he would not be swayed, Aquinas was released to resume his studies with the Dominicans.

Because of his slow manner, good nature and considerable girth, fellow students made him the frequent butt of jokes and bestowed upon him the nickname "Dumb Ox." One day after a particularly brilliant response to a question, Aquinas's teacher turned to his classmates and said prophetically, "You call him Dumb Ox. I tell you this Dumb Ox shall bellow so loud that his bellowings will fill the world." The teacher was Albertus Magnus, or Albert the Great, a brilliant Dominican scholar who pushed the envelope by exploring the ideas of a suspect philosopher—Aristotle. Up to this time, Aristotle's works had been largely lost to the Western church, but they were gradually becoming available again through new translations. However, most of the theologians of the time had a rather dim view of Aristotle's philosophy because, among other things, its this-worldly approach seemed to leave little room for God. Albert disagreed with this conclusion, and through his influence, Aquinas absorbed Aristotle's philosophy and used it as the framework for a revolutionary new approach to Christianity. In fact, so influential is Aristotle to the ideas of Aquinas that he is referred to simply as "The Philosopher" in Aquinas's writings.

True to Albert's predictions, Aquinas's "bellowings" were not only loud but also prolific. He produced over sixty works in his rather brief life, including commentaries on several books of the Bible and on many of Aristotle's philosophical works. The apex of his intellectual output consists of two *Summas* (a "summa" is a handbook or manual). The first is *Summa contra Gentiles*, intended for use as an apologetics text by those engaging nonbelievers, mainly Muslims, in intellectual debate. The second is Aquinas's *magnum opus*, the *Summa Theologiae*, a manual used for theological education on Christian doctrine. Both are massive works in terms of length as well as the depth of thought exhibited in them.

Throughout his career, Aquinas was constantly embroiled in controversies over the orthodoxy of his views, primarily because of his use of Aristotle. In 1274 he was summoned to the Council of Lyons, in part to respond to charges against his teachings. However, he died on the way. After his death several of Aquinas's doctrines were condemned and members of the Franciscan order were prohibited from reading his works. However, this was short-lived, and in 1323 Thomas was canonized (made a saint) and the ban on his works was lifted for all Catholics. In the late nineteenth century, he was proclaimed the patron saint of the schools, an indicator on his profound influence on Catholic thought.

FAITH AND PHILOSOPHY

In most cases, the first contact people have with Aquinas's philosophy comes through his proofs for God's existence. Because this aspect of his thought represents such a pivotal point in philosophy, we will examine these arguments later. Before we get there, however, it is important to see why he thinks such arguments are possible or necessary. This background is an important foundation because it shows how Aquinas addresses the sticky issue of authority. On the one hand, Aquinas was committed to a body of doctrine derived from Scripture and confirmed by the teachings of the church. However, Scripture *asserts* its truths without providing reasons for why we should accept them. For example, while the Bible assumes throughout that God exists, it makes no attempt to frame a rational argument intended to convince readers that this belief is valid. While the teachers of the church would often offer their own arguments to bolster why they believed the canons to be true, ultimately they revert to scriptural references as the final authority. On the other hand, Aquinas also respected ancient philosophical sources that sought to explain the truth about the divine, the world and our place in the economy of things. What is different in the philosophical writings is that reason was taken as authoritative, and they saw it as illegitimate to ground belief on assertions not backed up by rational argument.

As a teacher for the church, Aquinas has to decide how to handle truth claims that originate from these two very different sources of authority—revelation and reason. But this is also an issue that confronts every Christian. How are we to understand the relationship between rational arguments and the claims of Scripture? Do they have different spheres of authority so that we should follow revelation on matters of spiritual concern and rely on reason for navigating the questions of the natural world? Are they simply two different roads that provide different scenery along the way but, if followed to the end, dump us off at the same terminus? Are revelation and reason perhaps complementary, so that each has its own unique function and identity that contributes something important to a single goal? How one answers this question has major ramifications for understanding the role philosophy should play in Christian thought.

Aquinas opts for a version of the last view, which considers revelation and reason as partners rather than opponents. He writes, "The truths that we confess concerning God fall under two modes. Some things true of God are beyond all the competence of human reason, as that God is Three and One. Other things there are to which even human reason can attain, as the existence and unity of God, which philosophers have proved to a demonstration under the guidance of the light of natural reason" (*Summa contra Gentiles* 1.3). The second "mode" of knowing about God comes via "the light of natural reason," the tool upon which philosophy depends. Therefore, we see from the outset that Aquinas will argue that some information about God (e.g., that God exists) is potentially knowable by means of philosophical demonstration. Philosophy has its limits, however. The sphere of reality available to natural reason does not encompass the entirety of the Christian faith, but includes only what Aquinas calls the "preambles of the faith."

The first of these "modes" of knowing relies on Scripture's authority. This form of knowledge reveals what Aquinas calls the "mysteries [or articles] of faith." The major benefit of these mysteries of the faith is that they contain the entire message of the Christian faith. While he says that these "mysteries" fall "beyond all the competence of human reason," what he means is that such doctrines as the Trinity ("God is Three and One") cannot be *discovered* by unaided human thought. However, this is not to say that such ideas are irrational. Aquinas believes that once these doctrines are gleaned from Scripture, philosophy can articulate their truth and explain how they stand in relation to other ideas. Philosophy's ability to explain and synthesize theology is possible because God is the source of both modes of truth. If both philosophy and theology originate from God, "it is impossible for the truth of faith to be contrary to principles known by natural reason" (*Summa contra Gentiles* 1.7).

Aquinas's formulation of the relationship between faith and reason helps us avoid two common misconceptions of his philosophy. First, we can dispense with the claim that he reduces Christianity to a philosophical system. Aquinas is very clear that theology has a domain that is distinct and superior to the sphere in which philosophy and reason operate. Philosophy can be and should be used by theology, but it is not capable of unearthing most of the central doctrines of Christianity. Second, Aquinas provides a more nuanced model of how reason is related to revelation than is often recognized. By referring to both faith and reason as "modes" of knowing, he says that reason does not stand apart from revelation, but is a form of revelation. To be sure, it is not the only means or even the preeminent authority for understanding divine truths. At the same time, Aquinas claims that what people know through rational thought is not independent of God's self-revelation, but comes from the God who is the ultimate source of all truth.

NATURAL THEOLOGY

The vast majority of Aquinas's masterwork, the *Summa Theologiae*, exemplifies philosophy's broader role of providing tools to express truths that originate in Scripture. Our focus will now turn to the more narrow use of philosophy in the service of understanding God. This more limited role says that philosophy can discover truths ("the preambles of faith") that are consistent with Christian doctrine, but does so independently of scriptural revelation. This is commonly known as natural theology. It is "natural" in the sense that it works by capacities that all human beings naturally possess, the senses and the intellect. It is "theology" because it is a means by which we speak about God.

The first question that might arise is why God chooses to make himself known through reason if what we know through Scripture is more complete and is alone sufficient for salvation. Aquinas finds the answer to this question in the way God has created us. God has given us a natural sense of wonder and the desire to know.

> The knowledge of effects kindles the desire of knowing the cause: this search after causes set men upon philosophising. Therefore the desire of knowing, naturally implanted in all intelligent beings, does not rest unless, after finding out the substances of things made, they come also to know the cause on which those substances depend. By the fact then of pure spirits knowing that God is the cause of all the substances which they see, the natural desire in them does not rest unless they come also to see the substance of God Himself. (*Summa contra Gentiles* 3.20)

Thus, Aquinas says that philosophy is not arrogant rebellion in which we attempt to figure God out on our own terms. Instead, when we fully employ the faculties that God has given us, we will not be content to stop with the "effects" (by which Aquinas means the created order known through the senses). Instead, the mind that functions as God designed it to wants to go deeper to the specific causes of specific effects, to the ultimate Cause of the specific and intermediate causes (which, as we will see, Aquinas identifies as God) and finally to the "substance (essence) of God Himself." Our intellects are restless because God uses them to push us toward ever-higher levels of reality, of which God, in his essence, is the highest. Thus, our God-given natural sense of wonder directs us toward God, who alone satisfies the thirst for knowledge.

Viewed in this manner, natural theology can produce "demonstrative reasons that may serve to convince the adversary" (*Summa contra Gentiles* 1.9). This explains for Aquinas why many of the ancient philosophers have concluded that a perfect, eternal metaphysical Being exists without their having read about such a being in Scripture. Even though these philosophers did not equate this Supreme Being with the God of the Bible, Aquinas sees it as a sign of God's grace that Aristotle and other philosophers "saw through the glass darkly" by means of reason. As a further act of grace, Scripture clarifies and completes the knowledge that our rational investigations point toward. In this way, then, Aquinas reminds us that God never intended for natural theology to be his final word. As a sign of divine love, however, it is a first word that compels the intellect to look further.

DEMONSTRATING GOD'S EXISTENCE AND FAITH

We have already signaled Aquinas's belief that natural theology enables philosophers to determine that reason leads to belief in the existence of an absolute, divine being. However, before we get to the particular means by which philosophy arrives at this position, we need to ask how these rational arguments are related to faith. When I raise the question in class about whether God's existence is capable of proof, I can predict a response that will pop up every time. Even before we get to specific attempts at proofs, many students are convinced that any such project is doomed to failure. Moreover, those who are committed Christians are at least as likely to hold this negative view toward proving God's existence as anyone else. Why? Most often in the case of Christians, the assumption is that faith would be unnecessary if proof were available. If we can prove it, why do we need faith? However, Aquinas thinks that the "either faith or proof" position is a false dilemma that grows out of a lousy definition of faith.

Most Christians will have no problem with Aquinas's view of faith on two basic points: that faith involves both belief and will. We will look at Aquinas's view of faith first from the perspective of belief. By *belief* we mean the acceptance of a set of ideas as true. This seems to be a nonnegotiable aspect of any definition of faith. If individuals do not believe what they have faith in, it can hardly be called faith. What Aquinas would have us recognize, however, is that the intellect operates behind the scenes whenever we believe, even if we are unaware of it. For example, we do not simply believe, but we believe *in* something, and thus must intellectually understand on some level that in which our faith is invested. Moreover, we have some rational concept of the various beliefs from which we have to choose, so the mind comprehends to some extent what we choose not to believe. Also, Aquinas argues that we never simply adopt beliefs. Most people will agree that it is dangerous business to randomly opt for a set of beliefs. Instead, when we select them, we do so to achieve some goal that we consider good. Thus, intellect is involved in that we must think about our goals and how best to get there. We have reasons for selecting both our goals and the beliefs that we think will get us to those goals, even if we are not conscious of these reasons. In any case, Aquinas says, believing cannot be divorced from thinking, so faith itself presupposes reason.

When we look at faith from the perspective of the will, Aquinas would have us note an important phenomenon: our choices do not necessarily follow our beliefs. This can be true even when we are certain our beliefs are true. For example, I believe that I would be healthier if I made some modifications in my diet and exercised more. This belief rises above mere possibility for me. I have no doubts about the logical validity of these means of obtaining this goal and the goodness of a healthier life as a proper goal. Does this mean that I will take these logical steps? Maybe in the future, but my track record in the past has been pretty dismal. Where is the disconnect? Aquinas would tell us that even intellectual certainty requires another step before we get to what Christianity defines as faith. Once we intellectually assent to something, an act of the will, a choice, is necessary. Mere intellectual belief is not the same as Christian faith. Therefore, Aquinas argues that it is entirely possible for a person to attain intellectual proof for something without reaching the level of faith, because the will does not always act on what the intellect accepts as true.

We might sum up Aquinas's concept of faith in this way. On the most basic level, we must have information that the mind can grasp at some level. However, acquaintance with a certain level of information does not necessarily mean that you believe it. I am informed that some people believe that the Los Angeles Lakers will continue to dominate the NBA for the next decade, but this does not mean that I agree. Thus, the second rung on the ladder toward faith is intellectual assent. Faith requires that we trust that our beliefs are true. However, as stated above, Aquinas says that we only get to real faith when our will chooses to act on what which we trust intellectually. Faith requires a willful commitment. However, even though proof does not invariably move a person to faith, Aquinas says that it is of value in two ways. For those who do not believe, the greater the rational evidence, the easier it is to commit oneself to a set of beliefs. In this manner, intellectual demonstrations for God's existence may lead the nonbeliever toward faith in the God of Scripture. Evidences of God's existence can also deepen the faith of the believer. One can have true Christian faith without rational proof, but logical arguments that support intellectual certainty may lead to even greater trust.

THE "FIVE WAYS"

As noted above, Aquinas's best-known bit of philosophy is the very brief section (about two pages) of his *Summa Theologiae* that outlines his arguments for God's existence. These proofs are commonly called the "Five Ways," but this is misleading because most scholars agree that they contain only two basic arguments. The method employed in each follows Aristotle's idea that knowledge begins with what is grasped by the senses. These sense data are then processed by the mind, which allows us to get beyond the visible in order to understand some metaphysical truth. As Aquinas puts it, "When an effect [sense data] is better known to us than its cause, from the effect we proceed to the knowledge of the cause. And from every effect the existence of its proper cause can be demonstrated, so long as its effects are better known to us; because since every effect depends upon its cause, if the effect exists, the cause must pre-exist. Hence the existence of God, in so far as it is not self-evident to us, can be demonstrated from those of His effects which are known to us" (*Summa Theologiae* 1.3.2). In the Five Ways, the effect from which knowledge begins is the universe itself. Aquinas is convinced that this information, if properly filtered through the mind's rational functions, will reveal that we cannot understand how the physical universe came into being or why it operates in a logical fashion without believing that God exists.

The first four ways are variations on what has come to be known as the "cosmological argument." The cosmological argument rests on two principles. The first principle is not overly controversial in that it claims only that every effect depends on a cause. This simply seems like common sense because if we would see a broken window and ask what caused it to shatter, we would find it illogical if we were told that there was no cause. We might not know the actual cause, especially if the breakage resulted from something not immediately visible such as a sudden change of temperature. Nevertheless, we would still assume that some cause is needed to explain the effect since we are not acquainted with any examples of uncaused effects.

Aquinas would argue that the second principle is as obvious as the first, and perhaps it is, but it does require a little more explanation. This principle is that an infinite regress of causes is logically impossible. The language may be unfamiliar, but the idea is fairly simple. An infinite regress of causes is a causal sequence that runs backward infinitely without any absolute beginning point. I would guess that almost everyone at some time has set up a long line of dominos and started the chain reaction of cause and effect. From this simple experiment, we know that the last domino in the chain would not fall unless the next-to-last domino caused it to, and the next-to-last domino would not tumble unless the one prior to that caused it to by also falling, and so on until you get back to some beginning point such as a finger pushing the first domino in the chain. With an infinite series stretching into the past, we never get a beginning, and since each effect is dependent on a preceding cause, Aquinas says that current effects cannot be explained by an infinite regress of causes.

With these two principles in place, we can now examine the different forms of the cosmological argument, all of which approach the question of God's existence by asking "How did the universe get here?" I will replicate the first version of this argument in its entirety, and then briefly describe the other three. The "first way" is commonly known as the argument from motion. In Aquinas's use, *motion* refers not only to a change of location, but any change from one state to another (e.g., from potentially hot to actually hot).

> The first and more manifest way [of proving God's existence] is the argument from motion. It is certain, and evident to our senses, that in the world some things are in motion. Now whatever is in motion is put in motion by another, for nothing can be in motion except it is in potentiality to that towards which it is in motion; whereas a thing moves inasmuch as it is in act. For motion is nothing else than the reduction of something from potentiality to actuality. But nothing can be reduced from potentiality to actuality, except by something in a state of actuality. Thus that which is actually hot, as fire, makes wood, which is potentially hot, to be actually hot, and thereby moves and changes it. Now it is not possible that the same thing should be at once in actuality and potentiality in the same respect, but only in different respects. For what is actually hot cannot simultaneously be potentially hot; but it is simultaneously potentially cold. It is therefore impossible that in the same respect and in the same way a thing should be both mover and moved,

i.e., that it should move itself. Therefore, whatever is in motion must be put in motion by another. If that by which it is put in motion be itself put in motion, then this also must needs be put in motion by another, and that by another again. But this cannot go on to infinity, because then there would be no first mover, and, consequently, no other mover; seeing that subsequent movers move only inasmuch as they are put in motion by the first mover; as the staff moves only because it is put in motion by the hand. Therefore it is necessary to arrive at a first mover, put in motion by no other; and this everyone understands to be God. (*Summa Theologiae* 1.3.3)

Thus, as we have said concerning the movement of dominos, which are only potentially in motion while at rest, movement is only possible because something preceding it is actually in motion. At some point, there must be some power that is never potentially in motion, but is pure actuality. This original actuality that sets all subsequent things into motion is the first mover, or Prime Mover, which Aquinas says is what we call God.

The second way looks at efficient causes (i.e., a cause that brings about an effect). Aquinas notes, "There is no case known (neither is it, indeed, possible) in which a thing is found to be the efficient cause of itself; for so it would be prior to itself, which is impossible" (*Summa Theologiae* 1.3.3). At some point, as we trace the chain of causes backward, we must posit the existence of an Uncaused Cause, since, as we have seen, an infinite regress of causes is not logically possible. Here again, God is the originator of the causal chain. The third form of the cosmological argument builds on a distinction between two different types of existence, contingent existence and necessary existence. To have contingent existence means that a thing has been brought into existence and/or has the possibility of not existing in the future. With some thought, we can see that this is a broad category. Anything that has been created is contingent on something else bringing it into being. This indicates that nothing created could be the starting point for the existence of all other things, since created things rely on something prior to them to cause their own existence. Therefore, the ultimate cause of all other things must be a being that possesses what is called necessity ex-

istence. That which exists necessarily *cannot not* exist. And this is the type
of existence that is attributed only to God, whose existence does not rely
on anything prior.

The final variation on the cosmological argument is known as the argument from degrees of perfection. Aquinas observes that, "Among beings
there are some more and some less good, true, noble and the like. But
'more' and 'less' are predicated of different things, according as they re-
semble in their different ways something which is the maximum" (*Summa
Theologiae* 1.3.3). In other words, we are able to compare things in terms of
degrees only because we have some concept of a perfect standard to which
the lesser things are compared. For example, I can determine which of two
white cups is whiter because I already have an idea of the standard of
"whiteness." We still need one more element to make this an argument for
God's existence, which Aquinas provides: "Now the maximum in any genus is the cause of all in that genus; as fire, which is the maximum heat, is
the cause of all hot things. Therefore there must also be something which
is to all beings the cause of their being, goodness, and every other perfection; and this we call God" (*Summa Theologiae* 1.3.3). In short, anything that
has any reality or goodness must be caused by something greater, and
since in our comparisons we reveal that we have some concept of that
which is the greatest, God, the most perfect of all beings, must be the cause
of all lesser goods.

While the cosmological argument works from our present experience to
a first cause, Aquinas's final argument for God's existence, usually referred to as the teleological argument, looks to the design and purpose of
things. This takes its cue from Aristotle's idea that all things are designed
with a purpose, and thus things are good to the extent that they fulfill this
purpose. When something possesses intelligence, it comprehends its purpose and acts to achieve it. Thus, we can explain human activities in terms
of the goals that a person is attempting to attain. However, Aquinas says
also that

> things which lack intelligence, such as natural bodies, act for an end, and this

is evident from their acting always, or nearly always, in the same way, so as to obtain the best result. Hence it is plain that not fortuitously, but designedly, do they achieve their end. Now whatever lacks intelligence cannot move towards an end, unless it be directed by some being endowed with knowledge and intelligence; as the arrow is shot to its mark by the archer. Therefore some intelligent being exists by whom all natural things are directed to their end; and this being we call God. (*Summa Theologiae* 1.3.3)

The key to the teleological argument derives from the observation that physical objects do not act in random (fortuitous) ways. Their movements are predictable if we know the causes and understand the laws that govern nature. Aquinas argues that these laws that regulate physical movements are indicators of intelligence. Yet we know that matter itself does not possess the intelligence. Moreover, we recognize that while intelligent humans understand and make use of the order and structure made possible by the laws, we do not impose these laws on nature. This leads Aquinas to conclude that even though we cannot see a divine designer and intellect, the design manifest in the physical realm demands the existence of such an architect.

AQUINAS AND THE BIG BANG

Aquinas's arguments for God's existence come centuries before today's scientific theories about the origins of the universe. In the light of this, it is natural to ask whether these arguments still stand up against recent cosmological theories, specifically the idea that the universe originated from a massive cosmic explosion billions of years ago, what has been dubbed the "big bang." It is risky business to guess how a person who has been dead over eight hundred years might respond if alive today and brought up to date on current theories. However, Aquinas leaves some clues in his writing that may help us make an educated guess.

The main clue is found in the delineation Aquinas makes between science and theology. Because he believes that all human knowledge begins with sense experience, he has great respect for the natural sciences, which also begin their investigations from what we can access by perception.

However, he says that the natural sciences have their limitations. As long as we remain within the realm proper to the physical sciences, we only talk about physical objects and their interactions. In this sense, Aquinas says, "It is not the concern of physical science to study this first origin of all things: that study belongs to the metaphysician who deals with being in general and realities apart from motion" (*Summa contra Gentiles* 2.37). Thus, physical science, when acting within its field, looks only at changeable physical objects and "motion," the processes by which objects change. Once we move from the transient physical realm to that which does not change (e.g., God, the laws that govern nature), we are no longer making scientific statements, since the invisible and unchanging is not open to scientific observation directly. The latter is the world of metaphysics, the arena in which philosophy and theology operate.

If we apply this understanding of the relationship between science and the big bang theory, Aquinas *might* (and I stress might) say that we can accept both the big bang interpretation of the universe *as well as* his arguments for God's existence. I want to make clear that my aim is not to argue that the big bang theory is true. I don't have enough scientific background to weigh in on astrophysics. I'm also hesitant to presume to know what Aquinas would decide. The point is simply that if he were convinced that the science behind the theory of a big bang was sound, Aquinas *could* conclude that such an event occurred billions of years ago without modifying his Five Ways. This potential exists because he could argue that the big bang is not an explanation of the universe's *origin*. How does this fit together?

Aquinas would ask whether an explosion occurs from nothing or if such an event is the effect of preexisting materials that come together in such a way that an explosion results. Since Aquinas took it as self-evident that *ex nihilo, nihil fit* (out of nothing comes nothing), he would conclude that only the second option is possible. Some materials or energies, already in existence, combined to cause the effect we call the "big bang." If that is the case, the big bang does not explain how the universe began but merely describes an intermediate step in the process by which the universe reached its current state. In other words, since the big bang is an effect of preceding causes, it does not speak of the absolute origin. And, since Aquinas argues that an infinite regress of causes is impossible, there must be an Uncaused Cause (which he identifies as God) to account for the existence of whatever went boom in the big bang. In short, Aquinas might well argue that a cosmic explosion, a stage perhaps *close* to the beginning of the universe, still needs the cosmological argument to explain the universe's actual beginning.

Aquinas could also add another observation. Our theoretical big bang occurred long before any human beings were around to witness it. By what means, then, do some scientists conclude that such an event is a good hypothesis for understanding the current state of the cosmos? The answer is that they have observed the present alignment of the parts of the universe, traced its movements over a brief time and used their knowledge of physical laws to work back to an event in the distant past. Since Aquinas believes that this process of drawing conclusions is valid, he would have no objection to the method, although he acknowledges also that complicated theories are subject to error. He would, however, point out that science presupposes something that is often overlooked: the laws that govern nature remain constant and that they are accessible to human logic. At some point, Aquinas would say, we have to explain where these laws come from that science uses to develop theories about what is not directly observed. While, as we have stated, physical matter follows these laws, nature itself does not create or comprehend the laws by which it operates. Unintelligent matter cannot therefore be the source of the design apparent in its movements. Thus, Aquinas says that the orderliness, predictability and apparent design in the universe are evidence of the intelligent designer that his teleological argument leads to. He could therefore argue that the order and structure that the big bang theory depends on is not a refutation of his teleological argument for God's existence, but is an example of the universe's architect (God) in action.

DISSECTING AQUINAS

One frequent criticism from students attempting to wade through Aquinas's writing is that he is rather compulsive about definitions. Granted, all but the most devoted fans of Aquinas might admit that he goes a little overboard on defining terms. Nevertheless, while sorting through distinctions and nuanced classifications does not make for the most thrilling reading, this process is vital for clearing up assumptions and avoiding simple errors. Aquinas's definitions may put a spin on things that challenges our presuppositions and reshapes the way we look at some basic issues.

The first potentially useful distinction made by Aquinas is that we should think of reason as a mode of revelation rather than a competitor to revelation. An often-used cliché in Christian circles is that "all truth is God's truth." If that is the case, Aquinas would ask, why are Christians frequently fearful of employing reason to seek truth? If God is the creator of our rationality, why should we not see the fruits of rational investigations as God's truth? If Aquinas is correct in viewing reason as a form of revelation, it leads to two interesting implications. First, it means that God's revelation is broader and available to a greater number of people than we sometimes recognize. As a result, there may be common ground for discussion of the preambles of the faith with those who reject scriptural authority. Moreover, Aquinas would argue, if reason is not a valid route to truth, we are going to have a difficult time explaining how so many have used it to develop an accurate, even if incomplete, understanding of God apart from Scripture. A second implication is that Aquinas, in the process of broadening the idea of revelation, also expands the scope of God's grace. If reason is not a mode of revelation, it is easy to view philosophical activities as misguided and presumptuous. But if Aquinas is correct, God is the font of the sense of wonder that motivates philosophical investigation. Moreover, Aquinas believes that God graciously designs our intellects so that such investigations, if pursued properly, will point us toward God.

A close corollary to Aquinas's understanding of reason as a form of revelation is the type of connection he sees between science and theology. Many Christians have a tendency to see science and religion as an either-or choice, but Aquinas argues again for a middle ground. Each contributes something unique and important to our pursuit of truth. Science, he argues, is a useful tool for understanding how physical entities operate and the way in which they are interrelated. This is because God designs the laws that govern the natural world and provides us with a mind that allows us to understand these rules. Aquinas argues that our ability to understand the physical universe is an act of God's grace by which he makes it possible for us to take care of our physical needs. He would also say that science, to the degree that its conclusions are true, can inform how we interpret Scripture since truth cannot contradict itself. However, as we saw above, Aquinas says that if we limit knowledge to the physical realm, we only know effects. God's desire is that we get behind the effects to find the ultimate cause—God. Therefore, science, in a way that parallels natural theology, is good as long as we recognize and honor its limitations. In the end, Aquinas still views theology as the queen of the sciences since it includes all the other disciplines.

The third way that Aquinas challenges common assumptions comes in his definition of faith. By reminding us that our beliefs are fundamentally tied to our capacity to reason, he can help us avoid drawing absolute boundaries between thinking and faith. On the other hand, he points out that it is possible for us to grasp something by our intellect, even to the point of certainty, without a corresponding commitment of faith. To this extent, mental assent is not the end of the faith process because it does not inevitably bring commitment. Thus, he takes a middle path between the one extreme, which views faith as completely separate from reason, and the other end of the spectrum, which sees faith and intellectual certainty as identical. Reason is a part, but not the whole, of faith.

As we turn from Aquinas's general method to its application in the Five Ways, it is difficult to overlook the enormity of Aquinas's claim that natural theology can lead us to arguments that prove God's existence. As we noted at the beginning of this chapter, the question of God's existence has been central throughout human history. It is hard to think of anything more basic. Given the centrality of this question, we have to admit that, if nothing else, Aquinas has provided a useful starting point for attempting to understand why so many for so long have embraced belief in God. I believe that one of the reasons Aquinas's Five Ways have captured the imagination of philosophers is that he closely links belief in God with two of the other amazing mysteries of life. It is hard to imagine that a person could get too far through life without marveling at the questions of the origin of our universe and its intricate structure. The immensity of the known universe is staggering, and the natural question, given our experience that says that every effect is generated by a cause, is where the chain of causation leads us. Moreover, the complexity of even the simplest organisms is enough to boggle the mind. If we think of the vast numbers of elaborate systems that do not just function independently, but are profoundly connected, we have to ask the question of how this all came about. Aquinas is convinced that the link between the marvels of nature and God's existence is not novel, but it is God's intent. After all, Romans 1:20 tells us, "For since the creation of the world God's invisible qualities—his eternal power and divine nature—have been clearly seen, being understood from what has been made, so that men are without excuse" (see *Summa Theologiae* 1.3.2).

Because Aquinas's philosophical investigations take us to the heart of life's most essential concerns and inquiries, it will not surprise us that his Five Ways have drawn fire from many directions. Some Christian scholars argue that even if we concede that philosophy leads to the conclusion that there is a divine being that is self-existent, omnipotent and intelligent, this is still nothing but an abstract entity. Such a Being is a far cry from the God revealed in Scripture and incarnate in Jesus. Unless we can find a way to bridge the chasm between the Uncaused Cause or Master Designer and the God who reveals his love, grace and judgment in the course of history, we will have only an idol of the intellect, not the God of the Bible. In addition, they would indicate that while Aquinas points to Romans 1:20 as evidence of natural theology's possibilities, the next verse indicates that knowledge of God derived from nature leads to condemnation, not salvation. "For though they knew God, they did not honor him as God or gave thanks to him, but they became futile in their thinking, and their senseless minds were darkened" (Rom 1:21).

The position outlined above reveals not just a denial of Aquinas's proofs of God's existence but a rejection of natural theology as a whole. The essential problem Aquinas's opponents see is pride. When we start with what is known by reason, we fall into the temptation to worship what is within the limits of our own powers of comprehension. As a sign of this, it is pointed out that those who rely on natural theology often use reason as a standard for deciding what we should accept from Scripture rather than allowing the Bible to judge our reason. In the end, opponents of natural theology say that what is half-true (i.e., the god known by intellectual means) is more dangerous than what is completely untrue (that there is no God at all). Aquinas does not deny that reason alone does not fully comprehend the God of Scripture and that intellectual pride can become a problem. His argument is that reliance on reason can be kept within its proper limits so that it is not necessarily inevitable that natural theology leads to pride. The core issue that separates Aquinas from the opponents of natural theology, then, seems to take us back to the question of whether reason leads us to faith or away from it.

Apart from the criticisms of Aquinas's natural theology that arise from theological concerns, some view his specific arguments as logically flawed. For example, some have argued that Aquinas's five arguments may just as easily demonstrate that there are five separate divine beings instead of one. We can conceive of an intelligent Being with the ability to structure and design preexisting material, but not to create something from nothing. Conversely, the Uncaused Cause of the cosmological argument is not necessarily the Grand Designer described in the teleological argument. Thus, the argument might go, if the only characteristic revealed in the first way is that of being an Unmoved Mover, can Aquinas assume that this is identical to the cosmic architect of the fifth way? And is there justification for equating any or all of the Five Ways' gods with the God of the Judeo-Christian tradition?

Some scholars object that the cosmological argument engages in a philosophical sleight of hand that simply substitutes one set of mysteries for another. The cosmological argument starts with the assumption that matter cannot be eternal and that an infinite regress of causes is logically absurd. Therefore, without positing an Uncaused Cause, Aquinas concludes that we cannot explain how the universe came into being. Critics say, however, that this solution presents us with a new mystery: how can we conceive of a God who is eternal and exists without some preexisting cause? In essence, the issue is whether the new unanswered question (i.e., Where does an eternally existing God come from?) leaves us in a better situation than we had with the old questions (i.e., How can matter be eternal? How can we have an infinite regress of causes?).

Similar questions have been raised concerning the teleological argument. Many grant the presence of order in the universe, but point out that structure does not necessarily indicate design. For example, the fact that our bodies are able to digest various food products demonstrates order in the world. However, that is not the same as saying that what we eat was designed for our consumption. A second critique is somewhat more radical. It questions even the reality of order, arguing instead that order is not something we find in the universe, but is something imposed by our mind. Thus, we do not *find* an orderly universe, but we *make* it orderly by our thought processes (an idea we will find later in Nietzsche).

Much remains on both sides that could be said about Aquinas's natural theology in general and his arguments for God's existence in particular. Perhaps the greatest lesson in Aquinas's musings about natural theology is that they confront some of the most fascinating puzzles posed by life. Why do people find it so natural to believe in the supernatural? Where did this massive cosmos come from? What explains the order and complex interrelations between the various parts of the universe? The genius of Aquinas is that he finds ways to bring these questions, and others, into a systematic understanding in a way that leaves room for both faith and reason. Even if you finally conclude that he is not right, it is hard to find a better place to start the discussion of these important questions.

7

DESCARTES
Can I Be Certain of Anything?

If we think about it, most of us will admit that we live with a large degree of ambiguity. The choices we have to make are often decided with incomplete information. Questions that cry for answers are frequently complex, and we sometimes are left with a lingering uncertainty about whether we have tied up all the loose ends. We also have doubts about whether we have put the right kinds of knots in the ends we do manage to tie together. Over time, this constant uncertainty takes a toll. There is something in us that wants more than mere probability. We want to be 100 percent sure we are right, particularly when it comes to the foundational beliefs that all our other values and ideas depend on. I'm not talking about the type of certainty that one claims for a position simply by shutting out all contrary voices or by relying on the authority of an external source that claims to guarantee the validity of our views. What most people want is some bit of truth that could be proved to any reasonable person and can withstand any argument or objection.

If you have ever had such cravings for absolute clarity about basic truth, you would be in good company. This desire was shared almost four hundred years ago by René Descartes (1596-1650). Descartes was born in La

Haye, France, in 1596. His well-to-do family had the resources to make certain that their bright son received the best available education. To this end, they enrolled him in the Jesuit school of La Fleche, one of the most academically rigorous schools in the country. While there, he received instruction from some of the best teachers France had to offer in theology, philosophy and the other areas of the humanities. However, for the reasons we mentioned above, his studies in mathematics provided him the greatest level of satisfaction. While the conclusions of the liberal arts always seemed to be up in the air, if you did your math right, you got an answer you could trust. In short, he liked the certainty that mathematics and geometry seemed to supply and sought to rebuild philosophy in a way that it would have the same level of certainty.

After La Fleche, he completed a law degree at the University of Poitiers. He then supplemented this education by extensive travel throughout Europe for the next ten years, including two stints in the military. Concerned by the French Catholic Church's rather tight control on philosophical ideas, he moved to Holland. It was here that his most famous philosophical work, *Meditations on First Philosophy*, was published in 1641. By 1648 Descartes's philosophy had upset the traditionalists to such an extent that he feared for his safety. This danger motivated him to accept the invitation from Queen Christina to move to Sweden in 1649 and become her tutor. The queen provided protection and an income, but it came at a cost. She demanded that she receive her lessons in Descartes's "new philosophy" at 5:00 in the morning. This schedule was hardly compatible with his lifelong habit of remaining in bed, working on his writings, until midday. This change in schedule and the extremely cold Scandinavian winter may well have been responsible for the pneumonia that ended his life early in 1650.

GALILEO IN THE BACKGROUND

We mentioned above that Descartes's philosophy was viewed with suspicion by thinkers who were still rooted in the medieval tradition. This may surprise you when you discover that *Meditations on First Philosophy*, the book we will survey, arrives at rather tame and widely held conclusions. (*How* he gets there is more of an issue, but we will look at his methodology later.) When the smoke clears, *Meditations* concludes that we can be certain that we exist, the physical universe exists, God's existence can be rationally demonstrated, God is not responsible for human errors and the human being is a combination of a soul (or mind) and a body. This is not exactly radical stuff.

While Descartes's published ideas were not a point of contention for most people in his day, he did hold certain beliefs that, had they been published in his lifetime, would have made him even more controversial. One of those ideas was that the earth moved around the sun. Since the concept of a heliocentric planetary system is viewed as common knowledge today, it is hard to see why this would rankle so many. However, the fate of Galileo, a contemporary of Descartes, reminds us that the world is a different place today. In 1633 Galileo, in his *Dialogue on the Two Chief Systems*, expressed his agreement with Copernicus's conclusion that the earth orbited the sun. As a token of appreciation for his fine scientific work, Galileo was arrested by the Inquisition, required to recant his findings and spent the rest of his life under house arrest. Around that time, Descartes had completed a work entitled *The World*, in which he came to the same conclusions about the universe's structure. Although he was living in Protestant Holland and would have been protected from arrest by the inquisitors, this did not give him much comfort. He pulled his manuscript from the publisher, and *The World* was not published until after his death.

The reason for the Catholic Church's condemnation of Galileo was not scientific but theological. Scripture states that human beings alone are created in the image of God. The church interpreted this to mean that the place that humans inhabit, earth, must be at the center of all creation as a symbol of our primacy. Moreover, theologians had argued that, while human sin had infected the earth, God had preserved the rest of creation from contamination. Thus, the sun, moon, planets and stars remained in perfect orbit around the earth. When Galileo gazed through his telescope and declared that the earth was just another planet circling an uninhabited sun, the Catholic theologians interpreted this as a denigration of the human being's privileged place in the created order.

This puts Descartes in a bind. On the one hand, he is a dedicated mathematician and scientist, and he cannot deny that his own calculations put him at odds with the leaders of his faith. On the other hand, he disagrees that the heliocentric model of the universe conflicts with the Bible's picture of the human being as the crown of creation. As we have seen in his decision to stop the publication of *The World*, he concludes that confronting the church head-on is not the most prudent (or healthy) choice. Instead, his attempt to bring the church around to a new way of thinking takes a more indirect approach. Most of Descartes's writings, including *Meditations on First Philosophy*, focus on the methods by which we pursue truth. This allows him the opportunity to go public with only ideas that fit within the borders of orthodoxy. At the same time, however, Descartes subtly suggests a new approach to philosophy that will make it easier for future scientists to work without fear of reprisals. As he attempts to straddle the worlds of science and philosophy, Descartes proceeds cautiously. To help indemnify himself against the condemnation of the church, he dedicates *Meditations* to "the Dean and Doctors of the Sacred Faculty of Theology in Paris," assuring them that there is nothing in the book that contradicts the church's teaching. However, he also writes with an awareness that, when these theologians understood the implications of his book, he may well be on thin ice.

THE SEARCH FOR CERTAINTY

When I was in high school, I helped build a large garage and shop. The beginning part of the project was extremely frustrating. For what seemed an eternity, we worked with a transit, measured and leveled to make certain that the foundation was square and level. This is slow, tedious work and I became impatient. I wanted to do real construction work; it was time to get out the saws and hammer some nails. However, it soon became clear why it was so important to spend so much time on the foundation. If you are out of level, square or plumb at the bottom, it only gets worse as you go up. If you get the foundation right, it is easy to build on it.

The same is true for belief structures as it is for physical structures. Ideas that rest on a shaky foundation will never be sturdy. As he opens the *Meditations*, Descartes admits that his current intellectual foundations are not stable. "It is now some years since I detected how many were the false beliefs that I had from my earliest youth admitted as true, and how doubtful was everything I had since constructed on this basis; and from that time I was convinced that I must once for all seriously undertake to rid myself of all the opinions which I had formerly accepted, and commence to build anew from the foundation, if I wanted to establish any firm and permanent structure in the sciences" (*Meditations* 1).

To avoid being fooled again, Descartes resolves "to withhold my assent from matters which are not entirely certain and indubitable" (*Meditations* 1). In short, to weed out false beliefs, he sets up the most stringent standard possible. If he can find even one reason to doubt a belief, regardless of how improbable it seems, he will discard the whole thing. Moreover, rather than testing each particular idea separately, he will investigate the basic principles upon which individual beliefs rest. If the foundation collapses, what is constructed upon it comes down as well. This process of rigorously testing beliefs to find an indubitable beginning point is what is known as "methodological doubt."

Descartes begins by considering the process by which we gain knowledge. After all, we cannot say much about what we claim to know until we can be certain that our method of accumulating knowledge is trustworthy. The natural place to start appears to be the senses. Seeing is believing, if we believe what we have been told so often. However, Descartes admits that the senses often deceive us concerning objects that are very small or distant. We have all misjudged the height or shape of something viewed from far away. Therefore, sensation appears to be doubtful as a means of attaining certainty.

At the same time, it would be premature to give up on the senses so quickly. Descartes asks, can he not be certain that his sensory signals are correct in telling him that he is seated by the fire in a dressing gown holding a piece of paper in his hands? Then he remembers something important. "How often has it happened to me that in the night I dreamt that I found myself in this particular place, that I was dressed and seated near the fire, whilst in reality I was lying undressed in bed! . . . On many occasions I have in sleep been deceived by similar illusions, and in dwelling carefully on this reflection I see so manifestly that there are no certain indications by which we may clearly distinguish wakefulness from sleep that I am lost in astonishment" (*Meditations* 1). The sensory data in dreams can include sounds, smells, visual images, tastes and tactile sensations that are every bit as vivid as those experienced in waking moments. What is missing in the sensory experiences of dreams, however, is a direct correspondence to reality. Thus, if there is no independent way of knowing whether his perceptions match actual objects or if he is just dreaming, his senses are not a reliable source of information.

However, Descartes is still not willing to give up on the senses. Even if he is unable to find some foolproof way of separating mental images in dreams from perceptions of actual objects, Descartes states that the image in his dreams must come from something. Perhaps these perceptions can be reduced to the simplest truths to discover something that produces certainty. He then entertains the possibility that we can find a reliable touchstone in the truths of math or geometry, "For whether I am awake or asleep, two and three together always form five, and the square can never have more than four sides, and it does not seem possible that truths so clear and apparent can be suspected of any falsity" (*Meditations* 1). In other words, he returns to mathematics, the only thing that seemed to provide certainty.

At this point, we see how rigorous Descartes is in his resolve to doubt anything that can conceivably be doubted. He asks, What happens to the supposed certainties of math if there is "some evil genius not less powerful than deceitful, [who] has employed his whole energies in deceiving me; I shall consider that the heavens, the earth, colours, figures, sound, and all other external things are nought but the illusions and dreams of which this genius has availed himself in order to lay traps for my credulity" (*Meditations* 1). It is important to remember that Descartes is not claiming that such a demonic figure exists. Nor has he descended into a fit of raging paranoia in which he imagines himself to be possessed. From the outset, he resolved to methodologically doubt anything that was susceptible to question. Therefore, if it is at least *conceivable* (even if improbable) that such a malicious genius crosses the brain's wiring to the extent that all his thoughts are distorted and untrustworthy, certainty cannot be achieved. Thus, as Descartes ends his first Meditation, even the truths of mathematics, which seemed to be his only safe harbor for certainty, fall to doubt.

When he awakes the next morning to resume his meditations (although at this point he cannot be sure if he actually wakes up or simply dreams that he is awake), he examines the wreckage of his doubting process. Belief in physical objects and the verities of mathematics have been undermined. Surely, he says, he can at least be certain that he exists. But even his own existence presents problems. If Descartes defines himself in terms of physical attributes, this falls prey to earlier doubts about what we perceive through our senses, because bodies of all kinds are known by sensation. It seems that the only thing that cannot be doubted is that he doubts.

While doubt does not seem a promising means of attaining certainty, this slim thread provides a way out. *He is sure that he doubts.* What is doubt? By definition, it is a type of thinking. In turn, thinking requires a thinker, one who has thoughts. At this point, Descartes believes he has come to his first certainty. "So that after having reflected well and carefully examined all things, we must come to the definite conclusion that this proposition: I am, I exist, is necessarily true each time that I pronounce it, or that I mentally conceive it" (*Meditations* 2). Although he does not use the phrase directly in *Meditations on First Philosophy,* this idea is frequently summarized by the famous dictum "I think, therefore I am," or, in Latin, *cogito, ergo sum.*

Thus, Descartes says that it is not in sensation, but in all the forms taken by thought (e.g., doubting, understanding, conceiving, affirming, imagining) that we gain certainty of our existence. What is this "thinking thing"? Since thought itself has no physical attributes, the source of thought must also be nonphysical. The "I" that thinks must therefore be my soul or mind (but not the brain, which is a physical object). Thus, the truth of "I think, therefore I am" is not diminished by his remaining doubts about the reality of the physical world, because thoughts and the minds that produce thoughts are not physical. Neither is this certainty challenged by the possibility that an evil genius may be twisting our thoughts. We must, after all, exist in order to be deceived. Descartes thus is assured that we are a thinking substance. (The term *substance* in this case does not refer to physical stuff but to an essence.)

With his first certainty established that he exists as a nonphysical thinking thing, Descartes turns to a new problem. Although the mind is not tangible, it thinks about things that have sensory characteristics. What is the relationship between this nonphysical mind and things that have attributes that appear to be physical? Descartes envisions a piece of wax that has just been removed from a hive. The wax provides signals to all five senses. "It has not yet lost the sweetness of the honey which it contains; it still retains somewhat of the odour of the flowers from which it has been culled; its colour, its figure, its size are apparent; it is hard, cold, easily handled, and if you strike it with the finger, it will emit a sound" (*Meditations* 2). However, if we put a flame under the wax, "the taste is exhaled, the smell evaporates, the colour alters, the figure is destroyed, the size increases, it becomes liquid, it heats, scarcely can one handle it, and when one strikes it, no sound is emitted" (*Meditations* 2).

What happens to the wax when it melts? Obviously it is still there. But how do we know that melted wax is still wax, "since all these things which fall under taste, smell, sight, touch, and hearing, are found to be changed" (*Meditations* 2)? The senses know only changeable properties, so by what means do we know that which does not change—the wax itself? The essence of the wax is grasped by the mind. As Descartes puts it, "Even bodies are not properly speaking known by the senses or by the faculty of imagination, but by the understanding only, and since they are not known from the fact that they are seen or touched, but only because they are understood, I see clearly that there is nothing which is easier for me to know than my mind" (*Meditations* 2).

GOD'S EXISTENCE

Descartes now knows that he exists because he thinks. He has also demonstrated that thought is more reliable than sensation in grasping the unchanging essence of things. He wants to know if other certainties are possible, but before he goes any further, he needs to clear something up. While thinking guarantees the certainty of my existence, we must still find some way to determine whether my thoughts themselves are true. It is conceivable "that perhaps a God might have endowed me with such a nature that I may have been deceived even concerning things which seemed to me most manifest" (*Meditations* 3). If there is a divine power, such a being would be more powerful than human beings, and thus capable of confusing my thoughts. Moreover, even though Descartes has no reason to believe that a divine deceiver exists, neither has he given any evidence that a God of any sort exists. This presents Descartes with his next two tasks. "I must inquire whether there is a God as soon as the occasion presents itself; and if I find that there is a God, I must also inquire whether He may be a deceiver; for without a knowledge of these two truths I do not see that I can ever be certain of anything" (*Meditations* 3).

We are very familiar with the idea that every effect has a cause. If a ball rolls across the street in front of us, we know that this did not "just happen." Something caused this event, and we remain sure that there is an explanatory cause even if the actual cause of a runaway ball forever remains a mystery to us. However, we rarely think of the thoughts in our mind as effects of a cause. What does make it possible for us to think of a tree, for example? Don't we need to find some cause that can explain why we have the idea of a tree? Descartes, following many earlier philosophers, also points out that the cause must be sufficient to account for the effect. Dropping a grain of sand on Cleveland is not sufficient to cause the destruction of the entire city. Similarly, Descartes says, "the idea of heat, or of a stone, cannot exist in me unless it has been placed within me by some cause which possesses within it at least as much reality as that which I conceive to exist in the heat or the stone" (*Meditations* 3).

This brings us back to the God question. Descartes's mind possesses a very interesting idea: the concept of God. God, as Descartes understands him, is "a substance that is infinite, eternal, immutable, independent, all-knowing, all-powerful, and by which I myself and everything else, if anything else does exist, have been created" (*Meditations* 3). In other words, Descartes conceives of God as a perfect being. His idea of this perfect being is an effect, and the cause of that idea must have as much perfection as the effect. Descartes knows that he is not perfect because his earliest certainty was that he doubted. A perfect being would not only know all things, but would also have knowledge of knowing all things and could not therefore doubt. This means that Descartes himself could not be the source of the concept of God. Only a perfect being—God—could be the cause of our idea of God. Therefore, God necessarily exists.

Descartes now has come to a second belief about which he can be certain. God exists. Not satisfied with only one proof for God's existence, Descartes goes at it from another angle. He knows that he exists because he is a thinking being. However, while thought is *evidence* of our existence, it does not *cause* our continued existence. Similarly, the biological processes of my body keeps me alive, but what keeps the components of my biology in existence in order that I might continue to exist? Whatever that something is must exist at all times, and the only being that fits that description is God. Thus, we have a second proof of God's existence.

Once he has completed the first task necessary to determine whether his thoughts contained truth (i.e., to prove whether God exists), the answer to the second question (i.e., whether God is a deceiver) falls into place naturally. We know that God exists and that he is a perfect being. "From this it is manifest that He cannot be a deceiver, since the light of nature teaches us that fraud and deception necessarily proceed from some defect" (*Meditations* 3). Descartes now has the guarantee he realized he needed at the beginning of this section. God exists, and his perfection means that he cannot deceive our minds. Only an imperfect being would do such a thing. This also trumps the hypothesis that some evil genius may be constantly confusing our thoughts. Presumably a good God would not allow another being to distort truth so thoroughly that we would believe only error. Therefore, our thoughts, provided they are "clear and distinct," are trustworthy.

THE SOURCE OF HUMAN ERROR

The conclusion above makes it clear that Descartes has a new problem that must be confronted. If God's goodness and perfection certifies our knowledge, how can we make mistakes and believe falsehoods? Why would our rational abilities lead us into error by generating ideas that are less than clear and distinct? God would not want that to happen, so why does he not create us so we would not be deceived? As a point of reference for the discussion that follows, Descartes sets up two principles that follow from his finitude.

> In considering this more attentively, it occurs to me in the first place that I should not be astonished if my intelligence is not capable of comprehending why God acts as He does; and that there is thus no reason to doubt of His existence from the fact that I may perhaps find many other things besides this as to which I am able to understand neither for what reason nor how God has produced them. . . . It further occurs to me that we should not consider one single creature separately, when we inquire as to whether the works of God are perfect, but should regard all his creations together. (*Meditations* 4)

In short, an infinite God could have purposes that we do not understand and we finite beings see only a small part of the story, not the total picture. Our finitude, then, is the possible source of our error.

With these ground rules in place, Descartes then moves on to what he believes to be at the core of our mistakes. When we make choices, we employ two distinct faculties: our reason and our will. The faculty of will is rather simple to define. Will is the power to do or not do some act. This, in Descartes's view, is a power that is not measured by degrees. Either we can choose or we cannot. Since we can choose freely, the will in itself is a pure and perfect power. In fact, Descartes says that "it is for the most part this will that causes me to know that in some manner I bear the image and similitude of God" (*Meditations* 4). In other words, since we, like God, possess the unlimited power of decision, it is this ability in us that makes us most like God.

The problem is that the will does not function in isolation from our other capacities. God's will is harnessed to his perfect knowledge and power. Thus, he cannot err or fail to accomplish his goals. Our will, by contrast, is linked with a reason that is imperfect. To this extent, then, the perfect will is unequally yoked with finite and fallible rational power. Error arises, Descartes decides, when we extend our will beyond what we know. When we make decisions without clarity or certainty, we make mistakes. His antidote for this is to "restrain my will within the limits of my knowledge that it forms no judgment except on matters which are clearly and distinctly represented to it by the understanding" (*Meditations* 4).

In summary, Descartes's view is that God's goodness certifies the truths arrived at by reason, provided our reason stays within the limits of clarity and distinctness. On the other hand, when we make errors, God cannot be blamed. "For I have certainly no cause to complain that God has not given me an intelligence which is more powerful . . . than that which I have received from him, since it is proper to the finite understanding not to comprehend a multitude of things, and it is proper to a created understanding to be finite; on the contrary, I have every reason to render thanks to God who owes me nothing and who has given me all the perfections I possess" (*Meditations* 4).

GOD'S EXISTENCE: TAKE TWO

Descartes has proceeded in a very methodical and orderly manner in building his argument point by point. He began by doubting previous beliefs, established certainty of his own existence by means of thought, analyzed the fact that he could think of a perfect being and concluded that this provided proof of God's existence. From the definition of God, he deduces that a perfect God would not allow us to be completely deceived, and, as we have just seen, he attempts to explain why God is not to blame when we do fall into deception. At this point in his argument, however, Descartes does something that seems out of place. He returns to the question of God's existence and offers yet another proof for his existence.

This new argument is a modification of the first one Descartes developed. It begins with the recognition that we can conceive of various types of ideas. For example, I can grasp the idea of a triangle in my mind, understanding that by definition it must have three sides and the sum of its angles must add up to 180 degrees. However, for me to be able to grasp the essence, the definitive characteristics, of a triangle does not require that any actual triangle exists. We could also grasp the concept of a polygon with 561 sides, even if such a shape cannot be found anywhere in the world. The point is this: the essence of a 561-sided polygon, or the concept of any other finite thing for that matter, does not require its existence. Things do not necessarily have to exist in order for me to think about them.

While essence and existence can be separated in many things, Descartes says that our concept of God presents us with a rather different situation. As he pointed out earlier, when we think of God, we are thinking of a perfect being. By definition, a perfect being must exist. If we thought of a being who possessed all other perfections but existence, we would not be thinking of a perfect being because we could add something to it—existence. In other words, existence is one of the perfections, along with infinity, omnipotence and other such attributes. Thus, Descartes concludes, "While from the fact that I cannot conceive God without existence, it follows that existence is inseparable from him, and hence that He really exists; not that my thought can bring this to pass, or impose any necessity on things, but, on the contrary, because the necessity which lies in the thing itself, i.e., the necessity of the existence of God determines me to think in this way" (*Meditations* 5).

THE EXISTENCE OF BODIES

To this point, Descartes has proved the existence of an immaterial self that thinks and a God who possesses the sum of all perfections, but there is still significant chunk of reality whose existence is still open to doubt—the world of material things. He begins this investigation by pointing out that *if* he possesses a body and bodies in general exist, it must be a different substance (essence) than the mind. This is obvious because when two different entities have the same characteristics, they belong to the same class. Descartes defines the differences between minds and bodies in this way: "And although possibly (or rather certainly, as I shall say in a moment) I possess a body with which I am very intimately conjoined, yet because, on the one side, I have a clear and distinct idea of myself inasmuch as I am only a thinking and unextended thing, and as, on the other, I possess a distinct idea of body, inasmuch as it is only an extended and unthinking thing, it is certain that this I [that is to say, my soul by which I am what I am], is entirely and absolutely distinct from my body, and can exist without it" (*Meditations* 6).

A couple of definitions are in order before we move forward from here. When he speaks of "extension," what he means is that the body takes up (or is extended in) space. Regardless of how large or small, then, every body is a three-dimensional thing. Therefore, he is saying that if bodies exist, they do not think, but they take up space. Minds do not exist in space, but think. The second bit of vocabulary that needs to be introduced is the word *dualism*. Descartes is commonly referred to as a dualist because he believes that a person is a combination of two different substances: a thinking, nonphysical mind and a nonthinking, physical body.

As we saw early in the *Meditations*, Descartes found a number of reasons to doubt his senses when they appeared to communicate to him that physical objects existed. One of these objections, the idea that a malignant genius distorted our thoughts, was removed once we proved the existence of a good God who would not allow such an evil being to completely confuse our thoughts. This restores Descartes's trust in mathematical ideas since such truths are known clearly and distinctly in his mind. This has relevance for the question of whether he can trust his senses because mathematics and geometry can be applied to what he perceives as physical objects. When we combine two marbles with three marbles and count a total of five, this is visual confirmation of the mathematical equation of $2+3=5$, a truth known clearly and distinctly. If the marbles are an illusion, but the illusion matches our mathematical deduction, there is no way of escaping error. However, as Descartes points out, if God provides no possible way to recognize or correct this mistake, then God would be a deceiver.

The belief that the world contains material entities also seems to be confirmed by the fact that we have an innate concept of what Descartes calls "bodies." The common characteristic of bodies is that they take up space. They have mass and weight. This innate concept of bodies is also confirmed by our sense experience. I do not have to employ will to perceive sensible objects. They impose themselves on us. Thus, the categories that allow us to think about physical characteristics such as hardness and weight are confirmed when we see a rock, pick it up and drop it on a pane of glass. Once again, our senses seem to confirm a general concept in the mind that hard, heavy objects will break thin, brittle glass. If we drop the rock on the glass accidentally, we get the same result. Thus, our perceptions do not seem to be caused by our will, but are imposed on us by an actual physical world. And, as we said above, if what our sense experience told us about the rock's weight and hardness and its effect on glass was a deception, "I do not see how He [God] could be defended from the accusation of deceit if these ideas were produced by causes other than corporeal objects" (*Meditations* 6).

The tricky part of this is that Descartes concedes that when we rely on the senses, we can easily come to erroneous conclusions. If we recall, the very beginning of his *Meditations* reminds us of how often and in how many ways the senses can be wrong. How do we let God off the hook on the charge of being a deceiver if our senses so often lead to mistakes? Again, Descartes reminds us that sense perception is not always clear. It must be judged against the clear and distinct concepts in the mind. Now he expands on that point. While "we must allow that corporeal things exist . . . they are perhaps not exactly what we perceive by the senses" (*Meditations* 6). The qualities that can be calculated and measured—location, divisibility, movement, mass, weight—are actual characteristics of the object. Other qualities, such a color or sound, are certainly perceived by individuals. However, as a scientist, Descartes says that how these are perceived is not what they *are*, because light and sound *are* actually waves. Therefore, while we experience colors and sounds, we do not experience them as they really are. Only the scientist with the tools to measure and mathematically analyze light and sound waves experiences light and sound as they are. Once again, we see how Descartes places much greater trust in the powers of reason and deduction than in induction and sensation.

THE INTERACTION BETWEEN MIND AND BODY

Now that he has established the reality of bodies and defined their characteristics, Descartes moves to the question of the relationship between the mind and the body. "Nature also teaches me by these sensations of pain, hunger, thirst, etc., that I am not only lodged in my body as a pilot in a vessel, but that I am very closely united to it, and so to speak so intermingled with it that I seem to compose with it one whole" (*Meditations* 6). The idea that soul and body comprise a whole is usually called interactionism. Interactionism says that body and soul are unified in such a way that when a part of the body is injured, it is *my* injury, and if serious enough, it can damage my capacity to think. Similarly, my thoughts cause my body to do things, and when this occurs, the actions are not just those of my mind or body, but they are the actions that belong to me as a unified entity. In contrast, when a sailor notices a rip in a sail, it is not a rip in his being. Moreover, if the sailor thinks of home, these thoughts alone cannot turn the ship back to homeport. It is only when the thinking mind directs the body with which it is unified that the wheel of the ship can be turned.

Having *asserted* his interactionist position, which link the mind and body in a unified whole, Descartes must now explain *how* this interaction occurs. He begins by unpacking some of the implications of what it means for our body to be an object, or more precisely, an object made up of a collection of objects. The laws of physics govern all physical things. This means that our body operates in the same manner that a machine, with its collection of parts, functions. Thus, Descartes does not hesitate in describing our body as a "machine so built up and composed of nerves, muscles, veins, blood and skin" (*Meditations* 6). Like all causation in physical objects, the various parts are moved by connection to other parts. Thus, "when I feel pain in my foot, my knowledge of physics teaches me that this sensation is communicated by means of nerves dispersed through the foot, which [are] extended like cords from there to the brain" (*Meditations* 6). These sensations, then, are gathered in the brain, or as Descartes tells us elsewhere, in the pineal gland located within the brain, and communicated to the mind. This description of the way the body interacts with the mind is simply reversed to describe how the mind directs the body by means of its thoughts.

This completes the trip that began with radical skepticism. Descartes has moved from doubting everything to the conclusion that he could be certain of his existence as a thinking thing, the existence of God as a being whose perfection confirms the truth of our thoughts so that they are known clearly and distinctly, and the existence of bodies, including our own. As he reflects on his accomplishments at the end of the book, he concludes that "certainly this consideration is of great service to me, not only in enabling me to recognise all the errors to which my nature is subject, but also in enabling me to avoid them or to correct them more easily" (*Medita-*

tions 6). We might be tempted to pass this off as the less-than-humble evaluation of a thinker a bit too full of himself. However, the important question is not whether Descartes is an arrogant jerk but whether he has accomplished what he claims. If he has been successful in showing us how we can gain certainty about some of the most important truths, these ideas are invaluable. However, we cannot determine whether he has been successful except by dissecting the process.

DISSECTING DESCARTES

Descartes is commonly referred to as the "Father of Modern Philosophy." With such a lofty designation, we would expect to find something groundbreaking in his ideas. At first glance, *Meditations on First Philosophy* would seem an unlikely place to discover the beginning of an intellectual revolution. At fifty pages, the book hardly seems to have the heft required to kick off a new era. Moreover, there is nothing out of the ordinary about Descartes's conclusions. His basic beliefs simply echo those of many scholars in the preceding centuries. What is it, then, that sets him apart? Perhaps more than what he believed, it is his methodology and the implications of his approach that mark him as a trendsetter.

His use of methodological doubt as a beginning point is a significant contrast to earlier philosophy. Unlike the medieval thinkers, he does not appeal to the authority of Scripture, the church fathers or classical philosophers to establish his points. For him, the past is suspect. In fact, it might be said that suspicion, not faith, is central to his method. His unwillingness to place implicit trust in ancient sources was part of what makes Descartes suspect to many of his contemporaries. Moreover, we should notice what fills the "authority gap" once Descartes has discarded traditional sources. The first certainty, and the one on which all other beliefs are grounded, is of himself as a thinking thing. This provides a hint about why Descartes generated so much controversy among the traditionalists. It is no longer God, the church or faith at the center of philosophy. The finite, autonomous thinking individual now fills that role.

Even if Descartes does leave the beaten path by starting with the doubting (thinking) human rather than the eternal God known by faith, what's the big deal? If Descartes ends up with beliefs that are compatible with Christianity, why should it make a difference where he begins or what method he uses? To outline the implications of Descartes's method, we will examine a couple of cases. In the first instance, it is interesting to recognize that Descartes "borrows" his basic arguments for God's existence from a medieval theologian in good standing with the church, Anselm of Canterbury. While the argument for God's existence and the conclusion are the same, there is an important difference. Anselm begins his argument for God's existence by stating, "I do not seek to understand so that I may believe; but I believe so that I may understand" (*Proslogion* 1). For Anselm, reason is always under the authority of faith. To put it in a different way, Anselm and the medieval thinkers started from convictions (one of which is faith in God's existence) that are not open to doubt because they are grounded in divine revelation. Anselm's trust in any particular method, then, is determined by observing which method supports the beliefs that he begins with.

It is different with Descartes. His approach could be summarized as, "I *do* seek to understand so that I may believe." Because methodological doubt requires that he suspend belief in any uncertain idea, his method, not a preestablished set of doctrines, is the starting point for philosophy. Perhaps placing a particular method governed by rationality at the center of philosophy would not be problematic if we could be as certain as Descartes that his system was airtight. However, one does not have to look very far to find leaks. For example, Descartes's motivation to prove God's existence came at the point when he knew with certainty that he thought, but could not yet be sure that any of his thoughts were actually true. To certify the truth of his thoughts, he must determine whether God exists and if God deceives us. But something odd happens in this proof. Descartes's argument for God's existence relies on a logical principle: the cause of an idea of a perfect being must be sufficient to account for the existence of the idea in my mind. But how does Descartes know this principle is true until he proves that God exists and cannot deceive? If he does not know whether this principle is true, his argument for God falls apart. If his argument for God falls apart, he cannot know whether the idea that "the cause of an idea must have as much reality as the effect" (or any other idea) is true. So he finds himself in a vicious circle on this matter.

The point of this exercise is that when we sanctify a method, it can take us places we did not anticipate going. Although methodological doubt eventually led Descartes to beliefs that are in conformity with Christianity, later thinkers, who, like Descartes, stake their philosophy on a particular method, come to some very different conclusions. Many of his successors determined that nothing can be known with certainty and there is no proof for God's existence. Under Descartes's ground rules, this makes it impossible to embrace Christianity or any other belief system because beliefs must be grounded in rational certainty. This, in effect, makes reason the authority over faith, which is the opposite of the medieval approach.

The role God plays in Descartes's philosophy marks a second major departure from previous thought. Because it believed that God is the creator, sustainer and savior of all creation, medieval philosophy began from the concept of God and moved outward. After all, if God is the one who brings unity and coherence to creation, only God can bring unity and order to philosophy. Descartes, on the other hand, moves God slightly to the side. Knowledge does not begin with God but with "I think, therefore I am." To be sure, God's perfection is the key that confirms the validity of the mind's cogitations. However, this reduces God to the role of a philosophical tool that we pull out when we have a gap that can only be bridged by a perfect Being. In the end, the rational human mind is at the center of Descartes's philosophy. Given this point of departure, he opens the door for later philosophers to completely eliminate God when they determined that God was not necessary to ground knowledge.

A third significant ramification of Descartes's philosophy is the idea that theology and science should be kept separate. He does not come right out and say it, but implicit in *Meditations* is an invitation to the church to butt out of scientific matters. When he speaks of bodies as entities that are known solely by the rules of physics and mathematics, the message is that the theologians are not equipped to make pronouncements about such things as the movements of heavenly bodies. In other words, when the church condemns Galileo, it is meddling in the scientist's business. When theologians apply the rule of theology to science, they will inevitably make mistakes because the tools that one uses to understand God, the perfect substance, are different from those that allow us to comprehend bodies.

Descartes's separation of God, minds and bodies into distinct types of substances that are known by different methods cuts both ways. He also seems to say that scientists have no business applying the rules of science to the study of the human mind or to God. If thought (the mental realm) is not bound by the laws that govern things with size, shape and location (the physical realm), we cannot expect to come up with a science of the human mind. Similarly, since God is not a physical being, the methods used by the physical sciences are of no use in helping us understand God.

This separation between the physical world and the nonphysical realm presents a number of questions. First, if theology and science come to different conclusions on related matters, how do we handle the conflicts between these two fields? By stressing the distance between the physical and nonphysical, Descartes does not really seem to provide any way to pull them back together and show how they are unified. Moreover, many will later argue that since science offers a means of verification that follows constant and demonstrable laws, we should follow science when it tangles with theology. Second, while Descartes uses God as the basis for trust in our senses, many later thinkers go even further than giving priority to science. The naturalists argue that we can get rid of the ideas like mind and God, and science can get along just fine. If this is the case, why not examine everything by means of scientific law and eliminate anything (e.g., God, the soul) that does not fit scientific explanation?

Descartes's sharp separation between the nonphysical and physical also presents difficult challenges, only one of which will be pursued here, for our understanding of human nature. His dualism emphasizes the difference between bodies and minds. While bodies are "extended and unthinking," the mind is "thinking and unextended." About the only thing they share in common is that both are finite. However, after establishing the radical differences between soul and body, he must now bring them back together and explain *how* they interact in a unified human being.

The problem that Descartes's interactionism creates can be illustrated by attempting to imagine what would happen if we placed a soul in an automobile rather than inside a human body. Because the car's mind and its mechanism influence each other, the entire car would feel pain right down to the tires if the engine threw a ring. If the pain is intense, the connection between the car's soul and body might make the car's soul incapable of performing its thinking processes. In its impaired state, the soul might turn out the headlights, even though they were in perfect mechanical condition. Perhaps this automotive soul could contemplate its options and choose to cause the steering mechanism to turn the car at appropriate locations, eventually arriving at a shop where the engine could be repaired. Such a navigation process involves more than simply guidance by some computerized steering gadget. A computer is just a machine that does not choose, but functions as it has been programmed to function. A real mind would be free to make decisions, which it might then communicate to the steering mechanism through its electrical/mechanical computer.

Does the idea of a car with a thinking soul, emotions, will and other human functions sound ridiculous? If the idea of an ensouled auto seems absurd, perhaps we should ask why a human body with a soul does not also sound odd. After all, if Descartes is correct, our body is of the same mechanical nature as our Honda and follows the same physical laws. Why, then, would it be any more difficult for a mind to interact with sheet metal than our bodies, both of which contain a healthy dose of carbon?

Descartes's attempt to link our mind and body in the pineal gland does not help because it is self-contradictory. As he points out, only bodies, which exist in space, can be described in terms of location. However, the mind cannot be said to exist in a place because it has no spatial attributes. Since the pineal gland is a place, how can the soul reside in this, or any other organ? Moreover, bodies can be moved and changed, but only according to causes that obey the laws of physics. If this is true, how can a soul, which does not operate according to physical laws, bring about movement or change in a body? The same problem presents itself in Descartes's claim that bodies cause changes in our mental states. How can a machine, whose causes are exclusively physical in nature, impose itself on something that has no physical attributes? The difficulty in conceiving this explains why it sounds strange to speak of capturing a thought in a Ziploc baggie.

In many ways, Descartes's significance can be seen in the way he straddles two very different worlds. None of his conclusions would raise the ire of the doctors of theology to whom *Meditations on First Philosophy* is dedicated. In this sense, he is a child of the Middle Ages. However, the centrality of the autonomous individual for philosophical method is modern. He is a medieval in his belief that God's existence can be proved, but thoroughly modern in refusing to cite Scripture and ecclesiastical authorities to bolster his view, relying instead on the power of human reason alone. He embraces the certainty of foundational truth, but his starting point in doubt opens the door for skeptical philosophy. Like those in the Middle Ages, he affirms the human being as a composite of body and soul, but the questions he leaves unanswered pave the way for successors to deny either the body or the soul, leading to new understandings of human nature.

Similarly, while the basic truth of theology, God's existence, guarantees the validity of the natural sciences for Descartes, later thinkers use his paradigm to separate science from theology and, in many cases, to assert that science leaves no room for God. There is an ongoing debate concerning the extent to which Descartes recognized the ramifications of his methodological doubt for philosophy. Whether fully conscious of the implications or not, it is certain that "I think, therefore I am" puts the Western intellectual world on a new path.

8

KIERKEGAARD
Are Faith and Ethics Related?

Most philosophers give you something to chew on intellectually, but their ideas can be easily relegated to the category of "interesting" and quickly forgotten, except for readers who are uncharacteristically willing to allow their head to inflame their heart. Kierkegaard is different. He goes directly for the passions, evoking the emotions and prodding the reader to a decision. But aiming at the gut is more than just a method. It is part of Kierkegaard's message. As he sees it, if we wade through all the options in the philosophical marketplace, logically weigh their relative merits, successfully plug all intellectual leaks in our favorite system and only then dedicate ourselves to living by these ideas, we will never make the commitment. Perhaps more accurately, the only commitment we will make is to the intellectual search. Purely intellectual searches, by their nature, are eternally incomplete. There are always more angles to consider, questions to answer and counterarguments to address. Thus, dispassionate, rational consideration of ideas blocks our chance of committing ourselves to anything and building a life on it.

Kierkegaard's alternative to reason is faith. But what is faith? One might think that faith would need no explanation in Kierkegaard's nineteenth-century Denmark. Virtually every citizen was a baptized Lutheran in good standing with the church. This group should have a pretty solid grip on faith. However, Kierkegaard calls this assumption into question. When he examined the comfortable social conformity and clear rational theology of Danish Lutheranism, he saw little connection between what they called faith and the fear and trembling of an Abraham with the knife wielded above his Isaac's body. Surely Abraham's faith was something different.

This is the point of Kierkegaard's *Fear and Trembling;** Danish Lutheranism had removed the anguish and terror from faith and turned it into a mass-marketed commodity that anyone could be comfortable with. Since faith is the one precondition of Christianity, the Danish church, which replaced the full-bodied faith of an Abraham with a faded image, could not be called Christian. Instead, Kierkegaard refers to it as "Christendom," the institutional shadow of real Christianity that finds solace in moral and social respectability. Because it uses the same vocabulary as Christianity and represents itself as a community of the faithful, Kierkegaard considers Christendom, not pure unmitigated paganism, to be faith's (and Christianity's) greatest enemy.

From Kierkegaard's perspective, Christendom's perversion of faith had a willing philosophical accomplice in the ideas of G. W. F. Hegel (1770-1831). Hegel's highly systematic thought dominated the agenda and direction of the European intellectual scene for almost a century and exerted significant influence on the theology of the era. While we will not go into detail on his philosophy (a decision for which you should thank me), it is necessary to outline some of its key components since they form the backdrop for *Fear and Trembling*. Hegel believes that there is a reality that is above all things, is in all things and moves all things; this he calls the Absolute. The Absolute progressively pushes all things, human beings included, toward perfection. History is the story of incremental improvement.

---

*The version of *Fear and Trembling* cited in this chapter is the Alastair Hannay translation (New York: Penguin, 1985).

Hegel argues that humanity's increasing ability to understand the workings of the universe is due to an increasing reliance on our rationality. When we apply the tools of reason, our political systems improve, our medical knowledge grows and economic systems become more efficient. But Hegel looks at this also from the opposite direction. The fact that the universe's movements are comprehensible shows that the force within it, the Absolute, is a rational entity, or more precisely, rationality itself. Therefore, all answers to life's problems require that we tap into the rational power that permeates the universe.

This brief overview of Hegelian metaphysics reveals two elements of religious significance. First, Hegel conceives of a salvation that is collective and gradual, rather than individual and instantaneous. The universe, including all of humanity, goes through a salvation process. This corporate concept of salvation means that individual human action takes on value only as it benefits the whole. Our fulfillment is possible only within society, through which we corporately contribute to and benefit from an increasing improvement of our world until all reaches the perfection of the Absolute. Second, the various religious faiths, Christianity included, express the hope of future perfection. However, because religious doctrines are not fully rational, they express this expectancy in a symbolic manner that gives us only a hazy representation. Hegel argues that to get the clearest picture of the Absolute, which is rational in nature, requires that we employ reason. In other words, philosophy, with its anchor wedged into rationality, gives us a better handle on the divine than theology, which combines the reasonable with irrational elements. Thus, for Hegel, faith is a step on the road to reason, which is the more coherent means of expressing reality.

Kierkegaard believed that Hegel had so influenced Danish Lutheranism that the latter gave the impression that salvation is found in the fulfillment of social obligations. Christianity is transformed into something logical, orderly and systematic—something devoid of passion. When we fulfill moral duties to fellow citizens (who, in Denmark, are also fellow church members) the demands of the Absolute are satisfied. As long as individuals fit in and contribute to society by being good, they are heaven-bound. However, "fitting in" was impossible for Kierkegaard, both in his personal life and in his ideas. Not that he didn't try earlier in his life, when he convincingly played the part of a wealthy young socialite. However, this part of the story needs to be put into biographical context.

SØREN KIERKEGAARD (1813-1855)

Kierkegaard's father, Michael Pederson Kierkegaard, went from an extremely impoverished youth to wealth and social respectability in adult life. He was close friends with the ecclesiastical leaders of the Danish church and moved easily within the elite social circles of Copenhagen. However, two events from Michael's past haunted him. First, as a starving young boy tending sheep in the frigid regions of Denmark, he had cursed God for his circumstances. Second, after his first wife died, he impregnated the family maid and hurriedly married her. When five of his seven children and both wives preceded him in death, the elder Kierkegaard interpreted this as a sign that God had cursed him for the two earlier events. The fact that he had all the external trappings of success only intensified his inner, spiritual sense of condemnation.

This feeling of living under God's curse was communicated to Søren. Like his father, the son seemed a wealthy man about town, showing up at the theater, dining at all the right cafes and associating with all the right people. But an inner discontent gnawed at him to the point that he contemplated suicide. However, he went through a life-changing spiritual experience at twenty-five, the nature of which he leaves very vague, and came to see his life calling as that of the penitent.

Perhaps this calling explains his broken engagement to Regina Olsen. There is little doubt that Kierkegaard loved her deeply, but for reasons unclear other than his belief that God had demanded that he give her up, he broke the engagement about a year after she accepted his marriage proposal. Several of the illustrations that appear in *Fear and Trembling*, not to mention his other writings, speak of a deep love that must be sacrificed for the highest love. And while Kierkegaard is oblique about his own under-standing of the marriage that could not be, it is difficult to avoid the con-clusion that a significant amount of autobiography lies beneath his at-tempt to work through the story of Abraham and the demands of faith.

ABRAHAM'S JOURNEY OF FAITH

The demand of faith is the theme of *Fear and Trembling*. The challenge for Kierkegaard is that Danish Christendom thinks it has met the require-ments of faith. How can he compel his readers to reconsider something they believe they already know? Rather than confront Christendom head-on, Kierkegaard recruits some help. First, he uses the story of Abraham, the paradigm of faith, to remind his readers of the anguish that character-ized his journey. Second, he tells the Abraham story through the eyes of a character named Johannes *de silentio*.

Our storyteller, Johannes, is an ironic figure. The first irony is that Jo-hannes, "the silent one," speaks. However, when he arrives at a climax where we might expect him to define faith, he retreats back into silence. Over and over again, he makes statements like "Abraham I cannot under-stand; in a way all I can learn from him is to be amazed" (*Fear and Trembling* 66). Perhaps the deepest irony is that Kierkegaard portrays Johannes, who denies that he understands or has faith, as one who comprehends faith bet-ter than those within Christendom. Christendom tries to make faith logi-cal, transform it into ethics and equate it with social decency. From Jo-hannes's perspective, faith, when properly observed, evokes awe, not explanations. Even one who lives a life of faith cannot help others under-stand it. "The true knight of faith is a witness, never a teacher" (*Fear and Trembling* 107). Faith dangles before Johannes as something that draws and fascinates, but he simply cannot make the step of faith. He is certain, how-ever, that what Christendom calls faith is a pale counterfeit.

Fear and Trembling opens with a series of attempts to make Abraham's call to sacrifice Isaac comprehensible to reason. We could understand Abraham if he made himself appear demented to Isaac: "Better that he

[Isaac] believe I am a monster than that he lose faith in Thee" (*Fear and Trembling* 46). We might believe that, even though Isaac was spared, Abraham became a different, joyless individual. This would communicate remorse for daring to contemplate fulfillment of his horrendous duty. Abraham might have protected himself psychologically by concluding that he had loved Isaac too much and that God's command was a means of rearranging his priorities. We might make sense of Abraham if he dutifully goes through the motions with doubt and hesitation, but nonetheless resigns himself to his awful, God-given task. The problem is that these scenarios, although they make Abraham's actions coherent and rationally defensible, are not true to the biblical account. However, Johannes also believes that if we can make sense of the story, Abraham would not be who he is: a man of faith.

In an attempt to understand faith without adulterating the story, Johannes starts from the beginning to recount Abraham's pilgrimage. He does not simply restate the facts, but draws our attention to the between-the-line psychological factors that heighten the anguish and incomprehensibility of Abraham's faith. First, to abandon one's country renders a person of this time a nonentity, but when God calls Abraham to leave his homeland, he packs and goes. This social alienation is intensified by childlessness in a culture where parenthood was the ticket to full membership. Then comes the incomprehensible promise to the elderly couple that they would have a son through whom Abraham would bless the nations.

The irony of all this is hard to miss. The one through whom the nations will receive blessings by his offspring has no logical possibility of producing a child and will have no country of his own for the remainder of his life. Moreover, the promise is followed by many years of excruciating silence. This silence, punctuated only by an ill-conceived plan to conceive that resulted in Ishmael (Gen 16:1-4), is finally broken in Abraham's ninety-ninth year. God renewed his pledge that Abraham and Sarah would have a son. Then Isaac's birth, the miraculous impossibility, brings God's promise into view.

Abraham's faith through all these years was rooted in anguish. It was overwhelmingly clear to him that he was incapable of bringing God's vow to fulfillment. Yet his call required that he believe the impossible, even as the hope became more impossible with each passing year. However, now that Isaac was with them and advancing toward realization of the promise, one might believe that the anguish of faith would surely diminish. Then God, once again, calls to Abraham. This time he is commanded to sacrifice Isaac.

The biblical account of this story is tantalizingly compact. It does not pause to tell us how Abraham verifies the source of the message or the message itself. He knows, but he can't explain it. So Sarah, Isaac and Eleazar, the trusted servant, get no explanation. Abraham simply gets up the next morning, makes the preparations, takes Isaac and begins a three-day journey to Moriah. The trip offers plenty of time for doubts and second thoughts, but Abraham continues. The only recorded verbal interchange comes when Isaac notes that all the elements of a sacrifice are present except for the lamb. Abraham's simple response is that "God will provide the ram." The altar is built, the wood arranged on it, Isaac is bound, the knife raised. Then Abraham sees the ram trapped in the thicket. God has provided.

THE KNIGHT OF FAITH

Johannes is fascinated by the tenacity of Abraham's faith, but he struggles with how he should understand it. His initial inclination is to categorize Abraham's resolve as heroism. However, something doesn't fit. As Johannes puts it, "The hero I can *think* myself *into*, but not Abraham; when I reach that height I fall down since what I'm offered is a paradox" (*Fear and Trembling* 63). The paradox Johannes speaks of arises when we compare two different ways of evaluating Abraham's contemplated action. "The ethical expression for what Abraham did is that he was willing to murder Isaac; the religious expression is that he was willing to sacrifice Isaac; but in this contradiction lies the very anguish that can indeed make one sleepless; and yet without that anguish Abraham is not the one he is" (*Fear and Trembling* 60). This paradox—that Isaac's sacrifice is simultaneously murder and an act of deep faith—once again drives Johannes to silence.

Is Abraham a hero? Seen from the outside, heroism involves the sacrifice of something valuable, and Abraham certainly values the son he intends to sacrifice. However, Kierkegaard does not believe that all heroes can be dumped into a single catchall category. What is missing is an account of the inner mechanisms of heroism. What are the motives, goals and expectations of the one who sacrifices? When these internal movements are factored into the equation, Kierkegaard says that we will discover two categories of hero: the knight of infinite resignation and the knight of faith.

The knight of infinite resignation is the ethical hero, someone who performs a sacrificial duty for the benefit of many. One exemplar of the knight of infinite resignation is King Agamemnon, whose fleet is stranded at sea by the doldrums. If the winds do not pick up, food supplies will be depleted and his soldiers will die. Told by his soothsayer that the calm was a sign of divine disfavor that can only be appeased by sacrificing his daughter, Iphigenia, Agamemnon kills her. His awful duty is performed with resignation; the beloved one must be sacrificed for the good of the many.

While Agamemnon's sacrifice of Iphigenia looks similar to Abraham's, there is a decisive difference. When King Agamemnon kills his daughter, that chapter of his life is closed. Iphigenia is gone forever. However, Abraham, the knight of faith, after renouncing his claim on the loved one, takes another step. He believes that the impossible will happen. God will restore what has been sacrificed. This clarifies the difference between ethics and faith and their respective heroes. Both begin by surrendering that which is cherished. This first step, resignation, is a matter of discipline. One must make the tough-minded decision to give up something dear. But discipline is of no use in the next movement: the movement of faith. The knight of faith knows that no amount of will power and determination will bring back what has been sacrificed. Neither Agamemnon nor Abraham can reanimate their offspring. To believe otherwise would be absurd. However, while rational thought offers no hope for restoration, the hero of faith "admits the impossibility and at the same time believes the absurd" (*Fear and Trembling* 76). Abraham, through faith, expects the restoration of Isaac.

THREE PROBLEMATA: ETHICS AS A TEMPTATION

The background of Kierkegaard's contrast between the two types of heroes, the tragic hero of ethics and the anguished hero of faith, is Hegel's attempt to squeeze faith into his ethical system. While Hegel views faith and moral righteousness as next-door neighbors, Kierkegaard wants to argue that they are very different. Kierkegaard now builds on his earlier distinction between faith and ethics and their respective forms of heroism by outlining more specific differences in three *Problemata*. All three *Problemata* begin by identifying a basic element of Hegel's ethical philosophy. Each element reveals a characteristic an act must possess to be classified as ethical. Kierkegaard then shows how Abraham's actions fail to meet the requirements of ethics. Finally, he outlines why ethics does not move us toward faith but is a temptation *leading away* from faith. By breaking matters down to these three ethical principles, Kierkegaard wants Danish Christendom to recognize that faith is not an aspect of ethics, but something radically distinct.

In the first *Problema*, Kierkegaard attacks Hegel's idea of the Universal, the term he uses to express the idea that ethical principles apply to all people at all times. In Hegel's philosophy, the Universal "rests immanently in itself, has nothing outside itself that is its *telos* [goal/purpose] but is itself the *telos* for everything outside" (*Fear and Trembling* 83). In short, the ethical life is an end in itself. We can get no higher than this. Moreover, in Hegel's view, ethics is always social. What is good benefits the whole of humanity. Therefore, our ultimate purpose is bound up in how our activities advance the cause of others.

Given Hegel's definition, Agamemnon's sacrifice of Iphigenia is ethical. An entire nation benefits from her death. Isaac's sacrifice is a different story, however. Society will not profit from it. "It is not to save a nation, not to uphold the idea of the State, that Abraham did it [endeavored to sacrifice Isaac], not to appease angry gods. If there was any question of the deity's being angry, it could only have been Abraham he was angry with, and Abraham's whole action stands in no relation to the universal, it is a purely private undertaking" (*Fear and Trembling* 88). Reason tells us that Abraham's social duty is to protect his son and that Isaac embodies the hope that Abraham's descendants will bless the entire world. But Abraham is quite prepared to kill him despite the fact that humanity will be harmed by his death.

Johannes's conclusion is that "Abraham is therefore at no instant the tragic hero, but something quite different, either a murderer or a man of faith" (*Fear and Trembling* 85). These two options limit our choices in evaluating Abraham's status. If the universal is an end in itself, as is the case in ethics, Abraham is the worst kind of murderer imaginable. He can be a hero only if the goals of faith differ radically from those that govern ethics. Therefore, if Abraham is a hero of faith, we cannot, as Hegel does, view faith and ethics as contiguous realms. Instead, Abraham is a model of heroism only if faith has its own distinct standards. Agamemnon, the ethical hero, demonstrates the highest level of moral behavior in sacrificing his daughter for the sake of the many. However, "with Abraham it is different. In his action he overstepped the ethical altogether, and had a higher *telos* outside it, in relation to which he suspended it" (*Fear and Trembling* 88).

This "overstepping" of moral duties is what Kierkegaard refers to as the "teleological suspension of the ethical." The goal (telos) of ethical actions is the betterment of the world. While Kierkegaard acknowledges that ethical accomplishment won by wrestling with life's moral challenges is a great thing, "he who strove with God became greater than all" (*Fear and Trembling* 50). This is Abraham's claim to fame. When confronted with a choice between moral responsibility and his relationship with God, he determines that the latter is the higher goal, and thus his ethical obligations are suspended.

Two aspects of the teleological suspension of the ethical deserve clarification. First, ethical truths, according to Hegel, are inscribed in the structure of the world. They are eternal and cannot be superseded by anything. Suspension of the ethical would require that God (the Absolute) contradict himself. In contrast, Kierkegaard says that every moral value is arbitrary apart from God. Only God is absolute, and God alone confers value on people and actions. Therefore, the only right choice for Abraham, even when it violates the standards of ethics, is to sacrifice Isaac when God commands it. The second point follows from this. Abraham cannot take it upon himself to decide when ethical obligations can be suspended. That is God's call. Abraham's decision, therefore, is not whether he should sacrifice Isaac in violation of his moral duties, but whether he will fulfill his civic and moral duties or follow the divine mandate.

With this in view, Abraham can choose to do the ethical thing or follow God and allow the ethical to be suspended. In this equation, "the temptation is the ethical itself which would keep him from doing God's will" (*Fear and Trembling* 88). Thus, rather than being the apex of human obligation and achievement, as Hegel would have it, Kierkegaard maintains that the ethical tempts Abraham away from faith and his relationship with God.

GOD OR SOCIETY

Problema two deals with the question of who our audience is when we make our decisions. Viewed from the perspective of the Universal, "all duty is duty to God" (*Fear and Trembling* 96). Thus, social or familial obligations belong to the same category as divine imperatives. However, Kierkegaard counters that God and society—Creator and creation—are radically distinct spheres. Ethical action brings me into relationship with my neighbor because my neighbor benefits from it. However, it does not bring me into relationship with God, who cannot benefit from my feeble actions. So when it comes to the either-or choice between reconciliation with God or his fellow citizens, Abraham chooses God. This is the foundation of his heroism. Abraham is the one "who first saw and bore witness to that tremendous passion that scorns the fearful struggle with the raging elements and the forces of creation in order to struggle with God instead" (*Fear and*

Trembling 56). All other human tasks pale to insignificance alongside the terrible and wonderful opportunity to know God.

The paragraph above reveals a fundamental difference between Hegel and Kierkegaard concerning salvation. For Hegel, the Absolute is awesome by reason of its scope. All reality is eventually swallowed in a single gulp of salvation. This social dimension of salvation makes it a fearful matter for the Hegelian to be isolated from society. For Kierkegaard, however, the awesomeness of the Absolute is found in its specificity. God puts the individual above the whole. We will not all skip through the gates of heaven together singing "We Are the World." Salvation requires that we separate ourselves from the herd and stand alone before the Wholly Other God. This is exactly where Abraham found himself—isolated from society and incapable of being comprehended by others. Not even others with faith will be able to understand. While there is fear in social isolation for the person of faith, it is superseded by apprehension that our actions will run contrary to God's will for us. However, Kierkegaard wants us to be clear that faith does not exempt us from dread. The fear and trembling that consumes Abraham is his knowledge that he stood before God with no resources of his own to rely on.

Therefore, Kierkegaard once again concludes that the universal (ethical action) is not the route to salvation, but a temptation. "Abraham must have now and then wished that the task was to love Isaac in a way meet and fitting for a father, as all would understand and as would be remembered for all time; he must have wished his task was to sacrifice Isaac for the universal, so as to inspire fathers to illustrious deeds—and he must have been well nigh horrified by the thought that for him such wishes were merely temptations and must be treated as such" (*Fear and Trembling* 104). But Abraham does not receive salvation from society, and its rules do not constitute his ultimate concern. Abraham cannot approach God's call as a member of a group, but as an individual who "knows it is terrible to be born in solitude outside the universal, to walk without meeting a single traveler. He knows very well where he is, and how he is related to men.

Humanly speaking he is insane and cannot make himself understood to anyone" (*Fear and Trembling* 103).

THE DEMAND FOR DISCLOSURE

Abraham's apparent insanity—or what surely looks like insanity to everyone around him—provides the segue to the third *problema*. For the Hegelian the "ethical task is to unwrap himself from . . . concealment and become disclosed in the universal" (*Fear and Trembling* 109). In other words, ethical individuals have an obligation to explain their actions. Ethical explanation is possible because the universal is logical and orderly. In other words, ethical behavior is rational behavior, so it makes sense to rational people.

But God's mind does not conform to human canons of rationality. To be sure, Kierkegaard does not doubt that there is logic to the divine commands. What he doubts is the capacity of finite human reason to ascend the tower of Babel and discern God's logic. Thus, Abraham could explain to all why, as a father, he loves Isaac above all earthly things. A father's love for his own child is reasonable, responsible and ethical. What Abraham cannot do, given the limitations of our mind to comprehend God's ways, is explain why God would order him to kill his only son. When Abraham makes the preparations to sacrifice Isaac, he finds himself incapable of defending his plans to others. Rather than offering some futile explanation for his contemplated action, then, Abraham remains silent about his plans.

To this point, our focus has been fixed on two different approaches: the ethical life and the life of faith. However, Kierkegaard believed there was a third level that may describe more people than the other two. The state of immediacy, or what Kierkegaard calls the aesthetic life, is ruled by instantaneous needs, desires and concerns. This way of life does not see beyond one's self and, for this reason, sees no reason to explain its actions to others. In this sense, it bears some surface resemblance to the life of faith. But there is a decisive difference. The aesthete can conceal motives and goals, or can disclose these goals and motives so that others understand. If the latter is chosen, we enter the ethical realm in which our actions are laid open for others to judge. The aesthete, as Kierkegaard puts it, "can unwrap himself from this concealment and become disclosed in the universal," (*Fear and Trembling* 109) but the person of faith cannot. In other words, the aesthete has an option that is not available to Abraham. Even if Abraham wanted to explain his behavior, it would not make sense to others. Who can rationally defend the murder of an innocent?

The reason aesthetes can clear their reputation by disclosure is that explanations allow them to reestablish communion with those who have been wronged. However, Abraham does not seek communion with his fellow humans. He seeks a relationship with God, and the nature of this relationship requires his silence. Thus, the three significant others in Abraham's story—Sarah, Eleazar, Isaac—receive no explanation of his actions. As far as we know, Abraham said nothing to the first two. To Isaac's question about the sacrificial preparations, all Abraham can say is "My son, God will provide himself a lamb for a burnt offering" (*Fear and Trembling* 139). Even this is not an explanation, for neither Abraham nor Isaac knows what it means. Abraham, as a person of faith, cannot inform (or teach). He can only witness.

Kierkegaard makes an interesting observation about the function of disclosure. "The relief of speech is that it translates me into the universal" (*Fear and Trembling* 137). In other words, logical justification of our actions is our passport into the human family, which is why it plays such a central role for Hegel's ethics. But, as we have seen, Abraham's goal is not to be part of society, but to know God. As a consequence, Abraham lives in anguish because even those most intimately bound up in the story cannot understand what he is doing. Iphigenia can understand why Agamemnon does what he does, so she can also make the heroic step of resignation. Isaac, on the other hand, will never understand Abraham. Therefore, faith necessarily places one in a position of anguish, which can be relieved by disclosure. The cost of disclosure, however, is one's relationship to God. Once again, then, the universal's demand that individuals reveal their intent and goal is a temptation to retreat from faith.

FAITH AS AN ABSURD PARADOX

The conclusion Kierkegaard intends for us to draw from the comparison of Abraham's actions to the demands of the universal is this: faith is absurd. We must be very careful to understand what he means by absurdity, however. Kierkegaard does *not* mean that Christianity is untrue. Instead, absurdity means that Christianity does not fit within the parameters of human logic. It makes no sense (to us) for God to ask Abraham to sacrifice his son. This violates the moral standards God himself would later explicitly impose on his people. Even the most basic truths of Christianity are absurd by rational measures. The idea that the God who speaks the universe into existence would become a human, or that Jesus, God incarnate, would (or could) die for ungrateful, rebellious, finite human beings bursts the boundaries of reasoning.

Kierkegaard does offer a bit of logic to this seemingly illogical God and his demands. The key is found in the structure of human nature. On the one hand, we are finite, creaturely beings who experience all the limitations imposed by life in the finite realm. On the other hand, there is something that distinguishes human beings from the rest of the created order. An aspect of our being is made for, and longs for, a relationship with the Infinite. Thus, we straddle two worlds. The trials of the finite world can be navigated with some success by using the tools that are designed for it. The highest of these finite tools is reason, and to this extent, Hegel is on track. Our endeavors within the world of finite individuals, nonhuman creatures and inanimate objects are aided by rational action, and this is good as far as it goes.

As useful as reason is for our interactions with creation, it is of no help in fulfilling our need for communion with the Creator. This is the mistake of Christendom that Kierkegaard so strongly criticizes. Like a person trying to fly to the sun in a weather balloon, Christendom attempts to establish relationship with the Infinite God by the finite tools under our control. When these fail, Christendom solves the problem by redefining faith as a logically structured life of mutually beneficial relationships directed by rationality. Thus, faith is replaced by clear thinking, and God is defined by social acceptance. However, once faith and God are defined in such a manner, we lose all that is infinite in Christianity.

If rationality, self-discipline, living peacefully with neighbors and all the other things that are part of the ethical life do not bring salvation, how do we get there? Kierkegaard believes that knowing God requires a "leap of faith." It is as if we are standing on the edge of a cliff peering into complete darkness. A voice calls out to us: "Jump and I'll catch you." We know that behind us is the frustrating experience of trying to achieve salvation on our own. Even our attempt to see through the darkness to determine whether we will, in fact, be caught represents reliance on our capacities. Faith requires that we forsake all our efforts and jump. This is the paradox of faith. By the standards of logic, it makes no sense to go back. We know the futility of that route. At the same time, it does not make sense, by any objective measure of logic, to take the leap of faith.

The leap of faith cannot be made on the basis of reason, and there are no halfway measures. This is what Kierkegaard says that faith is: a passionate commitment of our whole being. Only passion can take us where logic cannot go. We can see from this, then, that Kierkegaard's definition of faith is a radical departure from the comfortable, logical and socially acceptable life of Christendom. Christendom is safe; faith requires that we bet the entire bankroll on something that is absurd and out of our control. But why not? Isn't our attempt at control what leaves us in frustration?

DISSECTING KIERKEGAARD

As mentioned at the beginning of the chapter, it is difficult for people to remain neutral about Kierkegaard. Some see him as a great danger. Others view him as the best thing that ever happened to philosophy. However, it is my experience that many are torn in their evaluation. In the same way that Johannes *de silentio* was both drawn to and repelled by faith, you may find yourself both attracted to and fearful of Kierkegaard's ideas. Regardless of your initial response, Kierkegaard raises some interesting questions about the relationship of faith and reason, the connection between salvation and ethics, how we should understand God, what human nature is all about and the proper interpretation of Abraham's story.

People in the Christian circles with which I am most familiar tend to be very comfortable in saying that there is much about God and his ways that are mysterious. If God is who Scripture says, why would we think that our knowledge of him could be squeezed into neat categories accessible to human logic? At the same time, these Christians would be very reluctant to describe God's ways as absurd. Instead, they would say that there is evidence (if not proof) of God's existence, the deity of Jesus, the reliability of Scripture and other foundational Christian beliefs. Since we can reasonably move from these foundations to faith, we do not believe in an absurdity. Kierkegaard's argument is that we cannot have it both ways. It is an either-or thing. *Either* we rely on faith *or* we rely on reason. Any attempt to build from reason to faith represents trust in our abilities for salvation, and results in the creation of a finite god that is easy to follow, such as the god of Christendom. The question Kierkegaard raises is whether this is an either-or situation. If reason represents a detour on our journey of faith, is any attempt to establish the validity of faith on rational grounds a deficiency of faith? On the other hand, Kierkegaard would ask how, if God is Wholly Other, our minds can be of any use in establishing a relationship with him.

Similar tensions arise for many Christians in working through Kierkegaard's understanding of salvation and ethics. Many Christians appreciate his warning that we should not equate a moral life with salvation. Even when we know better, we often fall into the trap of Christendom by using ethics as a barometer of our faith. The difficulty for many, however, is in believing that God would require unethical actions. It is one thing to say that ethics and faith are not the same thing. However, to assert, as Kierkegaard does, that the ethical life is a temptation that leads away from true faith seems to push the envelope. If the worlds of ethics and salvation are really so different, why does Scripture have so much to say about ethical expectations for saved people? However, Kierkegaard would remind us that this same Bible contains the story of Abraham. If his analysis of the call to sacrifice Isaac in *Fear and Trembling* is even close to correct, Kierkegaard makes it difficult to see Abraham as a model of morality.

One of Kierkegaard's most strident criticisms of Christendom was that, in its desire to make God accessible, it waters down the biblical portrayal of God and makes faith easy. I suspect he would also accuse the American Christianity of today of the same thing. We package God in a way that minimizes the demands made on those who follow him. There are, to be sure, some requirements. We are expected to avoid actions that would harm others and ourselves. Rules like those in the Ten Commandments are seen as guidelines for proper behavior. In short, we are counted on to be good people, the type of people that Hegel likes. However, Kierkegaard would say that we cannot define a moral lifestyle as faith if we compare it to the anguish of Abraham. The God who demands the sacrifice of Isaac is a far cry from the friendly, predictable and minimally intrusive portrayal of God so often offered today. To be sure, Kierkegaard argues that Abraham's anguished faith results in his salvation, so the story ultimately ends with a gracious God who is known by Abraham. Nonetheless, many wonder whether Kierkegaard's reading of this story reveals a God of grace and love or a capricious despot who plays games with us. Abraham is kept on the hook, waiting for a son for decades. After Isaac is born, Abraham is whiplashed between the joy of seeing Isaac grow and mature, having to find the resolve to carry out the sacrifice and finally experiencing the last-minute reprieve as the knife hovers over his son.

One final matter to consider in Kierkegaard's thought is the individualism implicit in his understanding of faith. Abraham cannot point to any external evidence that will justify what he is about to do as he leaves for Mount Moriah. All he can say is that, based on his inner relationship with God, he knows that this is what he is to do. However, any decent church member would (I hope) do anything possible to stop a father who claimed to have received a message from God to kill his child, no matter how convinced this father was about hearing God's voice. Even in less dramatic examples, Scripture seems clear that there are certain objective standards that people of faith are to be held accountable for. Thus, Kierkegaard's emphasis on the primacy of the individual over the whole raises tricky questions about how the church is to carry out its responsibility to discipline, exhort and correct individual members.

One of the most disturbing things about *Fear and Trembling* is what happens to our future attempts to read Abraham and Isaac's story. It now may be very difficult to hear it as an inspiring morality play. Morality stories call us to imitation. Surely we are not called to imitate Abraham's intent to sacrifice his son, and Kierkegaard clearly indicates that this is not his message. Instead of being an ethical hero whose actions are imitated, Abraham is a knight of faith. As Johannes *de silentio* tells us, Abraham is not a model of *what* to do since God (hopefully) calls none of us to the same action required of him. What will be demanded of us is out of our control. Abraham is simply a witness to *how* we should respond when God calls us away from the demands of everyday life, suspends our ethical obligations and requires an illogical leap of faith. If anticipation of this call gives rise to fear and trembling, Kierkegaard might say that you are on your way to faith.

9

MARX

Does Money Determine Our Beliefs?

Have you ever had a really rotten job—the type that makes you hate to get up in the morning and watch the clock all day as it slowly moves toward quitting time? If you haven't experienced this yet, odds are that you will. The sad fact is that many people have such jobs all their life. Chances are that most people in these crummy jobs believe that the problem is their particular occupation. Maybe, however, it is not just *this* job, *this* boss or *this* company that stinks. Perhaps the problem is bigger. Perhaps the entire economic system is responsible for their misery. Karl Marx is betting that the latter is the case, and built his entire philosophy around this concept.

You probably did not expect that a philosopher would spend much time talking about something as mundane as work. After all, isn't philosophy supposed to deal with impractical things? Marx, however, made work the centerpiece of his thought, and I think he is right in drawing such a tight connection between philosophy and what we do for a living. If one of philosophy's main concerns is how to get the most satisfaction and fulfillment in life, it seems natural to look at our jobs. During the prime years of our adult lives, we spend more of our waking hours at work than any-where else. If our job sucks the vitality out of us, it is difficult to have a positive view about other aspects of life. While most of us, with a little reflection, will recognize that what we do for a living is tied in with our entire outlook on matters, Marx says the integration between labor and life goes deeper than almost anyone imagines.

Many of us have been preconditioned to reject Marx's thought out of hand. After all, he was the intellectual father of Communism, and Communism's record on just about any important issue—economic output; freedom of speech, movement or worship; respect for the will of citizens—is rather dismal. In view of our preconceptions about Marx, a word of warning is in order, especially for Christians. Just as we would shudder at the thought of people drawing their conclusions about Jesus' teachings on the basis of what those claiming to be Jesus' followers have done, we ought to assume that, just maybe, Marx's teachings should be considered separately from the actions of those who have called themselves Marxists. Moreover, if Christians would read Marx's aims without knowing the source, I strongly suspect that they would find most of his aspirations commendable. The question is whether the worthy goals he seeks are attainable by the means he prescribes.

KARL MARX (1818-1883)

People often assume that Marx's ardent advocacy of Communism is the result of his own impoverished situation. While it is true that during his adult years he and his family endured a hand-to-mouth existence, this was a result of Marx's choices. He was so committed to promoting the cause of Communism that he spent every available moment on research and writing. As a result, his family financial situation was frequently in sad condition.

Marx's childhood was very different, however. He grew up in rather privileged circumstances. His father was a lawyer of some community stature and had the resources for young Karl to enter the university at Bonn. The early phase of his academic career involved more time in the beer garden than the library, providing little evidence that the world had a budding social revolutionary on its hands. Because of his lack of academic focus at Bonn, his father "encouraged" a transfer to the university at Berlin, and, while there, Marx encountered economic and political ideas that would shape his mission in life.

After college, he wrote and edited for publications that championed the cause of workers' movements and often was forced to move because of government suppression of his work. In 1844 he met Friedrich Engels, the son of a wealthy textile manufacturer. The two of them collaborated on many works, including the *Communist Manifesto* (1848), and Engels supplemented Marx's meager income frequently. Marx's activities with the Communism League made him unwelcome almost everywhere in continental Europe. In 1848 he moved to London, where he spent the remainder of his life, most of the time studying and writing in the British Museum.

HISTORY AS CLASS STRUGGLE

What makes people dislike their job? One reason, as a colleague of mine once profoundly observed, is that there are a lot of lousy jobs out there. No doubt about it, some jobs (possibly your current job) are boring, unimaginative, repetitive and downright humiliating. Quite often, there is more to it. A leading factor in work dissatisfaction is that we do not believe we are paid what our work is worth. The suspicion is that if we could follow the money trail to see what our labor produces and who actually gets it, we would discover that someone else is raking in big bucks from our sweat.

"Follow the money" is an often-prescribed principle for locating the source of a misdeed. This tenet observes that money, and the power that comes with it, is such a powerful motivator that scandals are illuminated by looking at whose financial interests are involved. Marx's key idea is that it is nothing less than scandalous that so many throughout history have experienced dire poverty, starvation and a denial of basic human rights while the fruit of their work lines the pockets of the wealthy few. When we learn the various ways in which the wealth produced by the lower classes has enriched the "haves," Marx claims, we will discover that the key to interpreting all human history is found in economics. Thus, the opening line of the *Communist Manifesto* states, "The history of all hitherto existing society is the history of class struggles" (1). In other words, the whole of history comes into focus if we follow the money to see how it is produced, why some people end up with lots of it and why others never have enough.

When Marx states that history is a story of class struggle, the one part that really needs little explanation is the idea that a disproportionate distribution of wealth creates opposition between classes. It is not difficult to see why this would be the case. The poor want what the rich have in order to improve their lot in life, and the rich want to preserve and increase their wealth. The goals of the two groups are thus in direct conflict. However, Marx's idea goes much deeper than simply a claim that the "haves" and the "have-nots" do not enjoy a harmonious coexistence. He says that the tension between these classes is *history itself*; we cannot understand the past (or predict the future) without comprehending the dynamics that exist between the rich and the poor. Why, then, does Marx draw such a close association between the events of history and economic inequity?

The first step in understanding how Marx connects the movements of history and class struggle is to recognize that money is not made within a social vacuum. Instead, wealth is always produced within the context of economic and social systems. For example, a number of entrepreneurs today have become amazingly wealthy (sometimes for only a few months) by creating ways that information can be organized and disseminated over the Internet. This is possible only because of the convergence of many factors. You need a literate population, a society with sufficient wealth to afford computers, the electronic infrastructure that allows data to flow from one computer to another, the computer hardware itself, electricity and a multitude of other elements, many of which did not exist anywhere in the world twenty years ago. In short, generation of capital through e-commerce is made possible by evolving social realities. No matter how ingenious the software, you could not have made money with a dot.com enterprise in medieval Spain.

Of course, people did become wealthy in medieval Spain, but the process of creating wealth in that place and time was determined by a different set of social realities. Thus, as Marx tells us in the second line of *Communist Manifesto*, the identities of the haves and the have-nots—"Freeman and slave, patrician and plebeian, lord and serf, guild-master and journeyman" (1)—change throughout history because the economic systems in which money is created are dynamic. However, there is one additional piece to this backdrop. Wealth is not *just* wealth. It is power, and in each period, the affluent, regardless of the fiscal structure of the time, also hold the reins of power. This not only allows them to make the rules by which society operates, which guarantees that they get to keep and increase their wealth, but perhaps more important, the wealthy can use their power to shape the ideas that rule the day. If the rich can influence the way people think about themselves, they can justify why they have all the toys and may even convince the have-nots that they are poor because they deserve it, because God has ordained it or because they have violated some rule about how the world operates. Ideas are power, and those who control this power govern the way we think.

To explain how economic imbalance comes into being and develops, Marx employs what was then a new tool: social science. Prior to Marx's day, social movements and transitions were not thought to be open to prediction or scientific analysis because they were viewed as the result of choices. If human decisions are free, they do not follow laws. But Marx was at the vanguard of a movement that argued that our decisions are not free. Freely chosen ideas do not create the way we govern, worship or make our money. Instead, government, religion and economics (what Marx calls our material conditions) determine our ideas. In short, social structures create the beliefs that rule any given age. These social realities are open to scientific analysis and investigation. Thus, Marx argues that we can understand social change in a similar manner to the means by which we understand the development of a fetus within a womb. Through careful observation of the changes in society, we can gradually recognize the laws that determine this process. Then we apply the laws to the present situation in order to predict future movements and to change things that are not right. In short, Marx is one of the pioneers of sociology, the scientific study of society. As such, he sees human history as data that provide the keys, if properly understood, that will allow us to change history's course.

THE STAGES OF ECONOMIC HISTORY

The biologist studies organisms that go through various stages of life—infancy, youth and adulthood. Marx believes that human history also develops through a series of stages, albeit longer ones. To know where we are going, we need to know the stages through which we have passed. Marx calls the earliest epoch of history the communal (or Asiatic) stage. This stage was characterized by basic hunter-gatherer societies in which virtually everyone was engaged in the same type of activity: trying to get enough to eat. The problem with such an economic/social structure is that people are left at the mercy of the things they do not control, such as weather and shifts in native animal or plant populations, which made food supplies highly unreliable.

The demise of the communal system occurs when a more dependable and productive economic system emerges. This second historical stage is characterized by slavery. The slave owner gains an advantage over hunters and gatherers, not only by having several people who do his or her work, but also by possessing workers who can specialize in certain tasks. This specialization allows for greater efficiency and the ability to take on large-scale projects. The most notable early improvement is cultivation of crops and domestication of animals, which makes tomorrow's lunch more likely. This stage also offers an additional new element not seen before. An economy based on slavery introduces a gap between the owner and the owned.

Slavery gradually fades away, not because of moral reasons (although moral reasons were offered by the wealthy people who would benefit from the demise of slavery in the next stage), but, once again, for economic reasons. From a purely economic perspective, slavery is flawed because it relies on a form of property—the slave—that can run away, be taken by others or die. Thus, feudalism, which is primarily based on ownership of land, replaces slavery. The serfs who farm the land for the feudal lords are essentially slaves since they are tied to the land. However, because they receive a percentage of the crop they raise, they have an incentive for greater productivity that is not present in slavery, an incentive from which the owner benefits. Similarly, those who were apprenticed are virtual slaves to guild masters for most of their lives, but have performance incentives that offer some slim hope of eventually becoming masters themselves. With the emergence of guilds, we get increased specialization and economic factors that favor the clustering of the guilds in towns and small cities.

Marx acknowledges that these different stages rise and disappear at different rates and times in different geographical regions. Since he is writing at the seam in European history between what he calls "the tottering feudal society" and the birth of capitalism, he focuses most of his attention on the characteristics and problems of the latter. He introduces his analysis of capitalism by stating, "The modern bourgeois society that has sprouted from the ruins of feudal society has not done away with class antagonisms. It has but established new classes, new conditions of oppression, new forms of struggle in place of the old ones" (*Communist Manifesto* 1). In other words, the opposition of the haves and have-nots remains. All that changes is the identity of the groups and the manner in which the wealthy oppress the poor. One of the newer factors, however, is that the distinction between the two social classes becomes much clearer in capitalism because the gap between the wealth of the bourgeoisie (the wealthy owners) and the poverty of the proletariat (the workers) is wide and growing.

THE EMERGENCE OF CAPITALISM

As noted above, Marx believes that social change is a matter of cause and effect. Therefore, his first step is to explain the social conditions that brought about the demise of feudalism and the appearance of capitalism. Impetus for this new economic system came from the discovery of the Americas, new trade with India and China, and colonization. Localized guilds were not prepared to enter new markets that demanded large quantities of goods that had to be transported great distances. These trade guilds were replaced by manufacturing processes that were rapidly revolutionized by the invention of massive machines. Thus, in a very short time, "the place of manufacture was taken by the giant, Modern Industry, the place of the industrial middle class, by industrial millionaires, the leaders of whole industrial armies, the modern bourgeois" (*Communist Manifesto* 1). This newfound economic power was soon translated into political power as the modern representative state replaced government by the nobility, which was occurring rapidly in Europe and America. However, Marx is convinced that representative government is not representative of all. Rather, those who possess economic power get to set the political agenda and will do so in a manner that allows them to achieve their interests.

As capitalism came to dominate the economic and political landscape in Europe, it changed the value system that had been in place during feudalism. Because the older system had wrapped occupations such as medicine, law, poetry, science and the clergy in the cloak of superstition and mystery, it viewed various professions with awe and respect. Capitalism changes all that by drowning our esteem for the professions "in the icy water of egotistical calculation" (*Communist Manifesto* 1). Because money alone determines what will be valued, capitalism "has left remaining no other nexus between man and man than naked self-interest, than callous 'cash payment'" (*Communist Manifesto* 1). The system turns everyone into a wage laborer, and the professions formerly esteemed because of the mysterious powers they possessed are now valued only because they generate lots of money. So far-reaching is the influence of capitalism that even family relations are determined by money. Marriage, childbearing and child rearing are all considered in terms of economic impact.

Since capitalism is built on competition, owners must continue to expand their businesses or they will disappear. Thus, "the need of a constantly expanding market for its products chases the bourgeoisie over the whole surface of the globe. It must nestle everywhere, settle everywhere, establish connexions everywhere" (*Communist Manifesto* 1). To preserve itself, capitalism breaks down national identities and undercuts what is unique in cultures by dangling the lure of cheap goods and the threat of insignificance. "It compels all nations, on pain of extinction, to adopt the bourgeois mode of production; it compels them to introduce what it calls civilisation into their midst, i.e., to become bourgeois themselves. In one word, it creates a world after its own image" (*Communist Manifesto* 1).

One aspect of capitalism's homogenization of society is centralization. At the beginning of the nineteenth century, the populations of Paris and London were approximately 500,000 and 800,000 respectively. At the end of the century, Paris had around 3,300,000 occupants while London grew to 6,500,000. This is paralleled by centralization of provinces into national governments with a single law code and system of taxation. This consolidation allows for economic efficiency and the ability to produce goods on a massive scale. Thus, Marx's beef with capitalism is not that it does not create enough wealth. He concedes that the bourgeoisie has generated wealth on a level never before seen in history. "Subjection of Nature's forces to man, machinery, application of chemistry to industry and agriculture, steam-navigation, railways, electric telegraphs, clearing of whole continents for cultivation, canalisation of rivers, whole populations conjured out of the ground—what earlier century had even a presentiment that such productive forces slumbered in the lap of social labour?" (*Communist Manifesto* 1).

WHAT IS WRONG WITH CAPITALISM?

This continuing subjection of natural forces looks like a gravy train that will generate ever-greater wealth for the bourgeoisie and thus solidify its grasp on power. Marx is convinced, however, that he sees something that others do not. "Modern bourgeois society . . . is like the sorcerer, who is no longer able to control the powers of the nether world whom he has called up by his spells" (*Communist Manifesto* 1). In other words, Marx believes that capitalism conjures up the very weapons that will bring it down. Moreover, by creating a huge proletariat, whose interests are at odds with the capitalists, capitalism creates the opponents who will use those weapons against it. However, before providing a full explanation of how capitalism eventually strangles itself, Marx wants us to know why we should be happy to see it die.

The answer, in a nutshell, is that capitalism dehumanizes humans. In this system, the owners incur certain costs in producing goods. They have to purchase raw materials and manufacturing equipment, and shell out money for utilities and a host of other expenses. For almost every enterprise, however, the largest cost of production is labor. As a result, Marx says, "These labourers . . . are a commodity, like every other article of commerce" (*Communist Manifesto* 1). Since a capitalistic system places value on money alone, the owner can no longer view the worker as a person, but as a business expense. Market forces determine the owner's survival. To stay in business, the owner needs a profit. Labor is a cost. Therefore, the owner cannot look at the employee as a human being, but as an expense that must be reduced as much as possible.

This dehumanizing process is compounded by the presence of the machine. "Owing to the extensive use of machinery and to division of labour, the work of the proletarians has lost all individual character, and, consequently, all charm for the workman. He becomes an appendage of the machine" (*Communist Manifesto* 1). As machines become increasingly "skillful," human skill looses its value. A single machine can replace hundreds of skilled workers at a fraction of the cost. The expertise that an artisan develops over years of training and experience—the type of workplace ability that one can legitimately take pride in—is no longer needed. The machine can do it faster and cheaper and with flawless uniformity. The jobs now available to these displaced workers are brainless, monotonous tasks.

As mechanical contraptions increasingly become the stars of production, "the repulsiveness of the work increases, [and] the wage decreases" (*Communist Manifesto* 1). The first element, repulsiveness, becomes a reality because humans play second fiddle to a machine and perform repetitive and mundane tasks that anyone can master in a couple of days. Given these conditions, it is impossible to see how work could be anything but repulsive. The second element, the decrease of wages, is the result of the first. Since skills developed through extensive experience were no longer needed, the factory doors are now open to those without specific workplace skills. In nineteenth-century Europe this meant that women and children entered the factories. This massive addition to the labor pool adds to the downward spiral of wages. As capitalism dictates, when the supply of a commodity is high, the price goes down. And, as mentioned above, since capitalism views workers as a commodity, an increase in the amount in the supply of this "raw material" forces low salaries lower. Even if the "bourgeois manufacturer" had twinges of guilt about a system that forced everyone—women, men and children—into inhumane factory conditions at dreadfully depressed wages, the same system forced the owner to minimize salaries or be swallowed up by competitors. No one survives if they pay more than market price for commodities, even if those commodities are human beings.

In sum, then, Marx says that factories built around highly efficient machines lead to a cold, oppressive uniformity that dehumanizes workers. "Masses of labourers, crowded into the factory, are organised like soldiers. As privates of the industrial army they are placed under the command of a perfect hierarchy of officers and sergeants. Not only are they slaves of the bourgeois class, and of the bourgeois State; they are daily and hourly enslaved by the machine, by the overlooker, and, above all, by the individual bourgeois manufacturer himself. The more openly this despotism proclaims gain to be its end and aim, the more petty, the more hateful and the more embittering it is" (*Communist Manifesto* 1). And, as if this picture is not already dreary enough, Marx adds that workers cannot even find relief when the workday is finished. "No sooner is the exploitation of the labourer by the manufacturer, so far, at an end, and he receives his wages in cash, than he is set upon by the other portions of the bourgeoisie, the landlord, the shopkeeper, the pawnbroker, etc." (*Communist Manifesto* 1).

THE END OF CAPITALISM

Marx does see a silver lining behind this dark cloud. In his view, capitalism, by its very nature, eats itself to death. This process occurs in stages. The first step is the loss of the middle class. As we saw above, when the skills of middle-class artisans are made obsolete by machines, they drop into the ranks of the common laborer. Similarly, the middle-class "mom and pop" shopkeepers cannot compete for long with Wal-Mart-sized businesses. They, too, are absorbed into the proletariat. The result is that the number of poor increases in dramatic fashion and the level of impoverishment of the entire class deepens.

As the proletariat's frustration grows, we move into the second stage, which is characterized by isolated pockets of rebellion against the bourgeoisie. The workers strike out by destroying equipment and burning factories, but accomplish little of lasting impact because their actions do not address the underlying cause—capitalism itself. In some places, unions begin to appear, but at the early stage they are controlled by the bourgeoisie for their own ends. Thus, "the proletarians do not fight their enemies, but the enemies of their enemies, the remnants of absolute monarchy, the landowners, the non-industrial bourgeois, the petty bourgeoisie" (*Communist Manifesto* 1). Slowly, however, the unions go through a transition that allows them to serve the interests of the workers rather than the owners. By means of improved communications (which, ironically, were created for the benefit of industry), individual unions begin to make contact with other unions. "It was just this contact that was needed to centralize the numerous local struggles, all of the same character, into one national struggle between classes" (*Communist Manifesto* 1). In short, workers begin to gain awareness that their problem is not limited to a specific factory, industry or even a single country. The fate of workers is everywhere the same, and thus the solution must reach across company, industry and national borders.

The final piece of the puzzle snaps into place when some members of the bourgeoisie join the workers in their struggle. These individuals "have raised themselves to the level of comprehending theoretically the historical movement as a whole" (*Communist Manifesto* 1). This theoretical understanding of history is important because earlier revolts originating in the lower classes have tried to resolve their suffering by turning the clock back to a (mostly imaginary) better time. However, Marx and the other intellectuals who will join with the proletariat know that the solution cannot be found in the past. History only moves forward, not backward.

These intellectuals also know that things will not get better simply by tinkering with the present system. The whole system is corrupt and corrupting. As Marx puts it, "Law, morality, religion, are . . . so many bourgeois prejudices, behind which lurk in ambush just as many bourgeois interests" (*Communist Manifesto* 1). The proletariat has been kept in subjection because they have been duped into believing that legal, ethical, political and religious structures were based on something divine or eternal. In reality, Marx says, these power structures (which Marx refers to as the "means of appropriation") are controlled by the bourgeoisie to protect their interests. When the proletariat, with the help of these intellectuals, realizes that these structures are not based on God's will or eternal truths, they finally develop the impetus to do what needs to be done: tear the whole system down. Marx says that capitalism's destruction will begin as a national struggle. "The proletariat of each country must, of course, first of all settle matters with its own bourgeoisie" (*Communist Manifesto* 1). It is inevitable, however, that revolution will sweep across national boundaries because the proletariat has been enslaved in every place where capitalism has existed.

AFTER THE REVOLUTION

Marx is confident that capitalism will produce "its own grave-diggers [and that] its fall and the victory of the proletariat are equally inevitable"

(*Communist Manifesto* 1). Then what? In Section 2 of *Communist Manifesto*, Marx attempts to persuade those of the proletariat class that they should align themselves with Communism. Communism shares with all labor movements the desire to be free of bourgeois oppression. At the same time, the Communists "have over the great mass of the proletariat the advantage of clearly understanding the line of march, the conditions, and the ultimate general results of the proletarian movement" (*Communist Manifesto* 2). In other words, all proletarian movements understand *that* they are oppressed, but, as Marx modestly claims, only the Communists know *how* oppression works and how to finally fix it. Past revolutions did not succeed in ending the oppression of the have-nots by the haves. Instead, the identities of the wealthy and poor have just changed. The way to bring a decisive end to "the exploitation of the many by the few . . . may be summed up in the single sentence: Abolition of private property" (*Communist Manifesto* 2).

As soon as Marx brings up the abolition of private property, he knows that critics will raise two major objections. The first is that loss of private property leads to the elimination of personal freedom. After all, many of our most important decisions deal with what we will buy or sell and how we will procure desired goods. The criticism is, then, if you take away property, you take away freedom. Marx's first response is that, "There is no need to abolish [private property for the proletariat]; the development of industry has to a great extent already destroyed it, and is still destroying it daily" (*Communist Manifesto* 2). In short, he says that if private property and freedom go together, then the vast majority in society, who are deprived of property by capitalism, have no freedom.

Marx's second response to this criticism comes from a slightly different angle. He points out that individuals do not create wealth independently. Instead, capital is created by large numbers of people working within a specific economic system, and is thus a collective product. Since money is created by people working together, it can only offer individual freedom for all people when society is restructured so that all people share in the capital that they generate. This, Marx argues, is precisely what Communism aims to do. Communism's goal is not elimination of freedom but precisely the opposite: the creation of a world in which all can be free. Stated from the other direction, Marx says that he is not against wealth. The freedoms that come by means of capital, a collective product, should be enjoyed by all who create it. Thus, he concludes, "Communism deprives no man of the power to appropriate the products of society; all that it does is to deprive him of the power to subjugate the labour of others by means of such appropriation" (*Communist Manifesto* 2).

A second criticism that Marx anticipates will be leveled at Communism's abolition of private property is that it will lead to laziness. If no individual receives additional compensation (private property) for hard work, why would anyone do anything? Marx's first response is that if we were motivated to work solely by the hope of individual gain, "bourgeois society ought long ago to have gone to the dogs through sheer idleness; for those of its members who work, acquire nothing, and those who acquire anything, do not work" (*Communist Manifesto* 2). Marx's second reply to this charge takes us to a pivotal element of his philosophy. In essence, he says that we have been misled by bourgeois powers to believe that it is an eternal truth that people are motivated only by self-interest and that those who work hard will get ahead. The reality is that such ideas benefit those who are already ahead. If the laborer works hard, the owner, not the worker, profits. The idea of enlightened self-interest is just a carrot dangled in front of the oppressed to keep their productivity high.

Marx says that Communism is not just a new way of doing business; it is a whole new way of looking at the world. This is the basis of Marxist philosophy. "Man's ideas, views and conceptions, in one word, man's consciousness, changes with every change in the conditions of his material existence, in his social relations and in his social life" (*Communist Manifesto* 2). Every transition in the way material goods are produced brings a corresponding change in the ideas that rule that age. And because money always brings power, "The ruling ideas of each age have ever been the ideas of its ruling class" (*Communist Manifesto* 2). When capitalism goes away, the ideas that have propped it up also disappear. The new idea that will come with Communism is that when all work together cooperatively, all benefit equally. Marx argues that using hard work as a motivation to material gain is more effective under a Communist regime because it is grounded in reality. While additional wealth for additional work is an illusion for most people under capitalism, Communism keeps its promise that a worker's increased productivity leads to a higher standard of living because it recognizes the social nature of wealth creation. Therefore, Marx argues, the workers will actually generate more wealth under his socialist system than through capitalism.

The shift in economic ideas is the most obvious ideological change in the transition to Communism. However, since Marx argues that all other aspects of ideology exist to justify economic systems, Communism's "development involves the most radical rupture with traditional ideas." Family, government, education, ethics, religion—all the basic structures that shape society and tell individuals where they fit in—are up for grabs and must be radically reinterpreted. Foremost among the so-called eternal truths that must be toppled to make way for Communism are those linked with religious doctrines. Marx says that religious ideas have always been used to make the oppressed comfortable with their lot. Elsewhere, he refers to religion as the "opiate of the people." Opiates kill pain and make people drowsy, and this is exactly what Marx sees as the function of religion. The pain of the masses is real, but it is only a symptom. Thus, when the here-and-now pain of oppression is treated with religious promises of salvation, well-being and comfort for an eternity in the hereafter, Marx says that the pain is numbed but all the patients die because the underlying disease is ignored. In his philosophy the pain is the result of economic conditions. Since economic pain creates the need for religion's narcotic effect, religion will have no function when the economic structure is set straight.

Obviously, those who have power will not simply hand it over. Therefore, Marx argues that Communism can only come into being with the seizure of wealth (and therefore power) from the bourgeoisie. One might ask why this has not occurred earlier since the poor have always constituted the vast majority of the population. However, as Marx states above, the numerical power of the proletariat has always been checked by the propaganda of the bourgeoisie. Mere numbers do not become power until the masses become conscious of what has been done to them, how it happened and who did it. Thus, once the intellectuals make the proletariat aware of the source of suffering, the overthrow of capitalism is inevitable.

Removing the systemic evil of capitalist economy and thought forms is only the removal of the negative. What must follow is the reconstitution of society, without private property. Thus, Marx outlines the various radical changes that go hand in hand with the elimination of private property. These include a heavily progressive income tax and abolition of inheritance to help guard against future imbalances in individual wealth. Banking, commerce and agriculture will be centralized under public power to make certain that the needs of all people are served by these basic economic engines. A similar centralization of communication and transportation is envisioned to guarantee freedom of information and movement for every citizen. In order to ensure that all the resources of a country are used to their fullest capacity and in a way that benefits all, population will be redistributed to revitalize agriculture, and the needs of agriculture will be combined intentionally with manufacturing. Finally, child labor will be ended and public schools will provide free education for all children.

In the end, Marx reminds us, all the steps outlined above are but a means toward a greater end. The goal is to radically redefine what it means to be a laborer. In all past systems, to be a worker was to be stripped of dignity. Whether the prevailing system was slavery, feudalism or capitalism, laborers have always been pawns in the power structure. The apex of Marx's Communist dream is a society in which a person's rights, dignity, freedom and needs are not determined by economic status. He believed strongly that no individual's opportunity should be held hostage to economic status. Since all jobs assist the goals of the people, no job should be dishonored by subsistence pay. This means that all will be free to pursue vocations that reflect their talents and loves rather than choosing jobs based on income potential.

This equality extends to the political arena as well. Because so many actual Communist political structures turned out to be dictatorships or dictatorial oligarchies, it is assumed by many that Marx advocated such a system. In reality, he envisions a pure democracy in which a person's voice would not be amplified by his or her wealth. In every society, some workers administer the affairs of state for the benefit of other workers. However, those who take care of the business of politics will not have greater power than other workers. They simply serve a necessary function in society with the permission of others. Marx sums up his vision of this new structure as one in which "the free development of each is the condition for the free development of all" (*Communist Manifesto* 2).

The remainder of the *Communist Manifesto* is a rather technical analysis of the various socialist movements in different countries during the nineteenth century. However, at the end of the document, Marx's rather turgid analysis gives way to the following stirring words: "The Communists disdain to conceal their views and aims. They openly declare that their ends can be attained only by the forcible overthrow of all existing social conditions. Let the ruling classes tremble at a Communistic revolution. The proletarians have nothing to lose but their chains. They have a world to win. WORKING MEN OF ALL COUNTRIES, UNITE!"

DISSECTING MARX

The introduction to this chapter mentioned that many of Marx's goals, once understood, might provide a considerable bit of common ground with a Christian view of life. One piece of intellectual real estate I share with Marx is the idea that work ought to be humanizing. A defining time in my life came some time ago when I spent two years in a job I disliked rather intensely. I discovered that when I didn't like what I did for a living, I also had a difficult time enjoying the other parts of my life. While it is true that our work should not define every other aspect of our life, it is also true that we cannot divorce our "real life" from work. Given this, it is hard not to admire Marx's aim of making our workplaces more humane and investing our jobs with dignity.

It is also hard to deny Marx's observation that capitalism, which emphasizes the dollar value of everything, can present hurdles to a humane and fulfilling vocation. I frequently see examples of one such obstacle in my office when I talk to students who have chosen majors in order to prepare for occupations that they really don't like. Why would anyone do this? It isn't hard to guess; they are going where the money is. It would be easy to accuse them of selling out to greed, but it is not really that simple. When you are immersed in a culture that keeps score by dollar signs, you must swim upstream if you want to follow a passion that society does not reward monetarily. If nothing else, such experiences illustrate how influential money can be in shaping one of our most important decisions.

Marx also has a great deal of insight about how money can reshape entire societies. Because capitalism is so efficient as a means of producing wealth, it puts great pressure on noncapitalist nations to change, become irrelevant or die. If a nation has something that is potentially valuable, whether it is cheap labor, skilled labor or a natural resource, it is very difficult not to use it (and exploit it) to create wealth. In order to do this, however, populations are often relocated, traditional practices or beliefs are undercut, old class systems undergo transformation and new languages may come to predominate. In short, decisions about social changes and what a culture will value are shaped by money. Therefore, it is difficult to go anywhere in the world without bumping into a McDonald's, Microsoft or Exxon logo. And in those rare locations where you can get away from them, you can be quite sure that the standard of living is pitiful or worse.

Marx's emphasis on the implications of the social and material aspects of our existence can help correct certain imbalances that are widespread in Christian practice (although I do not see these imbalances in Christianity itself). For example, it seems to be a common tendency among many

Christians to view all problems as individual. However, Marx's insight about the social implications of economic systems, capitalist or otherwise, stands as a reminder that some problems will never be resolved on an individual level. Many horrific social situations are so massive that people working by themselves will never make a dent. Moreover, some problems are systemic and require a complete change of the political and social situation. For example, in regions where starvation is a recurring pattern, we recognize that it is simplistic, shortsighted and even cruel to blame the starving people for their situation. In most cases, the problem exists because starvation benefits those in power in some way. The entire economic deck is stacked against the victims who are powerless to change things because they lack the wealth to do so. Thus, while we can (and should) feed those who need it, this only treats a symptom. Correction of the actual problem requires, at minimum, the reconstruction of the political and economic system. To this extent, Christians can agree with Marx that individualistic solutions alone are never enough.

A second one-sidedness in Christian practice is to view every problem as if it is strictly spiritual. Marx's concern about the physical and material well-being of people can help Christians remember that we are not just spiritual beings. God also creates us with a need for physical goods. Therefore, our definition of legitimate human needs (and therefore legitimate Christian ministries) cannot be limited to heaven and the hereafter, but must also include the earthly and the right now. However, Marx is similarly one-sided in his own theory by defining all problems as solvable by material means. Thus, he misses the mark when he interprets our spiritual yearnings as cleverly disguised economic problems. I do not believe that simple observation verifies his reduction of spiritual impulses to nothing more than an attempt to escape our dire earthly situation. Such impulses are not limited to the downtrodden. Instead, all people throughout history, wealthy and poor, seem to have a spiritual sensitivity and need that cannot be satisfied by political or economic resources alone.

Closely related to this criticism of Marx's disregard of the supernatural is that he never really offers an actual argument for atheism. I would certainly not dispute his observation that religion has been and is used as a tool of oppression. However, this does not mean that oppression is an inherent quality of religion. Moreover, even though there is often a one-sided presentation of Christianity that focuses attention solely on the other-worldly aspects of salvation, Marx must overlook a multitude of examples in which Christianity compels its adherents to work toward economic justice and provide care for the downtrodden in the here and now.

If Marx is wrong in his conclusion that the forces behind history's movements are exclusively natural and economic, this casts severe doubt on his belief that the course of history is predictable by means of social science and will inevitably resolve itself in the abolition of class struggle. In short, if God is involved with history, any method that excludes God from consideration is quite likely to be wrong in its predictions. Moreover, more than a century has passed since Marx's death and there are few indications that the tension between the classes is any closer to resolution. When we remember Marx's assertion that there are rules that predestine the course of historical development, we cannot explain why class struggle has not disappeared by appealing to faulty implementation of socialist theory by his followers. If human efforts are subordinate to historical forces, then Marx was either wrong in his predictions or was way ahead of his time.

Even if we accept Marx's view that history is not subject to divine intervention, it is not clear that his sociological approach is as scientific as he claims. For example, he cannot argue that his claim that class struggle is bound to disappear is based on any historical analogy. If history *is*, as he says at the beginning of *Communist Manifesto*, the story of class struggle, the Communist utopia he envisions is diametrically opposed to anything history reveals. In view of this, how does he discover from a history full of exploitation that a change to Communism will cause us to give up our oppressive ways? We can certainly dream that the optimistic ideal of a world without social strife will become a reality, but history would seem to provide little hope that this will happen to the extent that Marx envisions, apart from divine intervention.

My last criticism of Marx's philosophy revolves around his view that ideas are exclusively the product of social environment. To his credit, he is correct in recognizing that our social situation has a profound influence on our interpretation of reality, purpose, right and wrong and a host of other ideas. This is a particularly valuable reminder for Christians, because it is very easy to confuse cultural views with Christian concepts. Culture does provide the lens through which we see the world, and Marx reminds us that it is very difficult to step outside our culturally conditioned ideas. But he says more than this. Marx claims that it is impossible for people to get beyond the political, social and religious ideas the wealthy have established to keep everyone else in their place. This is his explanation for why the proletariat, despite its massive numerical advantage, has not rebelled and taken what rightly belongs to them. However, we might ask how Marx knows this. After all, isn't he also immersed in the same social environment that blinds the proletariat to reality?

Similarly, we might recall that the linchpin of Marx's philosophy is that the ruling powers have always claimed eternal validity for their ideas, when in reality they only reflected the economic structures of a particular period. In short, *all* of those who have claimed that their social, political, moral or legal theories are universal and objectively true for all time have been wrong. The only exception to this is, as Marx would have us believe, the ideas of Communism; the concepts upon which his philosophy is erected are the only ones with eternal validity. If Marx is correct that he alone in the course of all intellectual history has found the only beliefs that transcend cultural conditioning, he has accomplished something truly amazing. However, he never really explains how he alone is able to escape the influence of the prevailing power structures to see things as they "really are."

Christianity ought to share Marx's dream of a humane workplace and a social situation that protects the dignity of each individual. In the last analysis, however, Marx's assertion that human dignity can be restored only by rearranging the structure of economic forces seems to make him as much a captive to money as capitalism is. In both, dignity is measured in terms of dollars and cents. The only disagreement is in how the cash gets distributed. Christianity demands that we look beyond material forces (without ignoring them) to find a solid foundation for human respect and dignity. Without the idea that human beings somehow reflect the image of God, it is difficult to know what such a foundation would consist of. This is brought home in a powerful, although ironic way, by our next figure, Friedrich Nietzsche.

10

NIETZSCHE

Is Morality All About Power?

What is the origin of our ideas about right and wrong, good and evil, moral and immoral? Often, the first response to this question refers us to sources such as parents, educational institutions or churches. However, the actual question goes deeper than this. We are not asking for the sources that *teach* us about such things. Instead, the question is concerned with where the ideas themselves originate. What is the ultimate source of concepts such as good and evil?

With this clarification, a new set of answers emerges. Maybe certain acts are good because they are useful in some way. For example, some argue that truthfulness becomes a universal moral principle because social interaction requires that we can rely on the veracity of what others tell us. Without truth and trust, community comes unglued. Others might say that God's moral nature, communicated to us by some means, is the ultimate foundation of right and wrong. Another option is that ethical ideals are similar to axioms in geometry. It isn't clear where these eternal truths come from and you cannot prove they are true, but without them everything falls apart.

These three potential foundations for ethics, or some combination of them, represent very common attempts in the history of moral thought to find an ethical ground zero. While the differences between these various ethical approaches raise interesting questions that should not be minimized, they all have one point in common. As they are traditionally built out and applied to concrete circumstances, they almost always are thought to create a world where people are nice, considerate, kind and caring, provided that they conform to moral requirements. Stated otherwise, regardless of which of these starting points you select, the general agreement is that you will end up with familiar moral ideas like the value of honoring promises, the importance of respecting property and the wrongness of causing injury or death without just cause.

Just when you think that perhaps we have found something that everyone can agree on, along comes a dissenter who does not just want to nibble at the edges of conventional wisdom and time-honored moral ideals. Instead, he aims to turn everything on its head. Meet Friedrich Nietzsche. For Nietzsche, what is traditionally considered good is actually damaging to us. Sympathy, kindness, respect for others' rights should be replaced by a world where the strong free themselves of any limitations imposed by rules or conscience and create their own values. Obviously, this is moral thought that attempts to reverse what is taken by most as common-sense ethics. To use Nietzsche's vocabulary, this is a "transvaluation of all values."

FRIEDRICH NIETZSCHE (1844-1900)

This unique twist in Nietzsche's philosophy is paralleled by reversals in his biography, in which things did not end as one might have expected. For example, his father, a Lutheran pastor, died when Friedrich was very young. Nonetheless, his youthful piety led many to believe that he was destined to follow his father's calling, a supposition that appeared to be confirmed by his theological studies during the early period at the university. However, for reasons never fully explained, Nietzsche reversed course, renounced Christianity later in his college years and became a vociferous atheist and critic of the church.

Nietzsche's intellectual abilities were recognized quickly and he was mentored by Friedrich Ritschl, one of Germany's premier scholars. Through Ritschl's assistance, he was able to obtain one of he most prestigious university chairs in the country at the age of twenty-four, a virtually unprecedented feat. However, this promising start on the academic fast track quickly sputtered because Nietzsche despised lecturing and students, and his students reciprocated that sentiment. The situation deteriorated to the point that, after a decade of service, the university agreed to provide a lifetime pension in return for his consent to leave his chair.

The next two decades were marked by constant health problems, although Nietzsche still managed to write prolifically. The difficulty was that almost no one was interested in reading his work until the latter part of the 1880s. In a final ironic turn, just as recognition started to come for Nietzsche, he suffered a total mental breakdown and spent the final eleven years of his life in a state of complete insanity.

THE WILL TO LIVE/THE WILL TO POWER

No idea ever comes out of a vacuum, and this is clearly the case for Nietzsche's ideas in *Genealogy of Morals*. The attempt of ethicists to find logical reasons to act morally and account for the needs and rights of others is the broader background of this book. However, the narrower focus of his writing is located in the ideas of a fellow nineteenth-century philosopher named Arthur Schopenhauer. Schopenhauer's philosophical outlook, to put it into a nutshell, is that reason is not the most important of human capacities. Instead, our defining attribute is our will, the ability to choose. More specifically, it is the will to live, a blind impulse to extend life that governs our existence. The problem that the will to live creates for human beings is obvious; we are mortal, so this basic desire is always thwarted. What heightens this tension in our species is that we *know* that we are mortal. In short, we are cursed because we are aware that our most fundamental desire—the will to live—can never be satisfied. Death always gets in the way. For Schopenhauer, then, the key moral value is pity or sympathy.

Sympathy binds us to others who share the same fate of going down slowly in the leaky boat we call life.

Nietzsche has Schopenhauer's position in his sights in *Genealogy of Morals* because he believes that his fellow German is half right, but that the element of truth contained in his philosophy makes his error more dangerous than if he had been completely wrong. The part Schopenhauer gets right is that the world is governed by will, not rationality. In contrast, though, Nietzsche says that it is *not* a will to *live* that is basic to existence, but a will to *power*. The key to living is not simply perpetuating life, but to use our vitality to conquer and dominate. Thus, Nietzsche says that pity and self-sacrifice are ideas that Schopenhauer "had gilded, deified, and projected into the beyond for so long that at last they became for him 'value-in-itself' on the basis of which he *said No* to life and to himself" (*Genealogy of Morals* Preface 5). Nietzsche argues instead that the will to power—the desire to rule, to dominate and even to cruelly punish—is the "essence of life" (*Genealogy of Morals* 2/12). Rather than view it negatively, we should see the will to power as life affirming, fulfilling and even joyful.

Nietzsche is keenly aware that most do not believe that imposing power on others fits the description above. Instead, the individual who seeks to dominate is not often considered good and joyful, but evil. Sympathetic, caring people, on the other hand, are thought to be the good ones. As Nietzsche acknowledges, "One has hitherto never doubted or hesitated in the slightest degree in supposing 'the good man' to be of greater value than 'the evil man,' of greater value in the sense of furthering the advancement and prosperity of man in general (the future of man included)." He then follows up with the question that sets the agenda for this work: "But what if the reverse were true? What if a symptom of regression were inherent in the 'good,' likewise a danger, a seduction, a poison, a narcotic, through which the present was possibly living *at the expense of the future?*" (*Genealogy of Morals* Preface 6). In other words, Nietzsche suggests that we have inverted the ideas of good and evil so that our will to power is now misunderstood as something evil, and as a result we are slowly poisoning our future. He argues that this confusion concerning the proper meanings of right and wrong or good and evil has come about because recent philosophers "have bungled their moral genealogy" (*Genealogy of Morals* 1/2). His task in *Genealogy of Morals*, then, is to give a proper accounting of moral history and lead those who listen back to health.

MASTER MORALITY/SLAVE MORALITY

Most moral philosophers, Nietzsche claims, find the origin of "goodness" in unegoistic acts toward others. Because these acts were useful to the recipients, these beneficiaries called such actions good. As time went on, those who did the actions labeled "good" by others began to see goodness as a characteristic they possessed. Nietzsche has a different take on the genesis of the idea of goodness. Originally, "the judgment 'good' did not originate with those to whom 'goodness' was shown! Rather it was 'the good' themselves, that is to say, the noble, powerful, high-stationed and highminded, who felt and established themselves and their actions as good, that is, of the first rank, in contradistinction to all the low, low-minded, common and plebeian" (*Genealogy of Morals* 1/2). In other words, those of high rank used the term *good* to distinguish their status and power from the common people of the herd, the lower and slave classes. These earliest good people were individuals who possessed physical and mental strength and were unencumbered by guilt and conscience. Thus, their activities revolved around "war, adventure, hunting, dancing, war games, and in general all that involves vigorous, free, joyful activity" (*Genealogy of Morals* 1/7).

The current situation is different, Nietzsche sadly admits. "The people have won—or 'the slaves' or 'the mob' or 'the herd' or whatever you like to call them. . . . 'The masters' have been disposed of; the morality of the common man has won" (*Genealogy of Morals* 1/9). The reason for this temporary reversal, in a word, is resentment, or, because Nietzsche always leaves it in untranslated French, *ressentiment*. Since all people are governed by the will to power, the lower classes hate the fact that the nobility controls them. The power of the masters, which contrasts with the weakness of the slave class, gives rise to *ressentiment*. This, in turn, leads the slaves to seek a way to strike back in reaction, which they do in the only way the powerless can; they try to make the strong as weak as they are. "While every noble morality develops from a triumphant affirmation of itself, slave morality from the outset says No to what is 'outside,' what is 'different,' what is 'not itself'; and *this* No is its creative deed" (*Genealogy of Morals* 1 / 10). Thus, in contrast to the master morality, which "acts and grows spontaneously," Nietzsche says that "in order to exist, slave morality always first needs a hostile external world; it needs, physiologically speaking, external stimuli in order to act at all—its action is fundamentally reaction" (*Genealogy of Morals* 1/10).

In brief, the lower classes cannot control the truly powerful by imposing external force on the strong. The strength of the masters can be sapped only by internally imposed limits. Thus, if the weak can control the conscience of the strong, they can get the masters to say no to their natural impulses. This is exactly what has happened. The slaves convinced everyone that good is attained through self-denial, not self-assertion. They prevailed by hijacking the terms *good* and *bad* and assigning them to actions and morality, not people and power. This explains why slave morality is in the driver's seat—for now. However, we have to explore the genealogy of morals to understand *how* this reversal of values has occured. This occupies Nietzsche's attention in the Second Essay of *Genealogy of Morals*.

A Promise-Making Animal

Nietzsche opens the second major section of his book with the words, "To breed an animal *with the right to make promises*—is not this the paradoxical task that nature has set itself in the case of man? Is it not the real problem regarding man?" (*Genealogy of Morals* 2/1). The ability to make promises provides the raw material for our slide down the slippery slope to slave morality. The world is a dangerous place for wimps, in large part because it is so unpredictable. To reduce the danger, the impotent impose order, structure and regularity on the world, although they fool themselves into believing that they actually *find* it there. With regularity, they can anticipate what the future will bring. An important facet of regularity is responsibility. To know what will happen down the line, people make and receive promises and devise mechanisms to ensure that others remember their vows and fulfill them.

Nietzsche says that if people are to remember what they have promised, pain must be involved. "Man could never do without blood, torture, and sacrifices when he felt the need to create a memory for himself; . . . pain is the most powerful aid to mnemonics" (*Genealogy of Morals* 2/3). Therefore, he claims that the seriousness with which we view our pledges is not the result of some ingrained sense of moral responsibility based on the concept of human value. It is, for the one who makes promises, fear of the pain they will endure if they fail to fulfill the conditions of the contract. The one to whom the unfulfilled promise is made receives satisfaction by gaining "the pleasure of being allowed to vent his power freely upon one who is powerless. . . . In 'punishing' the debtor, the creditor participates in a *right of the masters*: at last he, too, may experience for once the exalted sensation of being allowed to despise and mistreat someone as 'beneath him'" (*Genealogy of Morals* 2/5).

To summarize Nietzsche's conclusions about the master morality stage of moral ideas, he claims that the original sense of responsibility arises in a creditor/debtor relationship. When a debtor is unable to make payment in land, money or some other form, the creditor gains the right to inflict cruelty on the one who owes. This is true compensation because, as Nietzsche puts it, "to see others suffer does one good, to make others suffer even more." He immediately acknowledges that "this is a hard saying but an ancient, mighty, human, all-too-human principle to which even the apes might subscribe" (*Genealogy of Morals* 2/6). Inflicting suffering, and enjoying this process, *is* our nature.

Given the current dominance of slave morality, which professes to find the idea of cruelty to another repugnant, Nietzsche finds it necessary to remind his readers of three things. The first is that this early stage was one in which people were not ashamed of cruelty, but celebrated those with the ability to inflict it. The second claim is that such an uninhibited expression of self-assertion led to a more cheerful life than one where conscience squelches our inner desire to dominate others. The final reminder, which Nietzsche develops later, is that we never really lose our desire to gain pleasure by causing injury to others. Instead, it simply is forced underground and disguised in the cloak of some other justification.

Before he looks to the next step in the degeneration from master morality to slave morality, Nietzsche returns to the most pressing problem that confronts weak people. Since they are helpless against the forces of nature and the strength of the powerful, they suffer. That is just the way the world works. The strong dominate; the weak suffer at their hands. We find, at this point, one of Nietzsche's basic criticisms against Christianity. Christianity, in Nietzsche's interpretation of history, originates in the slave class. Because slaves are powerless, they cannot act to end their suffering, so they react by convincing themselves and others that there is logic to suffering and pain. Moreover, Christianity elevates suffering to the level of virtue. After all, salvation is seen as the result of the suffering and death of Jesus.

In this manner, Nietzsche says, Christianity turns everything on its head. Rather than honestly acknowledging that the masters triumph by causing the weak to suffer, it placates sufferers (the Christians) by making up ideas about a hereafter in which toleration of pain leads to salvation. Moreover, *ressentiment* comes to the surface in the belief that those who inflict pain in the present will suffer an eternity of torment. The latter is also evidence for Nietzsche that the weak have not really forsaken enjoyment of cruelty. They just have to count on a God, who is bigger than the strong on earth, to put the hurt on their tormentors. Moreover, since God inflicts the punishment, they can enjoy the future, eternal punishment of the strong while claiming to be saddened by it. Nietzsche says that, in the end, Greek religion was more honest and healthy. "The Greeks still knew of no tastier spice to offer their gods to season their happiness than the pleasures of cruelty. With what eyes do you think Homer made his gods look down upon the destinies of men?" (*Genealogy of Morals* 2/7). The gods of ancient Greece did not keep their gods at arm's length from pain and cruelty. The Greek gods were responsible for our suffering and reveled in the arbitrary nature of its imposition.

THE EMERGENCE OF CONSCIENCE

Nietzsche now returns to the idea that responsibility originates in the creditor/debtor relationship to trace his moral genealogy. Eventually, the relationship of a debtor to an individual creditor undergoes a transformation with the development of society. After this, the community itself assumes the role of the creditor. Weak people like community because it offers security, but only on the condition that they fulfill their obligations. These obligations to society are expressed in terms of laws. This means that the privilege of torturing the debtor who fails to fulfill obligations now belongs to society. "The lawbreaker is a debtor who has not merely failed to make good the advantages and advance payments bestowed upon him but has actually attacked his creditor [society]: therefore he is not only deprived henceforth of all these advantages and benefits, as is fair—he is also reminded *what these benefits are really worth*. The wrath of the disappointed creditor, the community, throws him back again into the savage and outlaw state against which he has hitherto been protected" (*Genealogy of Morals* 2/9).

Most people believe that the purpose of punishing lawbreakers is found in the necessity of preserving the security of the community. Nietzsche says that the real truth is that most communities are powerful enough that the actions of individual transgressors are not destructive of the whole. Moreover, we cannot justify punishment by arguing that it benefits the lawbreaker. Generally, he observes, "it is precisely among criminals and convicts that the sting of conscience is extremely rare" (*Genealogy of Morals* 2/14). The actual purpose of punishment is as an outlet for our desire to see others suffer. There is, he argues, no purpose or utility in punishment beyond the will to power. To claim that an eternal reason and intent justifies punishment only means that "a will to power has become master of something less powerful and imposed upon it the character of a function" (*Genealogy of Morals* 2/12). However, the will to power is not a mere function; it is the essence of life. In reality, Nietzsche states, the justifications we offer for punishing others (i.e., dominating them) are merely interpretations. The fact that these reasons change over time is not indication of progression toward some loftier level of moral development. Changes in moral justifications merely signal shifts in who holds power in society.

The idea that what we call moral truth is only a cover for imposing power over others is part and parcel of a major theme in Nietzsche's thought. Truth is never neutral but is instead reflective of an individual's perspective. This explains why Nietzsche's theory of truth is often referred to as "perspectivalism." *Nothing* that we call "truth" is anything other than our perspective or interpretation, and those who successfully seize power get to interpret the supposed meanings and purposes.

The belief that those who hold power gain the right to shape how others see the world brings Nietzsche to a key stage in his genealogy of morals. Once moral truth is expressed in terms of uniform laws imposed by a community, it is only a short step to the internalization of these laws in the form of conscience. This is how it happens. The erection of a law-based society means that the function of punishment is taken over by the state. Thus, while law-abiding citizens of a society derive indirect pleasure from seeing violators punished, they are deprived of the joy of inflicting cruelty directly. Moreover, when society talks about laws in terms of goals and purposes, we have moved from the realm of actions (which laws seek to hinder) to motives (which are internal). As soon as people recognize that *they* want to do what others are punished for, and they accept an interpretation of the law's purpose, they begin to internally punish themselves for merely *wanting* to do what has been deemed wrong and harmful. The tool with which they do this is conscience, which Nietzsche sees as a means of self-inflicted punishment.

Nietzsche sums up this movement within moral genealogy by stating, "All instincts that do not discharge themselves outwardly *turn inward*—this is what I call the *internalization* of man: thus it was that man first developed what was later called his 'soul'" (*Genealogy of Morals* 2/16). Thus, as moral belief undergoes transition from the original master morality to slave morality, people "gain" something that the masters did not have—a soul, an internal life by means of which they reflect on their actions and motives. However, Nietzsche says that this internal consciousness works against us. It twists our will to power, which can no longer vent its dominance on others, and uses it as a club with which we beat ourselves. The masters were free of the self-inflicted pain of conscience, which is why Nietzsche views them as joyful and free. When conscience emerges, freedom to discharge our strength on others is repressed and then is turned against us.

The last step in this perversion of the will to power comes when God replaces the community as lawgiver and rule enforcer. If God exists, our ultimate debt is not to a human society whose power to protect us and knowledge of our inner motives is imperfect. We are now in hock to a Being who has no limits. On one level, the existence of such a God is attractive to weaklings. They do not have the resources to survive in a hostile environment, but an all-powerful deity can overcome any earthly power and allows us to rule with him in heaven. However, as Nietzsche sees it, salvation by an omnipotent God comes at a horrible cost. Because this God also knows all, not even our innermost thoughts are hidden. Since reflective people of religious conscience are acutely aware of their pride and desire to command others, and they know that God knows, they suffer intense guilt. Moreover, the fact that they do not actually act on their desires means that they derive none of the pleasure that comes from expression of the will to power. Therefore, Nietzsche says of the Christian, "Guilt before God: this thought becomes an instrument of torture to him. He apprehends in 'God' the ultimate antithesis of his own ineluctable animal instincts; he reinterprets these animal instincts themselves as a form of guilt before God" (*Genealogy of Morals* 2/23).

This puts Nietzsche's deep antipathy toward Christianity into focus. As he sees it, Christianity takes everything that is natural to our will to power—freedom from external and internal limits, pride, dominance through power, spontaneity and lack of reflection—and turns them into the most damnable of sins. In place of these original noble characteristics, it sets up humility, charity, equality and love as virtues. To put it into the language of Schopenhauer, Christianity calls us to sympathize with the weak rather than force them into submission. However, Nietzsche sees this as dishonest because we cannot rid ourselves of our nature. The weak, because of *ressentiment*, exercise their will to power by dragging everyone else down to the lowest common denominator. They say no to everything they cannot control, all the time denying that this is what they are doing, and then they justify it by calling it God's will.

While slave morality reaches its apex in the teachings of Christ, Nietzsche anticipates the arrival of another, an "Antichrist," who will be the "victor over God and nothingness" (*Genealogy of Morals* 2/24). Nietzsche's Antichrist is not the biblical figure who strives against God's kingdom and eventually loses, but one who is strong enough to survive without the illusion of purpose, moral limits and truth. This Antichrist becomes the creative spirit who once again values conquest adventure, danger and pain. This is a renewed innocence, in which this figure, whom Nietzsche calls elsewhere the "Superman" or "Overman," knows nothing of the conscience and thus is free of any inner sense of limitation. Because of this, the Superman can act without boundaries rather than simply react to the power of others. The "no" again becomes a "yes" to life.

THE ASCETIC IDEAL

The final essay of *Genealogy of Morals* is Nietzsche's development of what is wrong with the current take on ethics and those who promote it, the "ascetics." An ascetic is an individual who lives a life of self-denial in hopes that the earthly goods and pleasures given up will be replaced by rewards that transcend these transitory things. One group identified by Nietzsche as ascetics, not surprisingly, is the priests, who take a vow of poverty, humility and chastity. In a rather ironic turn, he also includes the philosophers, many of whom oppose the church and its priesthood, in this category as well. Like religious ascetics, these philosophers attempt to rise above the mundane distractions of life to contemplate the unchanging, the pure and the eternal. In this pursuit of timeless truth, they also take a de facto pledge to renounce temporal pleasures.

Nietzsche says that the problem with the ascetic life is that it is not a life at all. It is, in fact, opposition to life. "For an ascetic life is a self-contradiction: here rules a *ressentiment* without equal, that of an insatiable instinct and power—will that wants to become master not over something in life but over life itself, over its most profound, powerful, and basic conditions; here an attempt is made to employ force to block up the wells of force; here physiological well-being itself is viewed askance, and especially the outward expression of this well-being, beauty and joy" (*Genealogy of Morals* 3/11). Nietzsche's point is that the will to power, which is the essence of life, is precisely that which the ascetic opposes. In attempting to transcend the struggle of temporal forces, the grit and sweat of life, ascetics reject existence and attempt to replace it with something they can place under their control.

It is bad enough for Nietzsche that "the ascetic treats life as a wrong road on which one must finally walk back to the point where it begins, or as a mistake that is put right by deeds." The ascetic compounds this denial of life because "he *demands* that one go along with him; where he compels acceptance of *his* evaluation of existence" (*Genealogy of Morals* 3/11). Ascetics inevitably drag others down by an interpretation of the world that is passed off as immortal truth and a path to salvation. One might ask why a person who claims to have renounced earthly realities would be so enthusiastic about requiring others to do the same. This strategy, Nietzsche believes, is a manifestation the will to power. "The ascetic ideal springs from the protective instinct of a degenerating life which tries by all means to sustain itself and to fight for its existence" (*Genealogy of Morals* 3/13).

Ascetic individuals are too weak to deal with life itself, so, by means of *ressentiment*, they attempt to make everyone else weaker than they are. This is the purpose of the ascetic's message, which is, in essence, "You are sick and I have the cure." The secret of the philosopher and the priest is that they vent their will to conquest by becoming saviors. They "explain" to others why suffering exists, since the weak cannot survive without believing that pain has a purpose. Then the savior tells the herd how to overcome their suffering. However, in Nietzsche's assessment, the ascetic "combats only the suffering itself, the discomfiture of the sufferer, *not* its cause, *not* the real sickness: this must be our most fundamental objection to priestly medication" (*Genealogy of Morals* 3/17).

The question now is why Christianity has been so successful in selling its interpretation of suffering. After all, Nietzsche acknowledges, there are numerous philosophies and religions professing to provide answers to the question of suffering. Nietzsche explains:

> By prescribing 'love of the neighbor,' the ascetic priest prescribes fundamentally an excitement of the strongest, most life-affirming drive, even if in the most cautious doses—namely, of *the will to power*. The happiness of 'slight superiority,' involved in all doing good, being useful, helping, and rewarding, is the most effective means of consolation for the physiologically inhibited, and widely employed by them when they are well advised: otherwise they hurt one another, obedient, of course, to the same basic instinct. (*Genealogy of Morals* 3/18)

The genius of Christianity, then, is found in the will to power, disguised as love, so that those who act in loving ways, too weak to physically conquer others, can have a small taste of dominance over those they assist.

Nietzsche concludes with a warning to all who would be strong: "Let us be on guard against the dangerous old conceptual fiction that posited a 'pure, will-less, painless, timeless knowing subject'; let us guard against the snares of such contradictory concepts as 'pure reason,' 'absolute spirituality,' 'knowledge in itself'" (*Genealogy of Morals* 3/12). Even science, often the last bastion left untouched by subjectivism, is not free of interpretation. "Strictly speaking, there is no such thing as science 'without any presuppositions'; this thought does not bear thinking through; it is paralogical: a philosophy, a 'faith,' must always be there first of all, so that science can acquire from it a direction, a meaning, a limit, a method, a *right* to exist" (*Genealogy of Morals* 3/24).

Nietzsche's overarching point is that no knower or thing known is ever neutral or pure. The idea of a person with no perspective or agenda that determines what is considered knowledge is as unthinkable as "an eye turned in no particular direction" (*Genealogy of Morals* 3/24). There is nothing, which explains why Nietzsche's philosophical perspective is frequently described as "nihilism" (*nihil* is Latin for "nothing"). It is our drive for conquest and our relative ability to exert power within a world that shapes what we will accept as our interpretation of the universe. The weak will veil their will to power in words like love, truth, salvation and purpose. The masters honestly accept nihilism's conclusion there is no truth in or about the world. Because they are strong enough to impose their desires, nothingness provides the opportunity for them to create their own values. In them, the force of will, which Schopenhauer recognizes, is exhibited in a pure and innocent manner. However, the new master, the Superman, has no sympathy for the conquered who are sacrificed along the way. This would be a *reaction*. Those who will possess the fullness of the will to power will know only action, and will use their powerful activity to transvalue all previous values.

DISSECTING NIETZSCHE

It takes a while for the full extent of Nietzsche's nihilism to sink in. Once the implications begin to emerge, however, we can begin to see how far-reaching they are. Nietzsche does not simply deny God's existence. Instead, because he believes that every category traditionally of interest to religion and philosophy—purpose, truth, meaning, metaphysics, knowledge—relies on a divine source, these are all swept aside when God disappears from consideration. Even with divine revelation out of the way, we cannot count on an unbiased rationality or science that allows us to see natural world "as it is." Reason always works in the service of our will, and our will is governed by its insatiable quest for power. Moreover, Nietzsche goes so far as to deny the objective existence of the world. What we call the universe is not a static reality that exists in the same way for all, but a dynamic, ever-changing process that can never be experienced apart from our perspective. Because human nature consists of the will to power, and this will stratifies rather than unites us, no basis exists for the idea of democratic society or human rights. Debates about right and wrong are no longer about how power is used. Instead, power explains how "right and wrong" are used. Thus, all values that assume a moral truth must be "transvalued."

While we might think such a view of the world would be rather bleak, to a large extent, it is already here. If you superimpose Nietzsche's philosophy over our contemporary debates, it is amazing how prophetic he was. Perhaps the clearest example on the popular level is our society's skepticism about truth. While many are quite comfortable talking about "my truth," anyone who suggests that there is Truth with a capital *T* that exists for everyone encounters almost immediate and often hostile protest. Interestingly, the reason behind the protest is very Nietzschean as well. Appeals to objective Truth are perceived as thinly concealed attempts to impose one's agenda on others. Stated otherwise, appeals to Truth are filtered through Nietzsche's concept of perspectivalism, which says that truth is nothing more than an expression of what we believe will solidify our power.

While we find this skepticism toward Truth claims most often in ethical or religious discussions, Nietzsche argues that we cannot limit skepticism to these areas, and he has plenty of followers today in this conclusion. For example, people have often assumed that historical analysis can occur in a neutral, unbiased manner. We simply have to explain how one event or movement results from what comes before. However, Nietzsche says that the powerful, by means of their strength, get to write history in a way that determines how others will interpret the world. Indeed, one of the most heated debates in education today revolves around who gets to write the history textbooks and whom history should designate as the heroes. We could multiply examples in every field today as illustrations of Nietzsche's influence. While thinkers of the past assumed that Truth about religion, ethics, economics, political theory, law, mathematics and physical science was out there waiting to be discovered, that basic presupposition is increasingly challenged. It may not be an exaggeration to say that Nietzsche is the most influential philosopher today.

While, as I will explain below, I believe that Nietzsche's nihilistic view of the world cannot be sustained intellectually, he still offers some insights that I believe are worth consideration. One such area is his view of how an interpretation of the world functions as a means of shaping the behaviors of others. For example, I may not be physically capable of stopping a brute from beating me. Nevertheless, if I can convince my hypothetical brute that such an action is morally wrong, my goal, assuming I do not want to receive a beating, is accomplished. Nietzsche is also correct about how conscience is a means by which pain can be inflicted. If I persuade the same brute that he should be ashamed that he even considered causing me bodily harm, in addition to escaping my beating, I can get him to whip himself internally. The same thing is true on a collective basis. If we can convince a group to adopt a particular interpretation of right and wrong, real and unreal, or what constitutes the meaning of life, we can cause them to channel their energies in new ways and to experience the pain of guilt when they deviate from this worldview. In short, Nietzsche's idea that truth is a power-tool is hard to dispute. However, that does not necessarily mean that he is correct in his conclusion that every interpretation is *nothing but* an interpretation and an attempt to assert our power over others.

A corollary to this is a common theme in Nietzsche, which says that rather than imposing power honestly as the strong do, Christianity attempts to control by *ressentiment* and prohibition. I do not see this as characteristic of *Christianity*, but we have to admit that it is often characteristic of *Christians*. A friend of mine once observed that his church would have no reason to exist if all of its enemies disappeared because it defined Christianity in terms of what it was against rather than what is was for. It is hard to deny that we frequently get very nervous about what is new and "outside the box." In fact, it seems that many Christians view themselves as doing God's work by making the box as small as possible. Thus, Nietzsche claims that Christianity is primarily motivated by *ressentiment* and fear of what is unknown or what it cannot control, so it says no as a means of forcing its way on the world.

I disagree with the idea that we ought to automatically say no to everything foreign and unknown as much as I disagree with Nietzsche's view that we should never reject anything. It would take a while to fully explain what I see to be a more balanced view; for now, an illustration and a basic principle will have to do. At present, none of the more than one hundred schools in the Council for Christian Colleges and Universities offers a graduate degree in art, although a significant number of them have quite a list of graduate programs in many other disciplines. Why is this? I have to believe that much of the reason grows out of art's desire to explore the unknown and look at life in different ways. Christians often consider such excursions into the unknown dangerous. Therefore, Christians who would pursue art often face strong resistance from the church based on fear, and those who would pursue it into the graduate level are forced to do so in a secular setting. This seems a tragedy to me, and leads me to suggest the following principle. Instead of avoiding what appears at the outset to be an alien and dangerous idea, we ought to investigate first. "No" should not be the first word. If our investigations lead us to conclude that an idea should be rejected, we will then be in a position to explain "why not."

Perhaps I might best sum up my areas of agreement with Nietzsche by stating that he does seem to correctly recognize the implications of atheism. If God does not exist, it is difficult to understand what provides the bedrock for basic concepts such as purpose, truth and morality. In other words, nihilism leaves us with nothing objective or fixed to start from. If that is the case, Nietzsche's view that power is all that remains is difficult to avoid. What reasons could explain why you should not subject, oppress and enslave others if you are physically capable of doing so when your intended victims cannot appeal to purpose, truth and moral goodness? Notice, however, that this is conditional. The belief that human nature can be explained solely in terms of power holds *only if* Nietzsche's analysis is correct. The problem for Nietzsche, as I will attempt to explain below, is that he unable to get away from the very things he opposes—truth, reality, goodness and purpose.

We could cite numerous places where the very concepts Nietzsche wants to destroy are smuggled back into his philosophy through the side door, but we will limit ourselves to a couple of examples. First, it is not clear what Nietzsche believes he has accomplished in his genealogy by taking us back to the origin of morals. Even if his theory that the idea of goodness as rooted in power is correct, he does not explain why the "original" definition contained in master morality is in any way superior to the current slave morality. "Original" does not mean the same as "true" or "superior," so even if his dubious genealogy turns out to be true, the mere fact that master morality is original does not tell us why we should prefer it.

Likewise, Nietzsche's assertions that we should prefer the master morality are undercut by another common thread that runs throughout *Genealogy of Morals*. He says that the powerful have always interpreted things in ways that are suited to their purposes. What, then, is the basis for saying that the current expression of power by the "herd" is less good than the exercise of power by the masters? If power is what it is all about, why is one method of obtaining it any better or worse than another? At points, he claims that the expression of power by the masters is more honest than that of the slave, whose reaction is motivated by a *ressentiment* that they cannot or will not admit. However, what foundation exists in Nietzsche's thought that explains why honesty is superior to dishonesty and *ressentiment*? Similarly, he claims that conscience causes internal pain to those who possess it and obviously believes that this supposed self-inflicted torture damages us. Without some idea of purpose or goodness, however, it is unclear why Nietzsche believes that it is better to experience peace of mind than self-torture. In each of these cases, his evaluation relies on values that he undercuts elsewhere.

I believe that the examples below demonstrate just some of the ways that Nietzsche's idea of the will to power leads to self-contradiction when we attempt to examine its implications. In a similar manner, Nietzsche ties himself into knots of self-contradiction at a more basic level. It might be noticed that Nietzsche *asserts* that the essence of human nature is the will to power. However, when one begins to look for actual *arguments* that establish that all human actions can be reduced to a function of the will to power, you don't come up with anything. (The same is true of his case for atheism.) *If* you accept Nietzsche's basic thesis, then virtually everything we do can be interpreted as power games, and that is exactly what he does. However, *if* we accept the premise that all human actions are motivated by love, as Augustine does, or *if* we believe that human nature should be ruled by rationality, as Plato does, human behavior looks very different than it will under Nietzsche's interpretation. In other words, the definition of human nature that we start with has a great deal of influence on how we interpret human behavior. The question, then, is which interpretation is correct, and here we find an important difference. While Augustine, Plato and other philosophers offer some support for their idea of human essence, Nietzsche does little more than assert that we are inexorably driven by a will to power. Unless he provides some reason for us to believe that his fundamental view of human nature is correct, it is not clear why we should accept interpretations based on it.

So why doesn't Nietzsche simply accept the task of explaining why his interpretation of human nature is the correct one? Notice what this question requires. If Nietzsche attempts to establish that nihilism is true, he ends up with some really interesting problems. Since nihilism rejects the idea that anything is objectively true, then how are we to understand Nietzsche's claim that nihilism is true? It seems blatantly self-contradictory to argue that the statement "There is nothing that is objectively true for all people" is objectively true for all people. If, on the other hand, Nietzsche means that nihilism is true only for him, he cannot tell us why we should not simply dismiss it since it is not true for us.

Nihilism hangs itself on its own definition. If we get rid of truth, we cannot claim that nihilism is true. When Nietzsche claims that all statements are interpretation, we are left wondering what is being interpreted when he removes any world, truth or reality to interpret. If ideas of good and bad are dispensed with, why does Nietzsche feel compelled to set us straight about what good and bad really are? In the end, it is relatively easy to claim that nihilism is true and interpret the world accordingly, but it is impossible to make any sense of it. In spite of this difficulty, many of the same ideas show up in a different context in the ideas of our next philosopher, Jean-Paul Sartre.

11

SARTRE

Do You Really Want to Be Free?

How free are you? If we were to take a freedom inventory, most of us would ask this question against the backdrop of the obligations we have taken on, the rules that govern our life and work, and laws that define the extent of our liberty. We believe that we achieve a net gain in freedom when we pay off a debt, reach an age where certain actions become legal or, as I see often in the college setting, move away from home. These examples of things that increase or inhibit choice can vary widely, but we can observe a common thread that runs throughout this list. When we think of freedom, we often do so in the context of external elements—finances, location, rules, political structures, laws—that block or enhance our access to liberty.

A second general observation concerning freedom is that we almost without exception consider it a good thing. We work hard and save money for decades so we have the freedom to retire. The thought of being imprisoned for a significant portion of our life, and the loss of independence that comes with it, restrains the majority of us from what might otherwise be very tempting criminal options. Millions have sought professional help to find release from backgrounds, circumstances and illnesses that inhibit their lives and relationships. Millions of others have given their lives in the fight for freedom. In view of the tremendous sacrifices we make for the sake of self-determination, freedom must be incredibly desirable. In fact, the quest to maximize our range of choice seems to permeate our activities to such an extent that it does not seem an overstatement to say that it defines our lives.

When we recognize the huge role the pursuit of freedom plays in our life, it might hit us like a bucket of cold water when Jean-Paul Sartre tells us that we really do not want freedom as much as we claim. Instead, he views freedom as such a burden that we expend significantly more energy hiding from it than we do exercising it. And he argues that we have more freedom to hide from than we imagine. Regardless of the external situation, we can always choose and no one can stop us. The only thing we cannot choose to do is not choose. Whether slave, president, plumber, student or philosopher, we are not just free, we are condemned to be free.

JEAN-PAUL SARTRE (1905-1980)

To call freedom a condemnation certainly cuts across the grain of consensus, and this will tempt us to reject Sartre's claims before we hear him out. However, if autonomy is as big a deal as we assume, it would not hurt to see if his challenge can help us think through something we so naturally desire. Moreover, Jean-Paul Sartre's background was one that plunged him into fierce struggles over freedom, and gave him a unique and wrenching perspective on the subject. Born in 1905, he came of age in France during World War I, in which two million of his fellow citizens were killed in what was called a struggle for freedom. In the next couple of decades, Europe was immersed in turmoil as the various countries of the continent toiled to establish political systems that would correct problems that had led to the earlier war, all in the name of freedom. The attempts were ultimately dashed as the world became embroiled in a second, even more devastating, world war.

Between the two world wars, Sartre entered École Normale at the Sorbonne to study philosophy. In 1928 he became distracted during his finals and finished last in his class. He took the finals again the next year and received a first place. During preparations for this second shot at examinations, he met Simone de Beauvoir. De Beauvoir, who became a significant intellectual force in her own right, was Sartre's professional collaborator and lifelong companion. Following a brief stint in the military, he studied in Berlin and taught in several locations before being called back to the military in 1939. The next year, he was captured by the German army and was a prisoner of war for nine months. Sartre was released when he convinced the Germans that he had been taken prisoner by mistake, since, being blind in one eye, he could not possibly have been a soldier.

During the remainder of the war, he worked for the French resistance, taught, wrote and published what was to be his most famous philosophical work, *Being and Nothingness.** The remainder of his life was characterized by feverish literary output, which included philosophical works, novels, plays and film scripts. In 1964 he was awarded the Nobel Prize for literature, which he refused to claim. When Sartre died in 1980, existentialism, a philosophical movement whose name had been coined by Sartre, lost its most prominent advocate.

HUMANS AND OBJECTS

"Existence precedes essence." This, Sartre says, is the core doctrine of existentialism. To explain this rather cryptic claim, he begins with the mirror image—"essence precedes existence." A paper cutter, whose essence precedes its existence, "is an object which has been made by an artisan whose inspiration came from a concept. He referred to the concept of what a paper cutter is and likewise to a known method of production, which is part of the concept, something which is, by and large, a routine. Thus, the paper cutter is at once an object produced in a certain way and, on the other hand, one having a specific use; and one can not postulate a man who pro-

---

*The version of Sartre's *Being and Nothingness* used in this chapter is the translation by Hazel E. Barnes (New York: Washington Square Press, 1966).

duces a paper-cutter but does not know what it is used for" (*Existentialism*** 16). No physical object can be brought into existence without us first having a concept of its essence or nature. In short, an object's essence precedes its actual existence. This is what Sartre calls "being-in-itself." Being-in-itself is a nonconscious mode of existence. An object, whether a paper cutter or any other physical artifact, has no awareness of its existence and cannot become something else by its own decision. It simply is.

If physical objects are such that their definition or essence logically comes prior to their existence, what does "existence precedes essence" mean? A simple example will suffice to illustrate. A college student has the educational goal of becoming an engineer. As she progresses toward that goal, she occasionally wonders whether this will be a satisfying career or if she will later regret not pursuing her interest in sculpting. In a nutshell, this individual first comes into existence and then defines herself. The fact that she shows up on earth does not determine what she will become. After her arrival, she must choose her identity, her essence. Thus, Sartre sums up his basic idea of existentialism. "What is meant here by saying that existence precedes essence? It means that, first of all, man exists, turns up, appears on the scene, and, only afterwards, defines himself" (*Existentialism* 18). Our hypothetical student's essence will be shaped and constantly reshaped by decisions and actions. An engineer is different from a sculptor, a theist is different from an atheist, and a communist is different from a capitalist. Selection of one course of action eliminates other potential paths. Thus, contrary to common propaganda, we cannot have it all. Our identity is not determined from birth. Our essence *becomes* a reality as a result of the decision we make.

Why does existence precede essence in human beings? Sartre first points out that, while objects have no consciousness, the student does. The second step in his analysis of human existence, which he calls "being-for-itself," is to note that to be conscious is to be conscious *of* something. Thus,

---

**The version of Sartre's *Existentialism* used in this chapter is the translation by Bernard Frechtman (New York: Philosophical Library, 1947).

our student is not just a conscious being. She is also the object of her consciousness. She is aware *of* herself as a student. She does the scrutinizing and is the target of her own scrutiny. Third, our engineering student's consciousness of what she is can occur only in a context of her awareness of what she is not. In short, consciousness works through negation. In our awareness that something is this, we are also aware of what it isn't. To recognize that she is an engineering student, she must also know that she is not a psychologist or an art student. The latter two elements are certainly possibilities for her future, but these possibilities are not a present reality, nor do they necessarily have to become a reality in the future. These, and any other possibilities, are what Sartre refers to as "nothingness." As Sartre puts it, "Consciousness is a being, the nature of which is to be conscious of the nothingness of its being" (*Being and Nothingness* 47). In summary, Sartre says that being-in-itself is a knower that is aware of its present reality and its future possibilities.

While the idea of nothingness within our being does not sound too appealing at first glance, Sartre says that it is absolutely essential to our freedom. A paper cutter is complete as a paper cutter but is not free. Humans, on the other hand, are always incomplete and are conscious of this incompleteness through our awareness of nothingness. This nothingness represents our freedom to choose to become something else. This leads to another important existentialist concept: transcendence. Transcendence is simply a recognition that humans are never satisfied with what we are, since our awareness of nothingness reminds us that we are incomplete. Our engineering student does not want to remain an engineering student all her life. The nothingness (unrealized possibility) of engineering is her awareness that she has room to change. Her freedom consists in the ability to transcend present realities.

THE NATURE OF FREEDOM

Our first inclination may be to say that Sartre had provided nothing more than a convoluted description of something that is conventional wisdom:

that human beings are free to decide their future in a way that mechanical objects are not. There is much more here than meets the eye, however. The traditional definition views freedom as the ability to act in a way that varies from some standard. According to this definition, then, an engineering student's actions are judged against a measure of engineering-related competencies. In this view, the student is free to study hard in order to successfully demonstrate these competencies in order to move toward her career goals, or she has the option to blow off her finals and live with the consequences.

Sartre's definition of freedom goes deeper than this. He would point out that the traditional view assumes that this student has some objective reason for wanting to be an engineer. If she wants to be an engineer, studying for finals is a good idea. However, if existence precedes existence in humans, there is no preestablished essence (or goal) that determines that she ought to be an engineer. Freedom does not mean that she can decide whether she will conform to a given set of standards. Instead, it means that she must choose her essence, and this will determine what her standards will be.

The implications of Sartre's view of freedom are intensified by a couple of things. First, choice of one's essence is not a one-shot thing. Investment solicitations include a disclaimer that reads, "Past performance is not a guarantee of future results." The same is true for humans. If the engineering student decides to become an engineer, her choice is not the last one she will make. Future decisions will shape her life in radical ways. Just as she chose to major in engineering through an awareness of nothingness, a consciousness of all the things she might become, she will later make decisions about what type of engineering to do, where she will work, whether she should give it up and become a sculptor, or any one of millions of other possibilities available to her. No single decision completes the process. With each decision, one becomes aware of new possibilities from which one must choose. Therefore, the fact that this young woman exists does not define her. As Sartre puts it, we are hurled toward a future, and through our consciousness of nothingness, we see what we can become. Our identity is forever an open question.

A second element that ups the ante in Sartre's understanding of freedom is his atheism. In his view, how we answer the question of God's existence makes all the difference in how we think of freedom. If humans are God's creation, "the concept of man in the mind of God is comparable to the concept of a paper-cutter in the mind of the manufacturer, and, following certain techniques and a conception, God produces man, just as the artisans, following a definition and a technique, makes a paper-cutter" (*Existentialism* 16-17). Stated otherwise, if God creates us, we become objects; our essence precedes our existence. The very concept of creation assumes creation according to an essence in the same way the creation of a paper cutter presupposes a yardstick that determines whether the product is a good or bad paper cutter. Therefore, if we are a creation of God, our adequacy or goodness is judged by a standard that exists before we do, because the essence of human nature precedes our existence as actual human beings.

This illustrates why Sartre says that God and freedom are incompatible. Human freedom consists in our consciousness of nothingness (possibilities), and this openness in our being demands that we, not God, choose our own essence. "Human freedom precedes essence in man and makes it possible; the essence of human beings is suspended in his freedom" (*Being and Nothingness* 25). We cannot have it both ways. Either we exercise our freedom and choose our identity, or God creates us with a predetermined essence and we forfeit our freedom. The latter reduces us to the level of an object—being-in-itself—because it removes consciousness. Thus, he declares that even if God does exist it would make no difference. Being-foritself must shape its future through freedom.

If there is no God, there is no predetermined human nature provided by a perfect, divine Being to which we should aspire. As Sartre sums up the situation, "We are on a plane where there are only men. Dostoyevsky said, 'If God didn't exist, everything would be possible.' That is the very starting point of existentialism. Indeed, everything is permissible if God does not exist" (*Existentialism* 27-28). Freedom, then, means that nothing is off-limits. You can choose whatever you want. No God means no human nature as a target at which we aim our decisions. No predetermined target means there is no reason not to aim wherever we wish.

THE EXTENT OF FREEDOM

An expected objection to any view of freedom this radical is "No one can possibly be this free. Human choice is always limited by something." Sartre agrees but includes some important conditions. While, as we have seen, he rejects the idea that our freedom is limited by a universal human essence, there is a limiting universal human *condition*: "What does not vary is the necessity for [us] to exist in the world, to be at work there, to be there in the midst of other people, and to be mortal there" (*Existentialism* 45). Physical limitations keep us from walking through brick walls. Economic structures require that certain activities be performed in order to earn money so we can purchase things necessary to our physical existence. Other people limit opportunities available to us by their attitudes or the rules they establish, regardless of what we may want to do. Finally, we cannot simply decide that we will not die, at least not forever. In short, Sartre says, we are always "in a situation," and the facts of the situation will limit what we can do to some degree.

However, Sartre also wants to draw our attention to the fact that the features that make up a "situation" have something in common. They are external to us. However, no matter how constricting these external circumstances are, we are still free in an important way. Nothing outside us necessitates how we will respond to any given situation. For example, there are few situations more confining than what Sartre faced as a prisoner of war. Fences, guns, restrictive rules with harsh consequences, and imposed schedules would definitely qualify as daunting obstacles to action. Nevertheless, Sartre says that freedom is still a reality in this situation because none of these barriers determines what he must actually do. He could decide to cooperate with his captors, refuse to leave his bunk, attempt suicide or try to escape. While others could throw up roadblocks to hinder his decisions, nothing they do forces him to choose or reject any of the options above.

We may think that Sartre overlooks the obvious here. "How can you say that you are free to passively resist by remaining in your bunk or by actively attempting escape? They could kill you! Is that freedom?" Obviously, Sartre knew that some of his choices could lead to his execution, but this *in itself* is unimportant. To proclaim "They could kill you" assumes that life is a universal good. But what, Sartre asks, is our justification for putting such a high value on life? If God does not exist and heaven is empty, we have no objective basis for attaching value to life. "Before you come alive, life is nothing; it's up to you to give it a meaning, and value is nothing else but the meaning that you choose" (*Existentialism* 58). Therefore, if we take it as a given that life is good instead of choosing it as valuable, we have denied our freedom. Freedom to put price tags on everything means that even life is a choice.

When Sartre makes the claim that all values are absolutely subjective, he anticipates that people will suspect ulterior motives. After all, if we get God out of the way, we can do whatever we want without responsibility to anyone. In reality, Sartre says that existentialists "think it very distressing that God does not exist." Without God, "man is forlorn, because neither within him nor without does he find anything to cling to" (*Existentialism* 27). God would provide a standard against which we can measure our choices. Such a standard is a comfort because when our choices are questioned, we take refuge in saying "God commands it," and God takes the heat. If, on the other hand, we are the sole measure of our decisions, we bear the responsibility directly and alone. Thus, Sartre views existentialism, not as a means of escaping responsibility, but a philosophy that drops accountability squarely on our own shoulders. "We find no values or commands to turn to which legitimize our conduct. So, in the bright realm of values, we have no excuse behind us, nor justification before us. We are alone, with no excuses. That is the idea I shall try to convey when I say that man is condemned to be free. Condemned, because he did create himself, yet, in other respects is free; because, once thrown into the world, he is responsible for everything he does" (*Existentialism* 27).

CONDEMNED TO BE FREE

With the statement that we are "condemned to be free," we have turned an important corner in Sartre's philosophy. Responsibility is the burden that comes with freedom and, as long as we are free, we cannot stop from choosing. Since God does not exist, we cannot appeal to social conventions, biological or parental shortcomings, institutional guidelines, laws or divine commands as justifications for our actions. Even our past decisions will not justify our choices because, as being-for-itself, we cannot remain what we were in the past. Every decision shapes what we will become. Death ends the process, but the process is always incomplete. We, in our present state, are the sole justification for our actions. Freedom, then, is a condemnation and burden because it puts us on the spot. We own our choices; we become our choices.

Sartre's assertion of the depth of our responsibility brings a common feature of our psychology to the surface. Notice how quickly we look outside ourselves when we are asked (demanded) to justify our actions. "My boss said I had to." "I didn't want to upset anyone." "The Bible says." "My schedule requires." "It's against the law." The function of such statements is, of course, to take the pressure off us. What would happen, though, if we would simply say, "That was my decision." The latter creates a situation that Sartre refers to as anguish. Anguish occurs when we toss away the crutches of external demands, embrace our freedom and take personal responsibility for decisions.

Taking responsibility for choices without appealing to other authorities (which ultimately only have authority because we decide they are authoritative) is certainly enough to provoke feelings of anguish in us. However, Sartre keeps the pressure on by making sure that we do not confuse anguish with something more easily dealt with: fear. To explain the difference between fear and anguish, he asks us to imagine hiking on a narrow path above a deep chasm.

> The precipice presents itself to me as *to be avoided*; it represents a danger of death. At the same time I conceive of a certain number of causes, originating in universal determinism, which can transform that threat of death into reality; I can slip on a stone and fall into the abyss; the crumbling earth of the path can give way under my steps. Through these various anticipations, I am given to myself as a thing; I am passive in relation to these possibilities; they come to me from without; in so far as I am also an object in the world, subject to gravitation, they are my possibilities. (*Being and Nothingness* 30)

This is a description of fear. Fear arises in this situation because I recognize that, on one level, I am a physical object—being-in-itself—that is no more exempt from gravitational forces than a rock. Knowing that the path could give way, sending me hurtling to my death, generates fear.

Anxiety operates on a different level. It is an internal process. I would venture to say that anyone who has looked into deep emptiness from a high point has thought, "I could jump." Why do we do this? It is inherent in freedom. As we have said, freedom is our consciousness of possibilities, of nothingness. As potential future actions come to mind, we choose one while negating other possibilities. Jumping is a possibility that we (hopefully) negate. However, my negation of this possibility is an internal matter because no physical barrier compels me to do otherwise. When I attempt to navigate a narrow path along a precipice, I do not *have to* watch my step or stay on the inside of the path. I could choose to finish the rest of the hike walking backwards with my eyes closed. Moreover, even if I do not choose to do this now, walking backwards, jumping or lying down and refusing to move are still possibilities for me on down the path. "No external cause will remove [these possibilities]. I alone am the permanent source of their non-being, I engage myself in them; in order to cause *my* possibility to appear, I posit the other possibilities so as to nihilate them" (*Being and Nothingness* 31).

Sartre cites cases such as this to demonstrate why we are not as attracted to the idea of freedom as we might like to believe. A grasp of what freedom truly means is terrifying because it reveals the extent of our freedom. No objective standard prohibits bizarre or harmful actions, and, because the self is so radically free, there is nothing within us to guarantee that we will not indeed perform bizarre or harmful acts. Even my past decisions not to take a flying leap do not require that I remain in a safe position since, in our freedom, we are constantly reconstructing ourselves. Therefore, "if *nothing* compels me to save my life, *nothing* prevents me from precipitating myself into the abyss. The decisive conduct will emanate from a self which I am not yet" (*Being and Nothingness* 32). Anguish is the result of recognizing all the possibilities available to our consciousness and the awareness that nothing external to us can provide direction for our future actions.

BAD FAITH

Fear and anguish are both unpleasant emotions, and this unpleasantness pushes us to search for relief. Fear can be eliminated by exercising freedom. If I determine that death is no less preferable than life, and really mean it, walking on a narrow ledge above a chasm will not hold fear. Anguish, on the other hand, arises precisely from awareness of our freedom. This means, then, that the only way to relieve anguish is by "pretending that we are not free." This pretense is what Sartre calls "bad faith," and it is a form of lying. Lying is different from deception. I might, through ignorance, deceive a lost person by giving them bad directions to the closest hospital. In order for a deception to also be a lie, however, two things are necessary. We must intend to deceive, and, in order to do that, we must know the truth. What distinguishes bad faith from garden variety lying is the victim. Bad faith is a lie that we tell to ourselves. Thus, it is an odd type of lie because we are both the deceiver and the deceived.

Is it really possible to knowingly tell oneself a lie and, at the same time, believe it? Sartre says that it is more than possible. For most of us, it is a way of life. In a well-known example, he tells of a couple on a date. The man is trying to seduce the woman, and she knows exactly what his intentions are. However, she is afraid to make a decision about how she will respond to his seduction. Thus, "If he says to her, 'I find you so attractive!' she disarms this phrase of its sexual background; she attaches to the conversation and to the behavior of the speaker, the immediate meanings, which she imagines as objective qualities" (*Being and Nothingness* 55). In other words, she postpones a decision by lying to herself. She knows that "I find you so attractive" really means "I want to go to bed with you," but she tells herself it only means "I find you so attractive." She has lied to herself and she knows it.

She didn't say yes but she didn't so no, so her date makes his next move. "Suppose he takes her hand. This act . . . risks changing the situation by calling for an immediate decision. To leave the hand there is to consent in herself to flirt, to engage herself. To withdraw it is to break the troubled and unstable harmony which gives the hour its charm. The aim is to postpone the moment of decision as long as possible. We know what happens next; the young woman leaves her hand there, but she *does not notice* that she is leaving it" (*Being and Nothingness* 55). As her hand remains in his, "she speaks of Life, of her life, she shows herself in her essential aspect—a personality, a consciousness. And during this time the divorce of the body from the soul is accomplished; the hand rests inert between the warm hands of her companion—neither consenting nor resisting—a thing" (*Being and Nothingness* 56).

Sartre says that this woman's bad faith is evident on a number of levels. She disarms his attempts at seduction by taking them at face value rather than as statements of future intentions, even though she knows that is not what he means. Simultaneously, she likes the fact that he desires her, something that is only possible because she knows what his intentions are. In addition, the fact that she can speak in lofty terms about Life, which only being-for-itself can do, at the same time she treats her hand as being-in-itself, and *knows* this is what she is doing, indicates bad faith. She is trying to have it both ways. She wants to be a person with aspirations, thoughts and choices at the same time she mentally detaches *her* hand as if it were only a thing.

The story above may have just enough drama that we can recognize the woman's pretense while ignoring our own bad faith. However, Sartre would argue that bad faith is present even in the most mundane aspects of our life. For example, when my home phone rings at 6 p.m., I answer it. I don't want to, because the caller usually wants me to refinance my mortgage, sign up for a new credit card or donate to save the endangered three-eyed Peruvian nectarine worm. So if I know there is a 90-percent chance some obnoxious telemarketer is at the other end, why do I answer?

I am well aware that I do not have to answer a ringing phone. However, I also do not want to take responsibility for not responding, because I can just imagine this conversation three days later.

Friend: "What were you up to Tuesday night?"

Me: "Nothing. Home all evening."

Friend: "Oh. I called and no one picked up."

Since my friend would not have called unless he thought it was important, my failure to answer the phone seems impolite. I do not want a friend to feel insulted, so how do I justify my decision to let the phone ring? I would give a reason. "My wife was filling me in on her work day, and I didn't want to interrupt her." "I was reading to my daughter." "My two-year-old wanted to see if the toilet could handle a Teletubby and I was cleaning up the aftermath."

Even if the reason I offer is perfectly true, Sartre would say that I am in bad faith because I am trying to convince myself and my friend that the reason for not answering the phone is objectively good. It does not matter if my friend forgives me because he believes that spending time with a spouse, reading to a child or dealing with domestic disasters is good and decent. In the end, Sartre answers, nothing is good and decent in itself. Since values are completely subjective, I did not answer the phone because I chose not to answer it. My "reasons" are just a smokescreen to divert attention from my free choice and dump the responsibility elsewhere. Stated otherwise, Sartre would say that the only real reason free persons can give for a choice is that they decided, apart from anything else, to value or devalue something. Any other "reason" is bad faith.

Another common way we get trapped within bad faith is by the roles that society assigns to us. Sartre tells us, "A grocer who dreams is offensive to the buyer, because such a grocer is not wholly a grocer. Society demands that he limit himself to his function as a grocer" (*Being and Nothingness* 59). Rather than rebel against these socially imposed restrictions on our freedom, we find comfort in them because, when we obey them without question, we fit in. As long as we perform the tasks outlined in a job description, we do not have to justify our actions because we never make a decision. Our role dictates each move. Thus, Sartre says that the most everyday features of our lives, "alarm clocks, signboards, tax forms, policemen, [are] so many guard rails against anguish" (*Being and Nothingness* 39). Freedom, on the other hand, comes in the form of a question: Why should I do this? Is this *my* choice? When social convention squelches the question, we give up our freedom to be relieved of anguish.

SARTRE AND SALVATION

Sartre's crusade to warn us of the danger that bad faith holds for freedom helps us understand why his rejection of God's existence plays such a central role in his philosophy. If God exists, he is the ultimate justification for our decisions. If he does not exist, however, validation of decisions by appeal to divine commands is the ultimate in bad faith. The question that Sartre must then answer is why, when human beings claim to desire freedom, we continually immerse ourselves in the bad faith of theism.

For the answer to this, Sartre takes us back to the structure of consciousness. As we have said, our consciousness includes consciousness of what we are not, or nothingness. We know that we are imperfect. Through our decisions, we seek to negate nothingness or, in English, we desire to complete ourselves. We want to fill the void and become perfect, full and whole. This longing for perfection puts us in an impossible situation because the only type of being that is complete is being-in-itself. Objects, which have being-in-itself, are complete but are not conscious of their completeness. Consciousness—being-for-itself—is incomplete precisely because it is free. Ironically, then, if we attain the wholeness we strive for in our choices, we would become being-in-itself and thus cease to be free.

Sartre believes that this drive for transcendence and perfection is the source of our idea for God. The traditional concept of God includes the characteristics of perfection, in which no potentialities remain to be fulfilled. At the same time, God is also pictured as a conscious being, aware of himself and the world external to him. Sartre argues, as we have seen above, that this combination is logically impossible. To be conscious is to be incomplete and in process. To be complete is to lack consciousness. We cannot have it both ways.

In summary, Sartre believes that the idea of God is a product of our own impossible quest to transcend nothingness and become complete. Thus, even though Sartre insists that his existentialism is not a pessimistic philosophy, the inherent desire of consciousness to seek an impossible completion leads him to declare, "Man is a useless passion" (*Being and Nothingness* 615). "To be man means to reach toward being God. Or if you prefer, man fundamentally is the desire to be God" (*Being and Nothingness* 566). Because God is a logical contradiction, human existence is, in its most fundamental drive, an absurdity.

Sartre says that we can be free only when we accept the fact that heaven is empty. The absence of God means that we are forlorn. Coming to terms with our forlornness and accepting our freedom, with all its ramifications, is the only salvation available to us. "If man has once become aware that in his forlornness he imposes values, he can no longer want but one thing, and that is freedom, as the basis of all values" (*Existentialism* 53-54). Acceptance of our complete freedom, what Sartre calls authenticity, requires that we take over the task generally assigned to God; we determine what is right, good and important.

While he sets up authenticity as the goal we should strive to reach, Sartre is also pessimistic about the prospects for becoming authentic. For one thing, authenticity, like any other attribute, is never permanent. Our identity is always up for grabs in each decision, and the challenge we face is to exhibit authenticity as we make those decisions by accepting our freedom. In other words, the most we can hope for is authentic actions. Moreover, the pervasiveness of social expectations, cultural traditions and accepted authorities, in combination with the comfort we find in pushing off accountability on these third parties, makes consistent authenticity extremely difficult.

DISSECTING SARTRE

At the end of *Existentialism*, Sartre claims that his philosophy "is nothing else than an attempt to draw all the consequences of a coherent atheistic position" (*Existentialism* 60-61). I would argue that he has accomplished this goal very well. Sartre and I agree that for values, truth and goodness to be objective realities that exist outside our subjective decisions about them, they must have a supernatural basis. Without such a foundation, we have no objective, universal justification for our actions. Therefore, if Sartre is right about the absence of God, he is also correct that everything is permissible. Conversely, if he is wrong about God's nonexistence, as I believe he is, the idea that values are completely subjective encounters big problems.

Nevertheless, if we set the question of God's existence aside for now, his examination of atheism's consequences still provides a valuable service. First, he rightly demonstrates that our position on God's existence has important implications for many other beliefs. The nature of freedom, purpose in life, moral values and a host of other beliefs bring us around, at some point, to questions about God. Second, I believe he shows how difficult it is to get rid of God and, at the same time, maintain the idea that certain values are universal and objective. Sartre puts a heavy burden on his fellow atheists who try to maintain objective moral truths while denying God's existence.

In addition to his penetration into the logical ramifications of atheism,

Sartre is a master observer and analyst of our psychological processes and deserves credit for his insights into the nature of freedom and responsibility. For example, his diagnosis of freedom forces us to recognize that even if our circumstances include political repression, imprisonment or extremely limited financial resources, such factors do not necessarily determine our responses. These situations do make it difficult to choose, because our decisions bring consequences. However, Sartre illuminates the fact that we must still decide how much importance we will attach to various consequences.

Sartre's philosophy also reminds us that we cannot choose not to choose. Even if we allow external influences such as social expectation, fear, guilt or tradition to dictate our response to a given situation, "allowing" is itself a choice. In sum, he shifts our focus from things we cannot control to the internal dynamics of freedom. When this internal facet of freedom is acknowledged, it is difficult to avoid Sartre's conclusion that we have a lot more freedom than we generally admit, even if we disagree with his assessment that all things are permissible. In fact, it is not difficult to grasp his position that, given the vast array of choices at our disposal, freedom becomes a burden; it is more than we want because of the responsibility that comes with it. Finally, Sartre confronts us with how easily we fall into bad faith to avoid accountability for our choices. Give us half a chance to divert responsibility from our decisions, and we will take it.

Although I find Sartre stimulating and correct about a number of things, I also have some important areas of disagreement. Since most of these divergences ultimately lead back to the question of God's existence, this is the natural place to begin my more critical comments on his philosophy. One of Sartre's arguments against God's existence begins from the nature of consciousness. In sum, he says, God cannot be both perfect *and* conscious. Only physical objects are complete in themselves. In contrast, to be conscious is to be conscious of imperfection. Therefore, Sartre argues, consciousness and perfection are contradictory and incompatible.

Sartre's argument against God's existence seems to misunderstand the way language is used to speak about God. He is right in his analysis of the basic difference between objects and persons. To this extent, then, he is also correct that the concept of a being that is some sort of hybrid between an object and a person is incoherent. The fundamental problem with this argument is that almost no one thinks of God as such a hybrid being. God, in traditional thought, is not thought to be complete in the way an object is complete. The attributes of an artifact are always finite, and its definition is provided by a power external to it. By contrast, theists think of God as a being who possesses a perfect combination of perfect qualities from himself, not a collection of finite characteristics imposed by an external power. Similarly, the freedom that theists attribute to God is not just freedom of choice (Sartre's definition) but also freedom from limiting conditions, a form of freedom that human beings do not possess, as Sartre acknowledges. In short, then, when the theist speaks of God as simultaneously perfect and free, these terms mean something different when used of God than the definitions Sartre gives them when he speaks of a combination of being-in-itself and being-for-itself. And, I would argue, when the proper definitions are applied to God, the concept of a divine being who is both perfect and free is logically coherent.

A second argument Sartre employs to support his atheism begins with the human drive for transcendence. He claims that we recognize our incompleteness and endeavor to transcend this imperfection by actualizing options that are presently only possibilities. No matter how hard we strive for this perfection, however, finitude remains. So human beings are in a no-win situation, caught between our drive to become complete and the inability to do so. Sartre says that the concept of God emerges as an expression of this paradox. We have a need that we cannot ourselves satisfy. Therefore, we create, out of our impulse for transcendence, a God who possesses these perfections, who fulfills this need. A summary version of his argument, then, is that the idea of God seems too good to be true, so it is. We have simply talked ourselves into belief in God because this provides a happy ending to our story, Sartre claims.

Sartre correctly observes that we are quite capable of conjuring up imaginary answers to satisfy psychological needs or wishes. If we have a strong desire to be intelligent, good looking or funny, we can make ourselves believe that we are all these things, even if the beliefs have no connection with reality. Sartre's argument, however, goes further. Taken in itself, it assumes that any fulfillment of a psychological need is *nothing but* an expression of that need. Christians would not doubt at all that human beings, in our imperfection, have a need and a craving for a link with the perfect. However, they would also argue that this is one of those needs for which a fulfillment exists, just as food exists as a means of satisfying physical hunger. In short, Sartre supplies no reason to assume that the idea of God is *nothing but* wish fulfillment simply because it corresponds to a valid human need.

We should note that even if my criticisms of Sartre's atheistic arguments hold water, they do not constitute proof that God exists. Nor will any such proof be attempted here. However, one of the gaps Sartre leaves open above raises some interesting opportunities for us to think through the raw material of a case for God's existence. For example, Sartre makes it clear that, in some way, recognition of our limitations is a result of seeing what we are not (i.e., perfect). However, he does not explain why, given our inherent incompleteness, we would be capable of holding some concept of perfection. The latter is particularly puzzling since he argues that the actual existence of a perfect being is logically impossible. If we cannot logically grasp perfection, how does Sartre understand the concept well enough to know that we cannot logically grasp it?

Similarly, even though he provides some very thought-provoking ideas about consciousness, freedom, our desire for transcendence and our capacity for self-deception, Sartre makes no attempt to explain the origins of these functions. Why are we invested with this drive for transcendence? Why we are conscious being-for-itself instead of objects? Why are we here at all? Sartre simply decides up-front that these questions are unimportant, even though it seems that questions like "Why is there something rather than nothing?" and "Why are things the way they are?" are fairly basic philosophical inquiries. Sartre's decision has significant ramifications because understanding the source of something is usually linked to understanding its purpose.

Sartre himself acknowledges this connection when he says that the origin (existence) of the paper cutter is dependent on the purpose (essence) of the paper cutter. This makes it impossible to explore the origin of freedom, consciousness or existence without addressing the question of our purpose. Therefore, he says nothing about it. However, it seems arbitrary and a little too convenient to decide what you will attempt to explain (the mechanisms of human consciousness) and what you will simply leave as a given (the origin of consciousness), especially if those givens might get in the way of your conclusions. It is always possible to get the answers you want when you control the questions that get asked. Moreover, it is worth noting that, historically, most of the arguments for God's existence have been built on the very questions (e.g., Why can we conceive of perfection? What is the origin of our moral sense? Can conscious existence emerge from pure materiality? Why does anything exist?) that Sartre decides to ignore.

Another vulnerable point in Sartre's philosophy grows out of his assertion that we should avoid bad faith and embrace freedom. While he does a good job of explaining that part of the atheistic package is the complete subjectivity of values, I am not sure that he, or anyone else, can live in a manner that is consistent with radical subjectivity. For example, Sartre believes that everyone should avoid the self-deception of bad faith since it is a denial of freedom. Therefore, he appears to set out honesty and freedom as objective values, all the time denying the existence of objective values. He might respond that we have an obligation to maintain our freedom since it is the nature of consciousness to be free. Once again, however, it would be difficult to conceive of any reason why people have a duty to stay within the limits of consciousness. Moral subjectivity has a certain attraction, but it is hard to actually live it. At some point, values that are intended to be universal—authenticity and freedom in Sartre's case—keep sneaking in, as they did for Nietzsche.

In a related manner, I believe that Sartre's concept of freedom, while it contains some useful insights, leaves a very important question unanswered. As stated earlier, I give Sartre high marks for making us aware that we often avoid freedom in order to be free *from* responsibility and anguish. However, I find him much less helpful in his response to the question of what we should be free *for*. What is the purpose of freedom? Given his beginning point, Sartre's answer to why we should seek freedom becomes circular. Consciousness is consciousness of freedom, and the liberated individual is therefore one who lives consciously. In other words, consciousness and freedom are the same thing for Sartre. Therefore, we can seek no reason outside freedom itself as an explanation for why we should seek freedom. Sartre might respond that it is unfair to require that he explain the purpose of freedom. If God does not exist, no objective purpose exists for anything. However, he clearly argues that we should protect and maintain our freedom; yet, it is difficult to imagine why this is an obligation unless some purpose or reason exists for freedom. Since he does not seem to have a way to escape the circularity of saying that we should be free because we are free, the purpose of freedom is left hanging in midair.

From the Christian perspective, I would suggest that the type of freedom that Sartre worships—freedom from external standards or forces—is not an end or goal. Instead, it seems that the Bible views our freedom *from* sin, political oppression, hunger, imprisonment or some other type of limitation is to be used as a means and opportunity to use our freedom *for* service to God and others. As Martin Luther puts it, "A Christian man is most free lord of all, and subject to none; a Christian man is the most dutiful servant of all, and subject to everyone." Sartre was very open to the idea that truth could be found in paradox, but this is one of those paradoxical truths he seems to have missed. The door was open for him to see this when he recognized that human beings are, by nature, incomplete. Because we are, in ourselves, always finite and fallible, the only way to satisfy the desire for transcendence that Sartre speaks of seems to be in becoming free *for* the one who completes us.

EPILOGUE

The Examined Life

Now that you have been exposed to some of the basic philosophers and a few of their ideas, what is the next step? As you probably expect, my suggestion is for you to go deeper. The point is not so much to go deeper into philosophy itself as the issues that it concerns itself with. Philosophy books and classes, in my view, are only a means to a more important end. My suggestion for a worthwhile end is the examined life that Socrates speaks of and encourages. In short, the intent of this book is to motivate you to think more carefully about the ideas that will shape how you live, and this is an ongoing process for everyone.

On the first day of my Introduction to Philosophy classes, I ask my students to calculate how much of their life will actually be spent working in the profession they plan to enter. When you figure in the time lived before you enter the workplace and after you retire, you eliminate almost half the years of your life if you assume normal retirement age and life expectancy. When nonworking time is subtracted during the "working years"—vacations, holidays, nonworking hours, sleep, time off to raise kids, and so on—most people are rather shocked at what remains. Only about eight to ten years of their earthly existence will be spent at work.

The results of this exercise could be used to make a lot of different and significant points, but the observation I want to highlight is this: You are going to be a human being for a greater percentage of your life than you will spend in any profession you choose. Yet somehow we have been led to believe that education is more about that sliver of life that we call "earning a living" than it is about life itself. This is not to minimize what we do for a living. Our vocations are an important part of our life. But they are a *part* of our life, and if we identify ourselves completely with what we do for a living, we will live *partial* lives.

I'm not going to try to convince you that philosophy, rather than work, is life, because I don't think that is true either. Philosophers who see the intellect as the route to salvation have perspectives that are as out of whack as those who lose their lives in work. With this disclaimer, however, I want to add that I see careful reflection on life as vital. As I have attempted to demonstrate in this book, issues like the relationship of faith and reason, what it means to be good, what is true and whether we are free are natural, essential human questions. If we never deal with them, we may achieve success in the professions in which we are employed for those eight to ten years, but I don't see how we can have a successful *human* life in the average American lifespan of around eighty years.

One important point of reference I use for my life is Mark 12:30, which tells us to "love the Lord your God with all your heart and with all your soul and with all your mind and with all your strength." Because of all the *and*s in this verse, I assume that this is not a multiple-choice exercise, but is an all-inclusive guide for life. Thus, if loving God with our mind is not just a legitimate form of worship but a requirement for balanced spirituality, thinking seems to be OK with God. After all, God is the creator of the tools with which we think. And God has certainly created a world that is big and complex enough to provide plenty to think and learn about.

Thus, I do not separate the more philosophical type of learning from learning in general. To the extent that we discover how the world and the human beings that inhabit it function, we also gain some insight into what God is up to. But I also see a difference. I can be reasonably ignorant about things such as plumbing and accounting, and get through life without major problems. I can hire someone to take care of my plumbing and accounting, although it may cost me something. However, we shouldn't hire someone else to live our life and make our choices. The cost of that is incalculable. That is the point of an examined life.

As part of the process of examining life, I've encouraged looking at ideas that within Christian circles are often not considered "safe." The idea that life can be examined and adjusted as we go along provides a clue as to why I am not as apprehensive about exposing myself to ideas outside the boundaries of a Christian worldview as some Christians are. Many people seem to work with the assumption that ideas are like drugs. Once we swallow them, we lose control over their effects on us. If you passively absorb everything that goes on around you, there can be some truth to this. However, the fact that we can examine what we hear and read means that we have a say about the influences of the ideas that we encounter.

In reality, I agree that accepting some philosophical ideas we have seen in this book can make a mess of your life. This is the germ of truth in the warnings many Christians receive about philosophy. Ideas are incredibly powerful, and the wrong ones can lead you astray. In view of this danger, many have concluded that we should back away from the edge and stay where it is safe. Before we jump to that conclusion, we should acknowledge that the ideas found in any area of learning can be dangerous. Businesspeople can pervert their knowledge and use it in the service of greed. Those trained in fire science can become quite effective pyromaniacs. The fact is that any type of knowledge brings with it certain types of power. Thus, like any powerful tool, philosophical knowledge can be difficult to control and can leave unbelievable destruction in its wake if misused. However, if used properly, power, in any of its forms, can accomplish a great deal of good. Perhaps the power found in philosophical ideas is similar. If used correctly, good things will result.

A final word on what good things we should expect to come from the power of good ideas. I once had a discouraging discussion with a young

Christian who had chosen philosophy as a major so he could figure out how to beat pagans at their own game. I agree to the extent that we should have a clear and sophisticated understanding of non-Christian worldviews. I also buy the idea that Christian beliefs provide something important that pagan philosophies do not. However, I have two serious areas of disagreement with my fellow Christian's approach. First, I don't believe that philosophy belongs to nonbelievers; it's not "their game." It is a valid home for Christians, in the same way that history, math, music and physical therapy are valid disciplines for Christians. Second, an attitude that looks only at how we can "win" arguments seems arrogant. As the title of the book suggests, I'm convinced that Christians should learn from whatever sources of good ideas we can find. Beginning with the assumption that the purpose behind interaction with those outside the faith is to win arguments leads to the type of arrogance that made Euthyphro so unteachable. The power of reflective living does not seem to find a good solution in treating ideas like a stick with which others are beat into submission.

I prefer the approach we saw in *Theaetetus*, in which thoughtful wrestling with important ideas increases one's sense of wonder. When confronted with the marvels and complexity of truth, he developed an attitude of humility. As the next step in your pursuit toward the examined life, I suggest a careful reading of Book XI of Augustine's *Confessions*, a meditation on the nature of time. As is the case in many of the Socratic dialogues, at the end Augustine is forced to admit that his mind cannot fathom something as basic as time. The recognition of his intellectual limits, which cannot grasp even something that permeates every aspect of our existence, drives him to be astonished at the awesomeness of God. I can't help but believe that Augustine would be in a position to model the words of Socrates to Theaetetus concerning the beneficial effects of this sense of wonder. "You will be gentler and more agreeable to your companions, having the good sense not to fancy you know what you do not know" (*Theaetetus* 210c).